Target Language,
Collaborative Learning
and Autonomy

MODERN LANGUAGES in PRACTICE

The **Modern Languages in Practice Series** provides publications on the theory and practice of modern foreign language teaching. The theoretical and practical discussions in the publications arise from, and are related to, research into the subject. *Practical* is defined as having pedagogic value. *Theoretical* is defined as illuminating and/or generating issues pertinent to the practical. Theory and practice are, however, understood as a continuum. The Series includes books at three distinct points along this continuum: (1) Limited discussions of language learning issues. These publications provide an outlet for coverage of actual classroom activities and exercises. (2) Aspects of both theory and practice combined in broadly equal amounts. This is the *core of the series*, and books may appear in the form of collections bringing together writers from different fields. (3) More theoretical books examining key research ideas directly relevant to the teaching of modern languages.

Series Editor
Michael Grenfell, *Centre for Language in Education, University of Southampton*

Editorial Board
Do Coyle, *School of Education, University of Nottingham*
Simon Green, *Trinity & All Saints College, Leeds*

Editorial Consultant
Christopher Brumfit, *Centre for Language in Education, University of Southampton*

Other Books in the Series
The Good Language Learner
    N. NAIMAN, M. FRÖHLICH, H.H. STERN and A. TODESCO
Inspiring Innovations in Language Teaching
    JUDITH HAMILTON
Le ou La? The Gender of French Nouns
    MARIE SURRIDGE
Validation in Language Testing
    A. CUMMING and R. BERWICK (eds)

Other Books of Interest
Distance Education for Language Teachers
    RON HOWARD and IAN McGRATH (eds)
Quantifying Language
    PHIL SCHOLFIELD
Teacher Education for LSP
    RON HOWARD and GILLIAN BROWN (eds)

Please contact us for the latest book information:
Multilingual Matters Ltd, Frankfurt Lodge, Clevedon Hall,
Victoria Road, Clevedon BS21 7SJ, UK

MODERN LANGUAGES IN PRACTICE 5
Series Editor: Michael Grenfell

Target Language, Collaborative Learning and Autonomy

Ernesto Macaro

MULTILINGUAL MATTERS LTD
Clevedon • Philadelphia • Toronto • Adelaide • Johannesburg

For Jules

Library of Congress Cataloging in Publication Data

Macaro, Ernesto
Target Language, Collaborative Learning and Autonomy/Ernesto Macaro
Modern Languages in Practice: 5
Includes bibliographical references and index
1. Language and languages–Study and teaching (Secondary). 2. Immersion
method (Language teaching). I. Title. II. Series.
P53.44.M33   1997
418'.007–dc20   96-33004

British Library Cataloguing in Publication Data

A CIP catalogue record for this book is available from the British Library.

ISBN 1-85359-369-9 (hbk)
ISBN 1-85359-368-0 (pbk)

Multilingual Matters Ltd

UK: Frankfurt Lodge, Clevedon Hall, Victoria Road, Clevedon BS21 7SJ.
USA: 1900 Frost Road, Suite 101, Bristol, PA 19007, USA.
Canada: OISE, 712 Gordon Baker Road, Toronto, Ontario, Canada M2H 3R7.
Australia: P.O. Box 6025, 95 Gilles Street, Adelaide, SA 5000, Australia.
South Africa: PO Box 1080, Northcliffe 2115, Johannesburg, South Africa.

Typeset by Solidus, Bristol.
Printed and bound in Great Britain by WBC Book Manufacturers Ltd.

Contents

Acknowledgements

Many colleagues and friends have helped with the development of this book. I am especially grateful to Ros Stacey for the insight and the tact that she brought to the collection of data for the Tarclindy project. I would also like to express my sincere thanks to Irene Beatty, Julie Macaro and Kim Brown for their various contributions to the project.

I am indebted to Cynthia Martin, Wasyl Cajkler, Brian Richards and Janet Mellor for their comments and criticisms on the manuscript. Without their patience and, dare I say, perseverance, I would not have had the confidence to present it for publication. In this respect I am also indebted to Michael Grenfell, the series editor.

I was enabled to carry out the research and to write this book by the University of Reading Research Endowment Fund and I am grateful to the university for its generous award.

I would also like to thank Anne and Yves Feunteun, Alain Mathiot, Franco Greco, Edvige Costanzo and Gary Chambers for providing me with both written and oral information from the mainland about national curricula and teaching practices.

I owe a special debt to my friend and former colleague, Chris Leach, with whom I have had many illuminating conversations on language teaching and learning.

Last, but certainly not least, I would like to thank all the teachers and pupils who welcomed us into their classrooms and who gave up their time to fill in questionnaires and take part in interviews.

Although so many have contributed to this book, the responsibility for any of its failures is entirely my own.

Reading, UK
Spring 1996

Glossary

A level: External Examination generally taken by 18 year olds.

ALL: Association for Language Learning (in the UK).

AOE: Areas of Experience (in the NC, see POS).

AT: Attainment Target (in the NC) describes levels that pupils should reach.

Carousel: Where a class is divided into a number of groups (usually three or four) and these are offered a circus of activities in the same lesson.

CILT: Centre for Language Teaching and Research. A government funded organisation which supports language teachers and learners.

Comprehensive: A school which does not select pupils at entry according to ability.

DES: Department for Education and Science (now DfE).

DfE: Department for Education.

GCSE: General Certificate of Secondary Education. External examination (national) which 16-year-old pupils first took in 1988.

GOML: Graded Objectives in Modern Languages. A school or regional system of continuous assessment.

Grammar School: A school which selects pupils at entry according to ability.

HMI: Her Majesty's Inspectors.

HOD: Head of Department (or subject), responsible for all aspects of organisation of the subject.

INSET: In-service training.

KS3: Key Stage 3. Years 7, 8, 9. The first three years of secondary education.

KS4: Key Stage 4. Years 10 and 11. The final two years of compulsory education.

LEA: Local Education Authority.

Middle Schools: Some pupils transfer from middle school to secondary schools at end of year 7, year 8 or even year 9.

Mixed ability: Where a class is not selected according to the perceived ability of the pupils in that subject.

NC: National Curriculum.

NCC: National Curriculum Council set up to introduce NC.

O level: External examination replaced by GCSE. In MFL had strong grammar-translation basis.

OFSTED: Office for Standards in Education.

OHT: Overhead Transparency used on overhead projector.

POS: Programmes of Study (in the NC) describe what pupils should study, including AOE.

PSE: Personal and Social Education (Not an NC subject).

SAT: Standard Attainment Tasks (in the NC). Tests set to examine AT levels at end of KS3. Not in MFL.

SCAA: Schools Curriculum and Assessment Authority.

Top set: Where a year group is divided up according to ability in a particular subject.

Year 7: Pupils aged 11 approximately. Most schools transfer from primary at this stage.

Year 8: Pupils aged 12 approximately.

Year 9: Pupils aged 13 approximately.

Year 10: Pupils aged 14 approximately.

Year 11: Pupils aged 15 approximately.

Year 12: Pupils aged 16 approximately.

Introduction

Whilst there is a wealth of literature on second language acquisition (SLA) and second language learning this has tended to concentrate on:

(1) The learning of English as a foreign language.
(2) The learning of English as a second language for the purposes of communicating in an English-speaking community.
(3) Adults learning a foreign language (FL), or second language.
(4) Research in classrooms where the learning of English and, to a lesser extent other languages, is perceived by the learners as an essential part of their education.

This literature has emanated, for the most part, from the United States, Canada, Australia and Scandinavia. As a result, research into language learning may seem to have little relevance to some categories of FL teachers in the 11–16 secondary context. One aim of this book, therefore, is to help fill a gap in the literature by attempting to redress this imbalance in favour of EFL whilst at the same time not marginalising or denying the value of previous research and the role it can play in improving FL learning. Thus, as the reader would expect, the book combines an analysis of general L2 learning theory with FL practice. However, it sets out to do this within a recognisable educational framework. That is, one where political decisions and socio-cultural influences are recognised as having a real impact on teaching and learning. The book takes one nation's educational context (England/ Wales) as a framework within which to evaluate studies in language acquisition and language learning. It endeavours to operate, therefore, as a case study for other FL learning contexts. In order to break down some of these situational barriers, the book often references across the learning contexts.

The research, the teacher training and the in-service training I have been involved in over the past three years clearly demonstrates that the implications of the National Curriculum for MFL in England and Wales are only now being understood. Assessment and the rediscovery of creative writing are not featuring as prominently as was at first thought. Teacher and pupil use of the target language *is*. Teachers have

1

become increasingly aware that the relationship between the language that learners are exposed to and the development of their language proficiency is crucial as a background to any debate about approaches and methodology. However, the relationship between L2 input and L2 acquisition is too complex and unresolved to be examined only at the level of *quality* (e.g. input modification) as has generally been the case in the literature. Teachers' beliefs and actions regarding their *quantity* and distribution of target language need to be examined in the context of the 'modernist' approaches associated with communicative language teaching. Analysing the issue of quality and quantity of L2 input is a first step therefore in bringing together the fields of SLA and FL pedagogy. It is also one of the key elements which has to be examined within the socio-educational context in which it operates. In addition, teacher use of the target language cannot be divorced from current shifts towards less teacher-centred approaches. What are the implications for use of the L2 for teachers wishing to minimise the didactic nature of their role in the classroom? Can collaborative learning be encouraged in an atmosphere which excludes the mother tongue? Is foreign language provision's main objective to teach a language or does it also aim to prepare young people for future language learning?

The above are pedagogical concerns which, in recent years, have often been expressed to me by colleagues in modern languages departments. It has become evident that what is needed is a thorough reappraisal of L2 use within a syllabus design which promotes collaboration between learners, encourages independent learning tasks and leads to learner autonomy. The discussions with colleagues contributed greatly to the decision to carry out a research project at the University of Reading between 1993 and 1995. This book is therefore able to base itself on an empirical study of language teaching and learning in English schools as well as the author's own experience as a teacher and observer. It compares this data to other studies attempting to answer the same research questions in similar or different learning contexts. It relates principles resulting from the investigation to potential good practice in the classroom and good practice in the realm of managing change. It suggests avenues for future research and indicates a need for materials in a number of areas. At the end of Chapters 3 to 6 there are practical suggestions for teacher development. These can be used in pre-service, in-service and departmental training sessions.

The Tarclindy[1] Project

The research project's principal aims were to investigate four aspects, and their inter-relationship, of the National Curriculum (England and Wales) for Modern Foreign Languages. These were

(1) Use of the target language by teachers in order to carry out the business of lesson management and content delivery.
(2) Use of the target language by pupils as evidence of ongoing language acquisition.
(3) Collaborative learning through pair work and group work.
(4) Independent learning.

The project investigated the aspects via four sources:

(a) teacher attitudes and reactions;
(b) observation of classroom practice;
(c) learner attitudes;
(d) in-service training (INSET) providers: practice and beliefs.

Peripheral to this investigation, some small-scale action research cycles based on teaching techniques were planned and trialled. These are described briefly in Chapter 5.

The project began in 1992 with a pilot of the research instruments related to teachers. These were trialled with colleagues in England and, in order to broaden slightly the conceptual context of the study and to make comparisons, with teachers of English in Italy (Macaro, 1995). The project proper then started in 1993 and was funded by the University of Reading's Research Endowment Fund. This enabled a second researcher to devote time to the project. The project was completed in June 1995.[2] A detailed description of the project including research instruments[3] is given in the Appendix. As constant reference is made throughout the book to this project, readers are encouraged to familiarise themselves with this section before proceeding.

The Tarclindy project is a substantial study of target language use and effect involving high levels of triangulation. Attitudinal data, descriptions of beliefs and observation of practice provide a solid context in which to conduct the debate. What is of course missing from the project is any psychometrically acceptable measures of language proficiency related to L1/L2 distribution in the classroom. This would help to put some of the final pieces of the jigsaw in place. If this were based solely on teacher styles, however, the number of variables connected with any such test would be enough to deter any but the most determined and highly resourced investigator. Anything more rigorously experimental would be difficult to justify on ethical grounds. How many parents would agree to let their children be taught by a quantitatively different method to the rest of the children in the school? Yet a measurable causal link between quantity of teacher input and, say, vocabulary acquisition, would be welcome. On the other hand, as Paulston (1990: 191) points out, we need qualitative *and* quantitative approaches to understanding language acquisition and that any reliance on quantification and psychometrics, however rigorous, is not sufficient. The research strategy of the Tarclindy project concentrates on what practitioners say they believe and do and what observers say the practitioners do. Given the constraints, variables and difficulties attached to pre-test and post-test experiments on so fundamental a dependent variable as L1 and L2 use, it may be that this attitude-observation approach will provide the only reliable or achievable indicator for the optimal use of the target language for some time to come.

Structure of the Book

The results of the Tarclindy project are disseminated throughout the book according to the way that they inform relevant issues as they arise in specific chapters. The first two chapters are context-setting in that they provide a background, both national and international, to the main themes investigated in Chapters 3 to 6. Chapter 7, before offering some conclusions to the debate, reminds us that teachers are individuals with personal agendas and values. The following is a more detailed description of the chapters of the book.

Chapter 1 examines the educational framework within which language teachers in England and Wales have been operating since 1992 and compares this with frameworks and guidelines in other European countries. It notes that this framework is concerned much more with teaching and learning than with syllabus content. It asks what routes of inquiry and debate might have led to the design of this framework, shows how it was presented through official documentation and outlines the status and functions of agencies which were and are in place to ensure its implementation. It outlines the most salient issues related to teaching, learning and testing as contained in the official documents and examines the nature of INSET provision in its attempts to address those issues. It examines the difference between a general approach to language pedagogy and a prescriptive methodology. The chapter concludes with speculation as to the necessity for such a framework and the assumption of deficiences in classroom practice which the framework would appear to be making.

Chapter 2 explores the international phenomenon known as Communicative Language Teaching (CLT). It identifies a number of interpretations which teachers have made of this approach. It suggests that a communicative approach implies an eclectic taxonomy of learner activities in the classroom as well as different principles guiding the sequencing of those activities. This diversity necessitates a sophisticated level of teacher reflectiveness and integrity if s/he is to operate effectively in the enormous number of different national and international contexts in which CLT is being adopted. It asks whether teachers in the English FL context in 1992 were operating at that level of sophistication. Were they selecting appropriately for language learning, or were they selecting merely for the purposes of motivating reluctant learners? A brief examination of theories of motivation is undertaken and related to the secondary FL context. The chapter concludes with a suggestion that a number of concerns related to the eclecticism of CLT may have been justified.

Chapter 3 is in two parts. Part 1 describes the behaviours and language prevalent in the FL classroom. It explores the artificiality of the classroom, the artificiality of the teacher as the main input source, and the complexity of classroom discourse. Can teachers in the secondary FL context maintain a 'total immersion' atmosphere by pretending to be someone they are not? Is this pretence undermined by other, sometimes conflicting, inputs? By analysing a number of categories within teacher input itself, the chapter delves deeper into the complexities of classroom discourse: *message and medium oriented* input; *classroom language* and *content language*. Against this background, the argument of L1 exclusion is brought into focus. Part 2 explores the teacher's use of the target language. A number of studies are examined which demonstrate that recourse to L1 by teachers is an international phenomenon. In what aspects of teaching does recourse to L1 most occur? Are the variables to do with the experience of the teacher or the age, ability and socio-cultural background of the class of learners? Is another variable the teacher's ability to modify his/her L2 input? If so, can this technique be taught to teachers and can we be sure, in any case, that *comprehensibility* is the same thing as *comprehensible input*?

Chapter 4 investigates the person on the receiving end – the learner. What can SLA research tell us about how secondary FL learners actually learn? To what extent is L2 learning like L1 learning? Can the degree of 'likeness' inform the L1/L2 distribution debate? Implications are drawn from this discussion about overarching principles of language teaching and learning. These are compared to the views expressed by young learners in the Tarclindy project. Do they get frustrated and confused when faced with teacher L2 input? What *strategies* do they use to try to understand? To what extent should they be allowed to negotiate meaning? If negotiated meaning implies early language production, should learners be forced to speak in L2 from the start? What evidence do we have that *interaction,* including learner initiated interaction, is a necessary added ingredient for language *acquisition* and development? If learners use strategies to try to understand the teacher, it would suggest that they are actively involved in the learning process. Should other types of strategies be encouraged and should they be explicitly taught? What are the implications of this for teacher L2 use? The same questions are applied to the notions of predisposition to language learning and to informing learners about pedagogy. The chapter concludes with guidelines for optimal teacher use of L2.

Chapter 5 attempts an audit of the different ways learners in the secondary FL context collaborate. The chapter examines to what extent the beneficial outcomes of pair work and group work outweigh the possible detrimental effect of not receiving teacher input and teacher feedback. The chapter goes on to examine the strategies which learners can deploy in order to achieve or enhance interaction and communication. Do these strategies actually help the internalisation of a language system? What kind of interaction amongst learners is both achievable and at the same time beneficial? The chapter examines the Tarclindy data in order to ascertain to what extent teachers feel they can give learners in collaborative situations freedom to manoeuvre, whether there is a conceptual difference between pairwork and groupwork, what factors render this type of collaboration most successful and whether L1 or L2 should be used to prompt interaction among learners. Finally, the chapter reports briefly on a collaborative learning 'cycle' which formed part of the Tarclindy project.

Chapter 6 examines the various influences and different labels which have been attached to the notion of learner *autonomy.* It argues that we should be placing at the forefront a functional definition of autonomy which promotes emancipation from the classroom. The Tarclindy project data is examined to illuminate what are teachers' perceptions of autonomy, to what extent they are involved in promoting it and how much INSET they have received in this, as yet, underdeveloped aspect of language teaching. Can independent learning situations create the necessary conditions wherein individual differences are catered for? Can independent learning and autonomy be linked to what we know about age-related development? An age-related graduation towards learner autonomy is proposed as a model. Using a concrete example of a planned *unit of work*, the 'Practical ideas to try out' section asks to what extent can this functional autonomy be promoted in the learner by changing our teaching approaches?

Chapter 7 describes the teachers from the Tarclindy project as case studies. It suggests that examples of practice, to have credibility, should contain more than brief decontextualised descriptions of class activities. The book concludes by asking whether a national methodology, such as the one proposed by the National Curriculum for England and Wales, was desirable either from the point of view of the teaching profession or from that of the language learner. It suggests that, in terms of managing pedagogical change, valuable lessons can be learned from the case study contained in the book.

A note on terminology

To reduce some of the 'fuzziness around the edges' (Phillipson *et al.,* 1991: 43) of L2 research I propose the following definitions of the various types of L2 learning situations:

EFL1 – where all the learners in the classroom do not share a common L1 (and do not live permanently in the target country).
ESL1 – where learners do not share a common L1 (but live in the target country).
ESL2 – where learners do share a common L1 (but live in the target country).
EFL2 – where communities of learners do share a common L1 (but where English (L2) has a particularly special status – for example, India, Denmark).
FL – where learners share a common L1 (and do not live in the target country – for example Italians learning English, English learning French).

The above categories are neither exhaustive nor watertight. They would, however, seem to draw reasonable boundaries for the purposes of making major distinctions between learners. When no distinction is being made I will use the term Second Language Learning/Learner (or L2 learning).

A note on the style of the book

When I first started writing this book I set myself a number of objectives in terms of communicating with the reader – for example to avoid obscure terms, and to explain all technical terms. The book, after all, is not intended solely for 'experts in the field'. Far from it. I am now aware that this has not always been possible because of lack of space, for which I apologise. As a recompense I have provided a Glossary of British educational jargon and acronyms. I have also given in italics those terms which are used commonly in L2 literature in the hope that a baffled reader will at least be able to follow them up, without difficulty, elsewhere.

I have quoted teachers and pupils at length throughout the book. Given their energy and commitment to providing the data for the Tarclindy project I find this much more justifiable than my own summary of their views, anxieties and aspirations. I believe it also makes for a much more accessible and ultimately much more human piece of writing.

Where there is an implicit or explicit criticism of classroom practice this is made in the full knowledge that it is also a criticism of myself as a former and, occasionally, current practitioner. It is certainly done with precisely the humility often missing from 'official pronounce-ments' about good practice.

I have endeavoured to avoid the use of passives. An exception to this is in the description of the Tarclindy project in the Appendix and where in the main body of the book I felt it might endanger the anonymity of teachers or schools. Apart from in these instances, I believe a reader is entitled to know who the 'agent' is who is making a claim or a statement. Where the use of 'I' would have become excessive, I have used 'we' suggesting an exploratory journey together. I hope the reader will, as I have done, find the journey illuminating and worthwhile.

Notes

1. Tarclindy: affectionate abbreviation of target language, collaborative learning and independent learning.
2. There are two aspects of the project which are continuing: the action research cycles (described in Chapter 5); the attempt at a more sophisti-cated model of FL lesson description enabling a more accurate study of recourse to L1.
3. The teacher questionnaire is reproduced in Chapter 7 in the course of the description of three teachers' practice and beliefs.

1 A National Curriculum or a Framework for Methodology?

If a group of Modern Languages educators, in any country, were to sit down now and start to plan a national syllabus in their subject for pupils during the years of compulsory education, where would they begin? Would they begin by asking themselves '*Should* our youngsters learn a second language'? Or would they assume that the importance of learning a language other than one's own was self-evident and concentrate on 'for what *purposes* learn a second language'? Would they stop to question the concept of 'one's own language' first, ensuring that for their country the concept did not hold a number of unjustifiable pre-suppositions? Would they then proceed by matching the purposes they had come up with against a list of potential languages to be taught? Having selected a number of languages, they might then attempt to define the levels of competence one might reasonably expect from learners of differing abilities or success rates. Would they then start the slow, laborious process of what that syllabus might contain: words, expressions, idioms, structures, topics, being careful that the content matched both the purposes and the levels of competence?

Or would they come to the conclusion that this was far too complex and take a completely different tack? Would they disregard the content and start with what research says about how learners learn a second language? Here they might meet a bit of an obstacle. Not many linguists would want to fly in an aeroplane designed around the absolute certainties found in second language acquisition literature! But being practical people, the group would probably 'get down to it' and select bits and pieces from that literature which seemed reasonably OK. These bits might or might not conflict with one another. However, having taken this course of action, there would be nothing left but to soldier on. At this point, having made a stab at how learners learn, would they then turn their attention to how they should be taught?

9

Regardless of which of the two directions the group had embarked on, someone in the group might just pull them up short and start asking questions like: What sort of people are we? What political or ideological impetus might be guiding our decisions? Are we motivated by the interests of the nation? Are those synonymous with the interests of all the youngsters? What professional background might affect the judgements we are making and is that background the same for all of us? Is there a general consensus amongst practitioners about the direction we're taking? Are we sufficiently active if not expert in the field to be designing this syllabus? These questions might lead the group of educators to halt what they were doing and attempt first to research what the national consensus actually was on a potential national syllabus.

One of the conclusions of that investigation might be that there is a need to bring the fields of language acquisition, language pedagogy and language planning much closer together. Another conclusion might be that we must consider the specific nature of each language context and make the value judgements of the language planners explicit (Phillipson *et al.*, 1991: 45). This view, to some extent, echoes Paulston (1990: 187) who points out that national language policies are not based on research but primarily on political and economic grounds and that unless we account for the factors that lead to particular forms of language education we will not understand the consequences of that education.

In this chapter we shall be examining one nation's programme. We will examine the planning and implementation of the National Curriculum (NC) for Modern Languages in England and Wales.[1] We shall discuss to what extent this is a curriculum about *how* learners should learn rather than *what* they should learn and to what extent it is a programme *about the way* teachers should teach rather than *what* they should teach. This is not to pre-suppose that the *what* is more important than the *how*. Indeed it may well be that a curriculum, acting as a scaffolding structure for a national methodology or approach, was the direction that the planners needed to take. We will also examine how national agencies have combined in England to plan, implement and help deliver the NC. We will compare this structure with curriculum design and implementation in other countries. The questions raised will hopefully be of use to language curriculum planners elsewhere. For readers unfamiliar with education in England and as a reminder to those who are, we will start by examining which are the English agencies officially concerned with modern languages education and what is their function in relation to the NC.

The Status and Functions of National Agencies

In England, the Department for Education (DfE) replaced the Department of Education and Science (DES) in 1992. These departments are the ministerial institutions charged with carrying out official government policy on education. For the National Curriculum (all subjects), however, the National Curriculum Council (NCC) was set up by the then DES in order to oversee the design and contribute to the implementation of the NC of which Modern Languages officially came on stream in 1992. The first cohort of 11-year-olds started to learn a foreign language within the framework of the NC that year. Readers will thus be able to deduce that as I write (1995) not all pupils in compulsory education are learning within that framework. This is not an inconsiderable difficulty in discussions about content, methodology and policy both here and in ML departments in schools. At its inception it was envisaged that the NC would safeguard against overspecialised or idiosyncratic teaching and reduce the incidence of incompetent teaching (NCC, 1989). However (apart from the case of MFL, as I shall argue), the NC has not been particularly prescriptive about teaching methods.

The Secondary Education Assessment Council (SEAC) merged with the NCC in October 1993 to become the Schools Curriculum and Assessment Authority (SCAA). The chairman and the authority members are appointed by the Secretary of State for Education. Thus the Authority is now not only in charge of the curriculum but it is also the agency in charge of all assessment and examinations. That is not to say that it sets the examinations or tests but that it accredits all submissions from a number of independent examining boards. Exams are set externally and linked directly to the NC's attainment criteria. We examine proposals for these below.

The Office for Standards in Education (OFSTED) is a government appointed agency in the sense that it is financed by central government and private teams of inspectors apply to be trained and assessed by OFSTED. Registered inspectors can subsequently tender to carry out inspections in schools. Reports resulting from these inspections are in the public domain. Indeed, they can be accessed on the Internet. These reports may well be an important factor in guiding parents' choice of school for their children. OFSTED inspectors have a well documented framework of inspection criteria. However, the guidance for subjects in general states:

Teachers' work in the classroom will take many different forms, and it is important that judgements about effectiveness of teaching are based on its contribution to outcomes and not on inspectors' preferences for particular methods. (OFSTED *Handbook,* August 1993, part 4: 50)

The supplementary guidelines regarding Modern Foreign Languages, on the other hand, are much more prescriptive. Under the heading 'Quality of Teaching' we read:

Teachers should insist on the use of the target language for all aspects of a lesson. (OFSTED *Handbook,* section 37)

One of OFSTED's briefs is to ensure that the National Curriculum is being delivered. Thus, if that curriculum specifies the application of a particular methodology, the inspectors will be required to comment on whether that methodology is being applied. It is therefore not uncommon in inspection reports to attribute poor learner performance directly to a teaching approach with statements such as: 'the ML department has a policy on the use of the target language in teaching all aspects of the lesson. This is not consistently applied' (OFSTED, 1995).[2]

Local Education Authorities, having been by and large stripped of their former mandate as providers of education have, as we shall see, had an advisory/assisting role in the implementation of the NC rather that an influential one in the design of it. Responsibility for implementation of the NC rests squarely with the governors and teachers of the school.

The proposals for the MFL National Curriculum underwent a consultation exercise, carried out by the NFER/NCC[3] with teachers and other interested bodies. This resulted in the Consultation Report (NCC, May 1991). Examination of that document (in this and subsequent chapters) suggests that the validity of both the process and analysis of that consultation is questionable.

Judgements and Values in the National Curriculum

Statements about purposes

Some of the judgements and values inherent in the NC can be traced in the statements about what the purposes of learning a foreign language are. In order to understand fully the pedagogical implications of these here and in subsequent chapters, I list them fully:

- to develop the ability to use the language effectively for the purposes of practical communication;

- to form a sound base of the skills, language and attitudes required for further study, work and leisure;
- to offer insights into the culture and civilisation of the countries where the language is spoken;
- to develop an awareness of the nature of language and language learning;
- to provide enjoyment and intellectual stimulation;
- to encourage positive attitudes to foreign language learning and to speakers of foreign languages and a sympathetic approach to other cultures and civilisations;
- to promote learning of skills of more general application (e.g. analysis, memorising, drawing of inferences);
- to develop pupils' understanding of themselves and their own culture: (DES 1990a: 4; DES, 1990b: 3)

The fact that comments from the Secretary of State together with comments from '650 organisations and individuals' produced no changes whatsoever in the 'Purposes' from the Initial Advice (DES, 1990a) to the 'Proposals' (DES 1990b), might suggest an unprecedented and perhaps complacent consensus in a country not renowned for its language learning prowess. However, if we take the purposes individually it is actually very difficult to disagree with any of them. They are all very laudable aims. The problem arises when we take them as a whole or in juxtaposition to one another, when in fact we attempt to prioritise. For example, should we give more curriculum time to skills needed for 'further study work and leisure' or to 'encouraging positive attitudes' to foreigners. The two are of course not mutually exclusive, but the first emphasises instrumental goals and personal gain whilst the second emphasises international understanding and a predisposition to language learning. Should we concentrate on 'effective but practical communication' or on 'the nature of language' and other 'skills of more general application'? Again, these are not mutually exclusive but problematic if one is trying to establish whereabouts in the continuum between formal analysis of the language and functional use one wants to direct one's teaching.

Statements about pedagogy and good practice

The proposals state that within departments there should be consistency of teaching approaches (DES, 1990b: 58). It points out that, whilst we should not be seeking uniformity, learners in a school become confused when confronted with wide differences of approach.

It does not make clear whether there should be consistency *between* departments of schools with, for example, varying socio-economic intakes. It then lists 14 characteristics of good practice. As Westgate (1991) also points out, a number of things are unclear about these characteristics: who says they are good practice?; do they have a theoretical base?; do any conflict with one another?; what is their relative importance to one another?; as a set do they add up to a recognisable method or approach? If so how many can you take away before the whole edifice comes tumbling down?

There is not space here to examine all these characteristics[4] so we will confine ourselves to the three most relevant to this book. The first is:

• Characteristic 10.7: the target language is the normal means of communication.

In terms of official documentation it is illuminating to trace back the origins for the wording of this characteristic. In a draft statement of policy the DES (1986) advocated that:

from the outset, the foreign language rather than English should be the medium in which the classwork is conducted and managed.

It is interesting that this statement appears in a document which also suggests that part of England's poor showing in foreign language learning may be attributable to the way that foreign languages have traditionally been taught. What is confusing is that the document is published in precisely the year when the first cohort of students are embarking on a new course leading to a new examination at 16: the General Certificate of Secondary Education (GCSE), later to be much attacked for its extensive use of L1 for assessing comprehension (see below). It would be important to clear up the confusion not because of the machinations of one country's bureaucrats and educators but because of what it implies about language pedagogy's historical development. It would be helpful to know whether 'traditional' refers to vestiges of a grammar-translation method or whether it is to do with teachers using too much L1 in an eclectic communicative approach. The question of target language use is raised again in DES (1987):

In the classroom the foreign language should be the natural medium for teaching and learning

No explanation is given as to why the qualification 'natural' has been added. The paragraph in which it occurs clearly advocates the benefits of 'maximum exposure to L2 within the pupils' grasp'. Does the addition thus derive from 'natural' language acquisition hypotheses (see Chapter 2)? Is it about L2 learning being like L1 learning (see Chapter 4)? Is it to do with teachers and learners feeling comfortable using L2? Whatever the reason, it is noticeable that it is deleted the following year in *A Statement of Policy* and we return to:

> From the outset, the foreign language rather than English should be the medium in which classwork is conducted and managed. DES (1988: 12)

From now on the documentation appears to take much more confident plunges into second language acquisition literature:

> In communicating people interact with each other, negotiating meanings together thus affecting the way they each speak think and act. Communicating in a foreign language must thus involve both teachers and pupils using the target language as the normal means of communication. DES (1990b: 6)

The circularity of the above logic has already been signalled (Macaro, 1995). We can only conclude that what was meant here is that *learning* to communicate in L2 can *only* be achieved if teachers and learners practise doing so all the time. This interpretation is supported by the statement later in the document:

> The natural use of the target language for virtually all communication is a sure sign of a good modern languages course DES (1996b: 58)

We thus have the strongest expression of the L2 use issue through the reappearance of the word 'natural' and the additional 'virtually all'. I hope that the reader is sufficiently convinced of the power of the framework for implementation of the NC as described above, not to think that I am just playing around with words here. These are vital concepts both at a theoretical level and at a practical level and form much of the basis of the discussion in Chapters 3 and 4. Interestingly, the 'Advice' and the 'Recommendations' which followed from the 'Consultation' make only one reference to use of the target language, promising, instead, further clarification in the 'Non-statutory Guidance' (NSG) described below. Some may speculate as to precisely what status this vital methodological aspect has at this stage of the setting up of the framework. Has the 'virtually all' directive become non-statutory, in other words at the discretion of the individual teacher? Far from it. The reasons for this assertion are threefold. Firstly, 50% of the programmes of study, that part referring to listening and reading comprehension, are to be demonstrated via the use of L2. Since the other 50% is speaking and writing, which are obviously to be carried out in L2, we are still left with virtually all, L1 being designated only for the purposes of interpreting for others. Secondly, the Programmes of Study (POS) are mostly about the pupils' target language opportunities, not about words and phrases (see below). Thirdly, the quality of pupils' learning is to be judged, amongst other things, by the *quantity* of teacher use of L2:

the increased use of the target language by the teachers led to improved standards. (OFSTED, 1993b: 5)

and by the *comprehensibility* of the teacher's L2, as in this report by OFSTED on language teachers' performance (a Summary of Inspections) in 1993/1994:

Pupils were able to follow without difficulty lessons competently conducted in the target language (OFSTED, 1995: 5)

The Non-Statutory Guidance (NCC, 1992) provides a lot of useful and practical advice on using the target language in the classroom.[5] More importantly, for the purposes of later discussions, it shifts the emphasis to pupil use:

The NC ... extends opportunities and experiences for **pupils** (their emphasis) by promoting maximum use of the target language (NCC, 1992: B1)

We have therefore moved in this document from 'virtually all' to 'maximum' use. It also recognises that random use of L2 without recognition of learners' existing competence is inappropriate (NCC, 1992: C2). In a subsequent (non-statutory) publication (NCC, 1993: 1), the wording is again altered to:

optimum use of the Target Language by teachers and pupils is a central aim of modern foreign languages in the National Curriculum.

We have looked at this documentation in some detail because I shall be using the definitions *virtual, maximal* and *optimal* as a basis for discussing teacher L2 use in subsequent chapters. Note, however, the emphasis placed on the classroom. A central aim of the NC is stated not in terms of producing good linguists (outcomes), or of developing awareness and attitudes but in terms of observable processes in the classroom. One interpretation of the above quote might be that success in language learning is dependent on the successful application of a given methodology.

Let us now look at another of the 14 characteristics of good practice.

- Characteristic 10:1: (where) Learners often work co-operatively in groups.

Where does this belief come from? The series of official documents referred to above in the target language discussion also contain statements about the value of pupils talking to one another rather than simply reacting to approaches from the teacher. The advantages of this collaborative learning are stated in terms of:

- giving pupils greater opportunities for oral practice;
- opportunities for more spontaneous use of the language;
- opportunities for negotiated learning;
- greater flexibility for the teacher.

As we shall see in Chapter 5, this characteristic finds much greater substance in second language acquisition research than 10:7. However, it still raises many questions about pedagogy. In which language are pairs or groups of learners expected to organise themselves? What questions does it raise about: the age of the learner in relation to the types of tasks proposed; the relation of the task to the level of language competence needed to interact in order to perform the task? What theoretical assumptions does it make about the quality of learning from fellow learners' language, the role that feedback makes in testing language hypotheses, the fossilisation of error? A detailed discussion of these issues is to be found in Chapter 5. The last of the characteristics of good practice we will examine in detail is:

- Characteristic 10.14: (where) Learners become increasingly independent in their work.

Unlike 10:13, the issue of developing learner independence does not have as lengthy an official pedigree as the first two. Although there is a reference in DES (1987: 19) to moving beyond the stage of practising language in situations closely controlled by the teacher, it is not until DES (1990a: 131) that a clearer and more comprehensive definition of independence is arrived at. It is expressed in terms of:

- coping with unrehearsed situations;
- using more than the teacher as a language source and resource;
- learners being able to plan work on their own;
- learners choosing a topic or aspect to be studied.

This independence, we assume, is seen as independence from the teacher within the context of the classroom. We can make this assumption because homework in England plays a comparatively insignificant part in the learning process. I would estimate that the average weekly modern languages homework given to 'average' learners in year 8 to be about 30 minutes a week. This would hardly seem sufficient for it to be a context in which to develop the skills required for learner autonomy. We can assume that activities, such as planning work independently and discussing/choosing topics to be studied ('from quite an early stage' DES, 1990a, b), are to be carried out in L2. These issues are discussed in Chapter 6 and an attempt is made to link the three characteristics (target language use, collaborative learning and independent learning) via an age-related curriculum model.

If the above are statements and structures within which learning and teaching should occur, what does the framework say about 'content', about *what* learners should learn?

Statements about programme

In the DES Proposals (1990b) Programmes of Study (POS) are divided into two parts: Part 1: Opportunities, competencies and strategies; Part 2: The Content of Modern Language Courses. Part 1 is essentially yet another detailed exposé of the characteristics of good practice. The competencies which the programme is looking for in learners and the strategies they are expected to develop are directly linked to the 'frequent opportunities' which teachers are expected to offer them. They are described as 'skills and processes', 'comprehension and communication strategies' (DES, 1991b: 34). These opportunities are none other than defined classroom activities:

seek and give information; give and receive explanations and instructions. (DES, 1991b: 34)

If these skills are to form part of a compulsory programme of study rather than a description of desirable outcomes, it becomes clear that, when combined with other aspects described above, what we are dealing with here is a highly prescriptive programme based on a highly defined teaching approach. It does, moreover, differ considerably from similar documentation in other countries (see below). When this prescriptiveness is underpinned by the 'virtually all' use of L2, any claim that it is a general approach rather than a clear method becomes untenable. A consequence of this prescriptivism can be illustrated with a frivolous example. If a teacher found that s/he could successfully bring about an outcome such as 'spontaneous speaking skills ... initiating as well as responding to discourse' (DES, 1991b: 34), via a process of hypnosis, s/he could not be said to be teaching Part 1 of the National Curriculum programmes of study because s/he would not be providing 'frequent opportunities' for that kind of activity in the classroom.

In Part 2, the POS are about language content in that they describe the seven topic areas through which the above activities are to be experienced. (DES, 1991b: 39). These are virtually the only stipulation that the NC makes about what to teach, the 'language content' to be taught. An important point to signal here is that DES 1990a and DES 1990b do not have a reference to 'the language of the classroom' under Area A: Everyday Activities. This area 'concentrates on descriptions and narrations of specific activities and transactions which learners are likely to engage in, in their everyday lives'. It does indeed include school life but this is about language which can be used in communicating with youngsters from the target countries: timetable, lunch, preferences, etc. The recommendations for programmes of study, as arrived at in the Consultation Report (NCC, 1991) on the other hand, contain such a specification for the first time: 'Pupils should have regular opportunities to explore in the target language topics which deal with activities they are likely to engage in at home and at school,' this should include the *language of the classroom* (the wording is the same in DES, 1991). Is it possible that this addition came as a result of a request from teachers during the consultation period? It would seem unlikely. There is certainly no mention of such a request in the summary of the 'consultation'. The consequences of this addition, however, are enormous. The language that the teacher uses with the pupils becomes a formal part of the programme and is to be tested (see below and also Chapter 3 for a discussion on the nature of classroom language).

We have seen that both in the pedagogy and programme related elements of the NC framework, by far the greatest emphasis is on how teachers should set about teaching. What do the documents say about what learners should achieve?

Statements about outcomes and attainment

It is a feature of the NC in England that outcomes are expressed in terms of 'attainment targets' (ATs), of which in MFL there are four, corresponding to the four language skills. These targets are sets of statements of what learners should be able to do in order to attain a particular level. The DES (1990b) version has 10 levels.[6] The statements have no language content. They are, again, observable 'performances' which learners can either do or cannot do. I have at times felt this was like watching two actors on television talking with the sound turned off. In AT1 (the ability to understand the spoken language) for example, learners, in order to demonstrate level 2 competence, need to be able to respond to short phrases, instructions and information in familiar contexts, given visual support and repetition. (DES, 1990b: 16) This level then differs from other levels not in terms of what language (words and structures) is being used but in the fact that the phrases will be *short*, they will be about *instructions and information*, they will be set in *familiar contexts* (language and topics already encountered) and they will be given with *visual support and repetition*. Among the examples given are 'write that ... (pointing to board) into your books' and 'press this key (pressing key of a computer keyboard)'. This clearly is an assessment of competence in *classroom language* rather than of language competence projected to a future encounter with someone from the target country. Moreover, if this *classroom language* is being assessed, then it must be taught in a fairly prescribed way because we cannot separate the assessment of the 'performance' from the activity in which that 'performance' takes place. As if to emphasise that language competence will be evaluated through a process of observing certain (but not all) manifestations of performance, the OFSTED (1993a) observation guidelines confidently state that: 'good learning is characterised by a readiness to work in the language'.

Despite the revisions carried out to the NC attainment targets by SCAA (1994) and DfE (1995), revisions which transformed the level statements into level descriptors, this notion of the link between *what* is assessed and *how* the teacher teaches persists.

The last foundation stone in the NC edifice is the way in which learner skills (particularly listening and reading) will be tested.

Testing in the Target Language

The National Curriculum framework foresaw that all testing at the age of 16 (Keystage 4/GCSE) would be done in L2. The Consultation Report (NCC, May 1991) refers to the survey of teacher attitudes to this issue carried out by the NCC/NFER. A question put to teachers in this survey was whether they agreed with 'the use of the target language in relation to SATs' (Standard Attainment Tasks – or tests) (DES, 1991: 68). One of the key changes teachers were being asked to comment on was target language testing, i.e. testing listening and reading comprehension *through L2.* The consultation document reports that 'there was no consensus on the use of the target language in SATs: 24% agreed, while 16% disagreed' (DES, 1991: 11). What did the other 60% of respondents feel? Did they partly agree? If so, was there any qualitative follow up? Did they not reply to this question? If so, the presentation of the statistics is misleading. Yet on the basis of this very consultation process, the issue of target language testing seems to have been resolved in that we read:

> the target language must be considered the main language medium in which students will respond and express themselves, except where an interpreting exercise may require use of L1. The form of a Target Language exam assumes also rubrics in the TL. (Key Stage 4 criteria for MFL, SCAA, 1994)

There is scant reference in second language acquisition and pedagogy literature as to whether testing should be carried out in L1 or L2. Where it is mentioned, the issue tends to arise in discussions in journals on language testing, the arguments centring on validity, reliability, practicality and interpretability of answers. These themes, nevertheless, are the gauntlets thrown down by Brian Page (1993) and Woods and Neather (1994) in their almost acrimonious debate over target language testing. The Page v. Woods and Neather debate goes something like this:

Page: Tests have got to measure what they set out to measure. If the candidate misunderstands the L2 rubrics it invalidates the whole test.

W&N: GCSE L1[7] rubrics are silly anyway. They can be made simple and accessible in L2.

Page: Yeah, so simple and accessible that they lead to the setting of unimaginative tasks!

W&N: No they won't; look at the International GCSE and EFL exams.

Page: Look, if the questions are in the TL, the candidates will just lift the answer out of the text. It's not real comprehension testing.

W&N: You're getting hung up on questions, Brian. We've been using pictures and visuals successfully for ages!

Page: Where?

W&N: The International GCSE of course! Anyway, while the less able may only be able to recognise the right bit in the text, the more able can do lots of other things like deducing and reformulating language and drawing inference and evaluating.

Page: But that's my point! What will the test do other than test language manipulation and written language production? And don't tell me they're going to ignore errors in L2, that's impossible, too many grey areas between inaccuracy and lack of comprehension. And you're the ones that are hung up – hung up on mixed-skill testing. We do lots of single skill activities in the real world. Nothing wrong in that!

W&N: Oh dear, oh dear, so behind it all really there's the 'let's get back to translating' ... that's the hidden agenda. Well, no way, Brian ... that's absolutely not on.

Page: No hidden agenda. I'm just talking about authentic tasks and, Lord knows, it's taken time to get those introduced into the classroom and in exams.

W&N: Don't talk to us about authentic tasks. The rigmarole examiners have to go through to set authentic tasks is ridiculous. What's needed is educationally valid tasks. Maybe authentic texts but not necessarily authentic tasks. There's lots to choose from.

Page: Where?

W&N: The International GCSE and EFL. Also you might care to read a doctoral thesis by a certain C. Woods...

The tongue-in-cheek presentation of the above arguments *(pace* Page, Neather and Woods!) should in no way lead us to devalue the importance of what the authors are saying nor their genuine conviction. However, it is one thing to bat opinions across the net of a language journal, it is another when those opinions run the risk of becoming unquestioned official beliefs. Neather *et al.* (1995) were commissioned by SCAA to carry out a project on the testing of reading and listening without the use of English (L1). The authors of this document, from the outset, maintain their conviction that target language testing is desirable, feasible and reliable. They argue that the GCSE has had the undesirable effect of justifying or even increasing the amount of L1 use in the classroom. This view is supported by what a considerable number of teachers said in the Tarclindy interviews.

Neather *et al.* (1995: 6) point out that 'apart from traditional tests of translation, foreign language examinations in other countries also concentrate on target language testing'. The authors do not, however, divulge which countries they are referring to nor the percentage of marks awarded for translations. They also agree with the thrust of this chapter that: 'the most important feature of the National Curriculum in MFL has been the emphasis on increasing the use of the TL in the classroom' (Neather *et al.:* Introduction) and that the syllabus of the NC is 'a recommended methodology' (Neather *et al.*: 6). They argue, quite logically, that if the NC's prime objective is to bring about a change in teaching styles then the exams at the end of the programme must reflect that objective. Unfortunately the authors confuse this objective with the function of their report which is to examine the feasibility of testing through the target language. They do not set out to test *whether* target language testing is possible but to *prove* that it is. They recognise that the new comprehension exams, particularly at the lower end of the ability range, will have to contain many more multiple choice and true/false type tests. However, instead of arguing that these types of tests are an unfortunate consequence of wishing to create a more desirable backwash effect, the authors try to justify them with, for example, the following:

> no pupil in the current trials, or in a wide range of true/false tests with which the authors of this report have been associated, has ticked all the items of a task as true or false. Yet that would be the obvious response of a candidate with no idea and a determination to take the game of chance to its logical conclusion (Neather *et al.*: 13)

Clearly this would be a form of logic operating totally independent of human nature! Nevertheless, since the authors make a strong claim as to the validity of their tests it is upon these that we should judge them. Given the lack of space here I shall only concentrate on the reading tests which the authors claim are *less* problematic or even 'successful'. In other words, we will not examine the listening tests which the authors, in their conclusions, themselves describe as problematic. Pupils in the study were given a series of reading texts with questions and activities in L2. Rubrics were in L2. In order to ascertain whether L2 rubrics would invalidate the test (because pupils would not even be able to understand what the task was) they were also given L1 versions of the rubrics to refer to if they needed them. At the end of the tests, pupils were asked a number of questions among which were whether they had guessed any of the answers and whether they had used the L1 version of the rubrics. Readers interested in the issue of validity would do well to consult the original. However, the following give an idea of the findings:

Section 1, test 1. *Au restaurant* (text-only multiple choice). At least 20% of pupils found the L2 rubric 'difficult'. (N.B. respondents were not given a 'did not understand at all' category to choose); 45% claimed to have guessed some of the answers.

Section 2, test 2. *Béchamel Sauce* (picture to statement matching). As many as 88% guessed some of the answers; 29% used the L1 rubrics.

Section 2, test 4. *Plan de Caen* (visual to statement matching). At least 54% guessed some of the answers; 32% used the L1 rubrics.

Section 2, test 5. *Horoscope* (text to statement matching). At least 91% guessed some of the answers; 46% used the L1 rubrics.

Section 2, test 1A. *Tom Cruise* (true or false statements about a text). At least 75% guessed some of the answers; 21% used the L1 rubrics.

Section 2, test 1B. *Tom Cruise* (same text, matching data in text with statement). At least 53% guessed some of the answers. In this test the validity of real language comprehension is seriously undermined in another way. For example: *remarie* can easily be matched with *second marriage*; *New York* is only mentioned in the *1980* extract; This factor casts doubt on the purpose of five out of the seven questions as they appear to be testing (high level) candidates' ability to scan the text for words which match the questions.

Section 2, test 2. *Voyage dans le désert.* (L2 questions on a text). The authors, whilst claiming success[8] for this test, do not explain how it was marked. Yet it is perfectly possible to complete the test almost entirely by simply lifting text verbatim.

Neather *et al.* (1995: 50) conclude that 'many of the tests worked well' and that 'the clear conclusion from the evidence of both pupil performance and pupil comment is that this style of testing is perfectly feasible at GCSE'. From the point of view of test validity, I think we would have to conclude quite the opposite. This is unfortunate as the question of backwash effect has to be addressed. But the argument is a complex one. There is some evidence that tests have an impact on what a teacher chooses to do in the classroom and the amount of time s/he attributes to preparing for tests (Alderson & Wall, 1993). There is strong anecdotal evidence that teacher styles are affected by test types, indeed Table 1.1 gives (Tarclindy Teacher Interview Data) empirical evidence for this.

There is, however, little research on the backwash effect of test-types on learner proficiency, and this is urgently needed. If we do not have this evidence we can only speculate about the desirability of target language testing in bringing about increased L2 use however intuitive it may seem to be. Moreover, it could be envisaged that one backwash effect of such testing might be simply to increase the use of multiple choice, true/false and matching exercises in the classroom. This might have the effect of reducing what pupils actually say to numbers, letters, single words, etc. and work directly against the type of extended pupil use of TL that I am sure authors like Neather *et al.* would wish to

Table 1.1 Teachers' reactions to target language testing

Target language testing	Number
Doesn't show real comprehension; just copying; it's assessing different skills	9
GCSE exam makes it difficult for teachers to stay in L2	9
Limiting for the less able; intimidating	5˙
Misunderstanding rubric invalidates exercise	4
Limited number of ways of exploiting a text	3
Practicalities in classroom (e.g. can't leave set work when absent)	2
A good idea in principle	2
A bad idea in principle: not authentic; not natural	2
Impossible to negotiate meaning in written exam	2
Useful way to develop questioning skills	1

promote. Pupils interviewed in the Tarclindy project demonstrated anxieties about tests the procedures of which they might not understand. Teachers in the Tarclindy interviews, whilst claiming to recognise the undermining effect of comprehension papers in L1 on their classroom practice, were very anxious about validity, the effect on the less able and the practical implications. Teaching through the target language is made possible by virtue of the fact that the teacher knows the linguistic competence of individual learners and can modify the language input in response to lack of comprehension. Target language testing is not in a position to do this. Table 1 is a summary of teachers' reactions to target language testing in general.

The solution to the undesirable backwash effect of testing comprehension through L1 is not easily arrived at. It will certainly not be found, however, if we pretend that the problem of test validity simply isn't there. One of the underlying principles in this book will be that complex situations and multidimensional learners are best served by a variety of approaches and systems. Testing looks like being an area in which to apply this principle.

We can now see more clearly the framework of the NC and its fundamental tenets. We can summarise its design and implementation in the following way. The DfE, through SCAA, decides what is to be taught but emphasises *how* it is to be taught. SCAA broadly defines how that is to be assessed and ensures that assessment reflects how the foreign language is taught. OFSTED makes observations on the standards of teaching and learning in individual schools. It is not difficult to conclude that central government has a powerful hold on the methodology through which languages are to be taught in England.

We have looked in some detail at the scaffolding structure for the modern languages curriculum. It is now time to examine briefly how this was erected in schools.

Delivering the National Curriculum

Teachers have commented that the thing you most need to deliver the National Curriculum is a fleet of large lorries – a reference to the tonnes of documentation emanating from the agencies described above. In addition to a sense of humour and their own skills, teachers have been able to draw upon a programme of INSET which has helped them interpret, implement and deliver the NC in MFL. This has been provided mostly by Local Education Authorities, but also by Higher Education Institutions, the Association for Language Learning (ALL) the Centre for Information on Language Teaching (CILT) and the National Curriculum Council itself. The Tarclindy project surveyed the extent and the kind of provision which LEAs were able offer in the years 1991–94, that is immediately prior and just after the introduction of the NC. Did these advisers, usually ex-practitioners with a wealth of experience in working alongside teachers in their area, accept the NC's directives?

LEAs were asked which of a number of single issues related to teaching, learning and assessment they had concentrated on. These are shown in Table 1.2.

From Table 1.2 we can observe that by far the issue most preoccupying the minds of LEA advisers and, presumably, teachers was the new grading for assessment (i.e. grading of pupil achievement according to the Attainment Targets) being proposed by the National Curriculum. This is supported by a study carried out by Mellor and Trafford (1994). Experience of talking to teachers as well as the LEA projections for the future would suggest that this INSET issue is no longer salient and that the early importance placed on it was 'reacting to events' rather than one based on a reflection of true pedagogic need. One respondent described the prospect of an OFSTED visit and the New Orders as being items which Heads of Departments saw as 'urgent'! .

The least important issue is, somewhat surprisingly, choosing a new coursebook. It is surprising partly because hot on the heels of the

Table 1.2 Amount of INSET provision for single issues 1991–1994

Issue	A lot	Some	Little	None
Teacher use of TL	11	35	4	1
Pupil use of TL	5	29	12	4
Collaborative learning	5	19	19	3
Independent learning	6	25	16	3
Use of Information Technology	14	30	7	0
Low ability learners	9	26	11	0
Special Educational Needs	15	20	13	2
Choosing a new course(book)	2	9	28	8
Progression	3	28	11	1
Creativity	4	26	13	3
Assessment	23	23	4	0

publication of the NC has come a whole new arsenal of different coursebooks and materials, and partly because, given the extent of methodological discussion (not to say prescription) of the early documents, one would have expected a greater matching process of coursebook with intended pedagogy.

If we add together the scores for *lots* of provision with *some* provision (Figure 1.1) we find that teacher use of the Target Language and Assessment were the areas most covered by INSET programmes, closely followed by Information Technology. The last of these also seems to have recently lost some, although certainly not all, of its topicality. Collaborative Learning and Independent Learning do not figure very prominently, especially in Table 1.2, and pupil use of the TL lags some way behind the leaders. I shall be making some observations on this in the conclusion to the book.

LEAs were then asked what sort of approach they adopted in INSET sessions to the issue of teacher use of the target language. The following is, I hope, a balanced selection of responses:

(1) Encouraging and reminding them that the NC order is statutory and a reflection of good practice.
(2) Maximise it but with short blocks of English if required – clear markers for returning to FL.
(3) FL as normal medium – English as an exception. Use strategies to clarify and support understanding.
(4) Do not mix FL and L1 in same utterance or block of language.

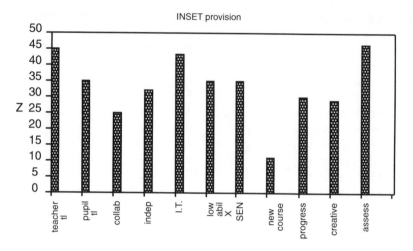

Figure 1.1

(5) Use mime, action and examples to support understanding.
(6) Start with a 'nice' class / start as you mean to go on with a new class of beginners.
(7) Use TL almost always but occasionally an explanation in mother tongue will facilitate an activity.
(8) Ensure that, through planning, there is constant use (of TL) by teachers within departments.
(9) Teaching some less able classes in KS4 sometimes needs English.
(10) How does TL teaching marry with teaching and learning styles and strategies? How does TL teaching accommodate input/intake for individual learners?
(11) Share experiences, accept differentiated progression, and don't pressurise teachers.
(12) Maximum use within realistic parameters.
(13) It should increasingly become the normal means of communication.
(14) Positive. Sustained. Convinced.
(15) To use the optimum possible.
(16) Aim at 95% plus but be pragmatic and realistic.
(17) As close to 100% as possible.
(18) Gradual development from Y 7 up.
(19) Unequivocal in principle but pragmatic in certain circumstances.

There are a number of themes in this advice which will be taken up in Chapters 3 and 4. However, one observation is worth making here and that is that whilst there are references to what is desirable and what is possible, not a single respondent expressed any pedagogical value in a teacher referring to the learner's own language apart from, possibly, the implied use of cognates in (iii). The learner's own language is clearly something that gets in the way of L2 learning.

The next question concerned the NC Area of Experience sub-topic *Classroom Language* and the nature of the advice that respondents gave to practitioners. Examples of possible approaches were given to respondents to consider: teach it as it comes up; plan it progressively in the schemes of work; start in year 7 with lots of phrases on the walls. It is perhaps a symptom of the complexity of this theme, which clearly is related to teacher use and pupil use of the TL, that it resulted in being more problematic to answer. Whereas the researchers intended the choices given to be, by and large, mutually exclusive, a number of respondents felt that all three were possible. By contrast, one respondent felt that it depended entirely on the classroom context: 'The question is too fundamental – too many assumptions in play. My advice depends on who you are, where you teach, what materials you have and what your desired outcomes may be.'

Another commented that it was still the most difficult to achieve, but 'We need to work towards the use of TL as the major mode of classroom communication. Floating phrase-cards[9] don't help much.'

For a large majority, however, planning classroom language progressively was by far the most recommended approach and starting with a sizeable chunk in year 7. The reader will immediately foresee where the problems might lay here and why some respondents were struggling with the issue. If it is planned progressively then what do you do if it comes up earlier and out of sequence? Do you revert to L1 or do you teach it on the spot, which is *not* planned and progressive? One respondent suggested a partial solution: 'teach an introductory package very early on, build on this as needed – involve pupils in expressing the language they need.'

We shall examine the issue of classroom language from the teacher and learner perspective in Chapter 3.

It is clear from the above that the majority of LEA advisers added their weight to the pedagogical thrust of the framework, but that they were realistic about the likelihood of achieving the 'total immersion' environment implied in the stronger of the NC directives on the issue of target language. The difference between idealism and realism is an important contributor to the discussion in Chapter 3.

We now have the curriculum edifice for England in place. We have examined its conception, its design, its fundamental tenets, the way it is to be assessed and the help teachers have had in its implementation. Are language curricula similar in other European countries?

National Curricula in Europe

France

The French curriculum for Modern Languages (CNDP, 1993) in the Classes de Collèges (years 7, 8, 9, 10) is provided in language specific documents. The MFL curriculum is conceived in terms of *Horaires* – curriculum time allocated; *Objectifs* – Objectives; *Programmes* – Content; *Instructions* and *Méthodes et Démarches Pédagogiques* – Guidelines for Teachers. Both the objectives and the content (and to some extent the guidelines) necessitate this language specificity. In the *Objectifs* of the English document, for example, the importance of English as an international language is stressed as well as a reminder that British English is the language variety most commonly taught in French schools. Other objectives refer to the practical nature of the language to be acquired, the emphaisis on Anglophone culture, the reflections that L2 learning bring on the learner's L1 and vice versa, and some criteria for language outcomes by the end of year 10: communication in simple situations; a base for further study at the lycée (upper school) and increased autonomy of language use.

The *Programme*, which is extensively documented in English (L2), is defined entirely in terms of functions, lexis and grammatical structures. It is, however, stressed that it is a content which serves the teacher as a 'sample' of the totality of language available (CNDP, 1993: 14). It is, on the other hand, a defined content in that it defines the maximum productive language that is to be expected of the learners.

The *Instructions* are brief, little over one page. The *Méthodes et Démarches Pédagogiques* (which are specific to year 7 only) more extensive, some four pages. Both start from the basic premise that:

> the teacher alone is responsible for the choice, the organisation and the conduct of the classroom activities taking into account the short and long term objectives defined by him, and according to what he knows or discovers about the needs and potential of the pupils. (CNDP, 1993: 13)

No difference in status is apparent between the *Instructions and the Méthodes/Démarches*. Furthermore, it is stressed that these are guidelines. They are not designed to be regarded as a body of methodological doctrine conceived in the abstract, but a 'collection of recommendations inspired by the reality currently to be found in the classroom. Their status, consequently, is transitory' (CNDP, 1993: 21). The guidelines then refer to the importance of:

- language resources other than the teacher;
- offering a variety of activities;
- creating a variety of learning groups;
- progression;
- the text as a language source;
- homework;
- differentiation;
- assessment.

Particularly for year 7 it signals:

- the usefulness of cognates;
- solving the mixed ability problem through differentiated activities;
- the importance of developing learner strategies.

Nowhere in the document is there a reference to the exclusion or inclusion of L1 other than that the learner must be 'led gradually towards distancing himself/herself from the mother tongue' (CNDP, 1993: 11). Nowhere in the document is there a list or a reference to specific language activities which are to have a direct causal link with outcomes, nor to the types of microskills described in POS Part 1 of the NC in England. The reader may be surprised at this lack of Gallic prescriptivism given the continued existence of traditional educational stereotypes. Does the prescriptivism therefore reside elsewhere? Another source of official documentation is the *Bulletin Officiel*. Here too the recommendations and amplifications stay well clear of prescriptivism in the realm of methodology or approach. Here too the emphasis is on pupil outcomes, on general orientations, on classroom activities 'likely to bring about', on distinctions between formal and informal language. Even in the documentation relating to the experimental introduction of primary modern languages (BOEN, 1991, Nos. 9 et 10: 18) where one might expect tangible methodological implications, the direct references are scarce. The closest is probably a recommendation for a shift away from text as source, placing the emphasis more on 'the execution of movement, gesture and manipulation, tasks where language appears to be merely an extension of the activity itself'. Since there is no externally set exam before the Baccalauréat, the backwash effect is not likely to be very powerful. In any case, at higher levels (year 11 upwards), the skills involved in translation are positively encouraged (BOEN, 1994, No 8: 170).

Is the structure and nature of official French educational agencies likely to contribute to a methodological prescriptivism? Education in France is divided into regional Académies charged with carrying out the policies of central government. Is the recteur d'Académie (a sort of Chief Education Officer for the area) able to dispense instructions or more stringent guidelines about approach or method? The answer again is 'No'. Are the Inspecteurs d'Académie in a position to do so? The answer here is: only partly. Firstly, reports of lessons observed go only to the teacher concerned and the Chef d'Etablissement (head-teacher). Secondly I have not, despite the help of French colleagues, been able to trace any official guidelines on what is good classroom practice (for example of the OFSTED type). No doubt, I am told, they exist in the minds of the inspectorate and consequently they may well be variable and form the basis of discussions if not heated debate at inspectorate meetings. What competencies exist refer more to professional competencies of the teacher (preparation, punctuality, relationship with pupils, own L2 competence) rather than method. Influence in France in terms of classroom practice is exerted via the MAFPEN (Mission Académique à la Formation des Personnels de l'Education Nationale) and IUFM (Institut Universitaire pour la Formation des Maîtres). Although these are government dependent organisations, their services are by invitation.

Italy

A no more prescriptive documentation can be found in sources emanating from the Italian ministry (Ministero Della Pubblica Istruzione, 1979). The objectives and purposes of foreign language learning for the Scuola Media (years 7, 8 and 9) are articulated in five short paragraphs. The emphasis is on communicating and on the role that FL learning plays in developing an understanding of the 'socio-cultural reality' of the target country and in particular within the context of Italy's membership of the European Community.

The guidelines on methodology (Ministero Della Pubblica Istruzione, 1979: 38) are certainly more specific than is the case in France. The document proposes that the teacher will want to, 'from the outset, through the constant use of the foreign language, both his/hers and that of the pupils', develop the fundamental skills of listening, speaking, reading and writing. Examples are given of classroom activities which use the language communicatively: giving and understanding information; describing places and people; understanding and writing letters. How these activities are to be introduced, conducted, sequenced is not stated, but in the guidance for year 7, teachers are encouraged to offer pupils roles in active dialogues in situations which the pupil is most likely to encounter and without having recourse to translation. One assumes, given this statement, that comprehension is to be demonstrated in L2. The whole of these guidelines take up one page of A4.

The reality is that Italian teachers do not regard the documentation as anything but general guidelines.[10] In fact, Italian education is characterised by an almost total absence of constraints at the methodological level (Adelman & Macaro, 1995). The Ministry of Education's policy is interpreted and implemented at the local level by the 'provveditore'. This, as the title suggests, is a post concerned more with the provision of education than reflections on good practice. Exams at the end of the compulsory age of education (currently 14), exert little influence on methodology given that they are based on so little documentation. The inspectorate appears to function more at the level of troubleshooter than disseminator of pedagogical guidance and information. The single most discernible influence in determining teaching styles is the selection of the textbook or coursebook by groups of languages colleagues within a school (there is no head of department). As this has to be achieved with the consent of parents (who are paying for it) the criteria for its selection or rejection may include non-pedagogical considerations. Since formal pre-service training does not exist and in-service training is optional, teachers turn to local autonomous organisations for new ideas and approaches where good practitioners often emerge by reputation.

Germany

By contrast, the syllabus for teaching English in Schleswig-Holstein (Kultusminister, 1986),[11] offers much more detailed recommendations. Since secondary schools in Germany are differentiated according to general ability, it is not surprising that recommendations on use of L2 by the teacher should also be differentiated by ability. Thus, in the Gymnasium (grammar school – high ability), L1 should only be used on those rare occasions where the learners' knowledge would require excessive L2 use to make an explanation comprehensible. L2 is permitted in grammatical explanations where contrasts between the two languages are being highlighted. L1 is not permitted on the grounds that it saves time. Competency in authentic comprehension situations is only possible if pupils are systematically exposed to constant L2 use. If the L1 has to be used when mime and contextual clues have failed to put across the message, a gloss should be given in L2. In slight contrast the recommendations for the Hauptshule (secondary modern – lower ability), suggest that the L1 can be used when putting across the meaning of abstract words or expressions of for the explanation of grammar. Even in this school, however, frequent language switching is to be avoided and translation should only be used as a strategy in situations where interpreting would be justified. Similarly, in the more technology oriented Realschule, the L1 is permitted but only when the L2 would be beyond the language capabilities of the learners or for grammatical explanations.

To what extent these recommendations are statutory or are enforced by an inspection system is not obvious from an examination of the documentation alone. Chambers, G. (1992: 66) reports on informal discussions with language teachers and teacher trainers in Germany. They have, he claims, a 'common sense approach – aufgeklärte Einsprachigkeit' to use of L2.

By expanding our perspective of national curricula we can now assert with a fair measure of confidence that the NC in England is extremely prescriptive in terms of the methodological principles it advocates and enforces and in terms of the actual classroom activities that it wishes to see occurring. But when does an approach become a method and within that method what flexibility or choice of activity remains?

Approaches and Methods

What distinguishes an approach from a method? A useful framework is the one proposed by Richards and Rogers (1986) where an *approach* is qualified by *design* and *procedure* in order for it to become a *method*. An approach is a set of axioms deriving from theories of language and theories of language learning. An approach may not necessarily lead to a given method. An approach does not specify procedure. Thus two teachers might say 'Our *approach* is based on the belief that the functional *theory of language* is most likely to be true. It is also based on the *theory of language learning* that suggests you have to have natural processes and conditions in order to learn.' The two teachers may, however, perfectly logically, offer a very different menu of activities in the classroom. Richards and Rogers propose that *design* includes the following: objectives; language content; tasks and activities; the roles of learners and teachers; the role of materials. They propose that *procedure* includes techniques, practices and behaviours (Richards and Rogers, 1986: 26).

The NC is clearly more of a method than an approach for two reasons: (1) It defines at an explicit level the design requirements above, skimping only on the language content. Many of the techniques, practices and behaviours expected of teachers are implicit and often explicit in the POS and the ATs. (2) When (as I shall argue in subsequent chapters) the characteristics of good practice (which in their totality might suggest a flexible eclecticism) conflict, they are immediately prioritised by the directive on the virtual exclusion of the mother tongue. Yet, as Richards (1984) argues, proponents of methods must address the issue of accountability and very few method developers or their supporters have made any attempt to gather evidence which might support their claims.

This chapter has tried to demonstrate the processes by which a national methodology can be officially put into place, promoted and monitored. Are nation states justified in moving towards a national methodology? Particularly, are European countries, such as England, sufficiently homogenous as to be able to identify national needs which can be met with national solutions through a designated pedagogy? Indeed, what justification can there be for subscribing to international methodologies, importing pedagogy and didactic principles? There is an increasing body of literature (Debyser, 1989; Phillipson, 1992) which is now warning educators of the dangers and hidden agendas of exporting pedagogy to the Third World. An international pedagogy in L2 teaching (for example TEFL) brings with it, they argue, the export of a dominant national economy and culture. Ideas do not float around in the international atmosphere, they emanate from people and institutions. Grafting a national approach on the plant of an international pedagogy with its roots in this historical process may lead to fruit which bears no resemblance to the indigenous strain . What are the implications, therefore, of adopting such a pedagogy for learners in England struggling to come to terms with the concept of dual or even multiple identities (Adelman and Macaro, 1995)? Byram (1992: 12) reminds us that tolerance and insight into the foreign culture will not emerge automatically as a consequence of concentrating on communicative skills. Hawkins (1987) argues strongly for a UK specific language curriculum, one which would include an awareness of language as well as language learning, an emphasis on the learning of several languages rather than a monolithic single language. Bauckam (1995: 4) argues for a theoretical framework for FL teaching which will locate it in a 'broader understanding of language education'. A number of respondents in the Tarclindy project refer to the isolation and marginalisation of foreign language learning from the rest of the school curriculum if too much emphasis is placed on skills which are foreign language learning specific. We will attempt to find answers to some of these questions in later chapters.

The above considerations would tend to pertain to learners in English schools – the consumers in the current political jargon. What of the teachers – the providers? Is the national methodology aimed at bringing about a change in the Modern Languages teaching profession? To judge from the tone and content of the documentation we have moved a long way from Wilga Rivers' contention that:

> truly successful teachers are highly idiosyncratic. From the plethora of information and recommendations, they select. They take from the new what suits their own personality and their teaching style and what is appropriate for the personalities and aspirations of their students, thus forming their own approach. (Rivers, 1983)

What are the explanations for this methodological prescriptivism in the English NC? One possible explanation is the self-congratulatory one, which might go as follows. We have probably one of the most extensively trained teaching forces in Europe, a comprehensive system of in-service training, a comparatively high output in pedagogical and practitioner journals. We are therefore ahead of the rest along the road of pedagogical development. We have a high level of consensus of what good practice is and we can, as a consequence, accommodate a rigid framework seeing that it is what we do and like doing anyway. Another explanation is the self-castigatory one. This says that traditionally languages have been taught badly in the UK. This has been both a consequence and a cause of the lack of motivation amongst our language learners. The changes brought about by the GCSE have made some difference, but the courses and tests were badly flawed methodologically and conceptually. They have brought about a plethora of irreconcilable teaching styles. We therefore deserve to have a methodology imposed on us and this has to be achieved by the short sharp shock of directives such as the 'virtually all'. We need to be dragged screaming into the international mainstream. There may be other explanations which are more to do with political forces wishing to impose constraints on a profession having recently experienced a long period of industrial action, or explanations more to do with the composition of the group of NC designers, the brief they were given and the time they were allocated for the completion of their task. These latter explanations I will leave the interested reader to pursue and reflect upon elsewhere. The next chapter, therefore, will examine interpretations of the communicative model in order to ascertain what deficiencies a national methodology might be trying to address.

Notes

1. Readers outside the UK may not know that Scotland has its own education system. As all my teaching experience as well as the research project relates to English schools and, as there are important differences between the English and Welsh documentation for the National Curriculum, Welsh colleagues will forgive me if I do not constantly make reference to both countries.
2. As this is a quote from a particular school's report, readers will understand why I do not give the complete reference.
3. National Foundation for Educational Research (NFER). The Consultation Report states, however, that 'the conclusions drawn and the advice and recommendations presented to the Secretary of State for Education and Science ... are those of the National Curriculum Council NCC, May 1991: 9).
4. Other characteristics worth noting are: giving learners an insight into their own and the foreign culture; learners should read extensively for information and pleasure; assessment is integrated with teaching and learning.
5. However, it has recently been attacked (Harris, 1995) on a number of other topics, notably progression and differentiation.
6. These have now been reduced to eight level descriptors.
7. General Certificate of Secondary Education – currently uses essentially L1 questions on L2 text, except in part of oral test where examiner's questions are in L2. All rubric, instruction and scene setting is in L1.
8. Neather *et al.* (1995), in their analysis, often confuse success in pupils' achievement in the tests with success of the test in terms of validity.
9. Many classrooms in England have developed the use of dangling classroom language phrases from the ceiling so that pupils can refer to them.
10. For a more detailed account of the views of Italian teachers of English on use of the target language see Macaro, 1995. See also Chapter 3.
11. The German *Länder* have virtual autonomy in educational matters and I have no evidence as to whether these recommendations are replicated throughout Germany.

2 Interpretations of Communicative Language Teaching

In the last chapter I described in considerable detail how a fairly rigid methodological framework, based around the tenet of L2 exclusivity, has been established in England for teaching foreign languages in secondary schools. Readers from other countries are invited to make comparisons with their own curricula. We now need to ask what might motivate the design of such a framework. In order to answer that question we shall examine the NC against the background of the development of an international approach to language teaching – the communicative approach. In so doing we will be in a better position to understand the interaction of target language use, collaborative learning and autonomy.

There are two historical lines of development leading to the phenomenon which over the past 20 years has come to be known as communicative language teaching (CLT). They are distinct in that they have their tap roots in different theoretical cultures. The methods and techniques that they have spawned, however, tend to resemble one another sufficiently for them to be generally classified under the term 'modern teaching methods'.

The first historical development leading to CLT has an affinity with theories and hypotheses about *language learning*. It can be traced back to the Direct Method which was the nineteenth century's break with the grammar-translation tradition. This tradition had been based on a virtually unchallenged belief[1] that a modern language could and should be taught in the same way as Latin and Greek and for the same purposes. It did this in two ways. The first was by focusing on words and bits of words in L2 so that the rules of the language could be learnt and compared and contrasted with the rules, words and bits of words in L1. The learner was then able to carry out translation exercises into L2. The second was to focus, once sufficient mastery of L2 had been achieved, on classical texts in L2 and translate chunks of these into L1.

The learner's two major outcomes were, supposedly, the development of logical thought and an understanding of the classics. In fact it could be argued that this wasn't language teaching at all but a quite different subject.

By contrast, the Direct Method's fundamental tenet was that learners acquire L2 in the same way as they acquire L1. Even in a formal setting such as a classroom, therefore, a second language could be learnt *through* the target language, without comparing and contrasting it with the learner's L1. This is what can be called the *intralinguistic* as opposed to the *interlinguistic* hypothesis[2] of language learning. Although L2 learning was claimed to be like L1 learning, the direct method retained features which pertained to the *forms* of the language rather than *natural acquisition*. Thus while guiding principles might include: make a direct link between the object or action referred to and the new word; allow only the L2 to be spoken; delay writing, the method would also advocate principles such as: require that all answers be in the form of complete sentences. In Direct Method classrooms, moreover, true information giving was subordinated to continuous rapid-fire exchanges between teacher and learner (Richardson, 1983: 39). Realising that L2 learning differed from L1 learning in one vital aspect, the amount of time available to the L2 learner, quantity of exposure was made up for by intensity of exposure. Nevertheless, grammar was to be learnt inductively from use of the language itself. The Direct Method, as well as undergoing a variety of reactions and attempts at syntheses within itself (Compromise Method – the compromise being the removal of the shibboleth of L2 exclusivity), gave rise in the twentieth century to a number of marketed courses and internationally recognised techniques: Berlitz, Suggestopaedia, The Natural Approach, Total Physical Response, the Silent Way (Skinner, 1985).

The second development leading to CLT has more affinity with theories about *language*, both philosophical and linguistic. Austin's now famous *How to Do Things with Words* (1962), demonstrated just that. Language is not merely a series of statements which record or impart information, but a tool that the user operates in order to persuade, cajole or even mystify. Searle (1969) took up the baton with his hypothesis that any theory of language has to be inextricably linked to a theory of action. If when we speak we abide by rules, we cannot study the rules of language without also studying the rules of the behaviour in which that language is being used. This rapprochement gave rise to the notion of *Speech Acts*. Halliday's research (1973) into child language development indicated that at a basic level, language could be classified in terms of seven functions, categories of speech acts each with its subset of structural exponents – bits of language which fitted the aims of that category. Hymes (1972) gave the development even more impetus by observing that language use in a particular language community could not operate outside that community's social norms. These social norms included the rules of *discourse*. For speakers to have real competence in a language they would have to acquire more than the vocabulary and grammatical rules of that language. Communicative competence thus became the fundamental objective of communicative language teaching. Rationalisation of how communicative competence could be achieved through a syllabus was proposed by Wilkins (1976). This development brought about a situation where, in the early stages at least, language learners could operate at a level where a functional model of linguistic structure could serve them as a means of producing speech that put across meaning. This line of development however, whilst accounting for how an L2 learner might go about classifying language and operating within that classification, does not account for how the learner takes in or acquires that language in the first place.

Krashen's acquisition hypothesis (1981 and 1987) upset the complacent applecart that might have developed out of the vagueness of the single goal of communicative competence. For Krashen the goal could not be achieved other than by a number of specific means. If the philosophical and socio-linguistic line of thought might have led practitioners to incorporate into their lessons reflection about language in context, Krashen was to remind them sharply of the hypothesis that language is only truly learnt *through* the language. If communicative competence might have led teachers to attempt to achieve outcomes solely through the completion of a content syllabus, Krashen was to insist that content could not be acquired without process.

There are five elements to Krashen's proposal and it is useful to remind ourselves of them. (1) There is a fundamental dichotomy between *acquiring* a language naturally, through sub-conscious absorption and assimilation and *learning* a language through the formal study of its rules. Only the former will bring about true competence. The two approaches cannot interrelate or overlap for the purposes of language production. (2) There is a *natural order* of acquiring the structural features of a language. Some features are acquired early, some later. It doesn't matter which L1 you have even though there may be similarities between the L1 order and the L2 order. L1 is not the starting point. The L2 is. It is therefore fruitless for teachers to 're-order' through a structural syllabus these grammatical features. (3) The L2 student can only acquire language if s/he is exposed to a steady stream of comprehensible language (*comprehensible input*) from the teacher. The (effective?) teacher is the best person to do so, better even than native speakers outside the classroom because, in most cases, only s/he can moderate the input to make it comprehensible. It doesn't have to be *finely tuned* input (acquired language + 1 not-yet-acquired element), it can be approximate, *roughly tuned* to what the teacher knows the student can understand. Students need not understand everything. The important thing is to provide an input rich environment. (4) Whilst L2 utterances are only initiated through the acquired system, the learned rules can act as a checking device, *a monitor*, on whether the utterance is correct or incorrect. But the monitor system is limited in two ways: in real time dialogue there is sufficient time for the speaker to monitor *only the most simple rules*; the monitor system cannot initiate a communicative utterance. (5) The processes of input and acquisition can only come about in the appropriate conditions: little or no hostility to language learning; no hostility to the target language or culture, through limited use of the 'monitor'. In other words, high levels of motivation and low levels of anxiety coupled to an unwavering belief in the acquisition process. This Krashen calls lowering the *affective filter*.

Clearly Krashen's proposals on the primacy of L2, together with their practical application documented in Krashen and Terrell (1988), would indicate an exclusion of L1 use in the classroom (at least on the part of the teacher) as well as an inevitable teacher-centred approach.[3] The primacy of L2 teacher one-way input has been disputed for example by Long (1983b: 214 quoted in Allwright and Bailey: 121) and Swain (1985), such that input without interaction is generally not accepted as being sufficient to lead to language acquisition.

We have seen that the goal of communicative competence can be traced back through two lines of development. If we accept and absorb both these lines, therefore, the notion of communicative competence would seem to entail both implicit learning and explicit understanding. For example, an L1 speaker of English needs to know both *how* to use and the functional implication of using *Lei* or *Voi* instead of *Tu* in formal situations in Italy. In accepting the eclecticism of CLT we are also taking on board the inherent tension between theories of language and theories of language learning. It is this tension which gives CLT both its strength and weakness. The tension has given rise to pendulum swings in methodology. I would argue that these pendulum swings are a natural and healthy result of the tension. They are an inevitable result of the dual lines of development. We should not therefore be cynical about the fact that the pendulum might swing (in fact we should worry if it didn't) but we should be wary of huge swings. Let us explore this a little further.

CLT is inevitably different in range and status from any other method or approach. It is an international phenomenon incorporating learning contexts as different as adult Spanish speakers learning English in California and 13-year-old Italian speakers learning French in Calabria. As Richards and Rogers point out (1986: 66) there is no single text or authority on it nor any single model that is universally accepted as authoritative. Consequently coursebooks being used in the UK and claiming to incorporate a communicative approach can span from the quasi-structural Tricolore (1978) to Auto (1992) with its emphasis on developing learner autonomy. Both, however, do not have exclusion of L1 as their primary strategy. Textbooks aimed at EFL1, on the other hand, have perforce to exclude any L1 as they are designed to be used in any language learning context. It is noticeable that EFL2 learning contexts have recently been developing more country-specific teaching materials. In these materials the inclusion of the L1 is a controversial issue.

CLT, through its different contexts and through its materials, displays an enormous eclecticism. It is the same eclecticism which produces, with some justification, the following axiom:

As a general rule in the early stages:
The class should **say** only what they have **heard**
The class should **read** only what they have **said**
The class should **write** only what they have **read**. (Smalley and Morris 1992: 17)

As an axiom, it is a clear offspring of the Direct Method. Indeed, it can be found in Alexander's *New Concept English*, (1974), and yet it does not sit uncomfortably in Smalley and Morris's book for the 1990s and claiming to take into account the two major influences of GCSE and the National Curriculum. The resolution of the eclecticism of CLT comes through the notion of communicative competence.

Facilitating Communicative Competence

Most practitioners who have espoused CLT would tend to have the following beliefs about what facilitates the goal of communicative competence:

(1) An emphasis on speaking and listening rather than on reading and writing.

(2) An emphasis on communicating new information rather than 'already known' information.

(3) An emphasis on active involvement rather than passive learning.
(4) An emphasis on meaningful bits of language rather than well formed sentences, individual words or bits of words.

It would be perfectly possible for a practitioner to argue that the above four principles about the route to communicative competence can be achieved with very little teacher use of L2, relying entirely on, for example, taped and written materials in the foreign language. This would be to deny the importance of a number of processes which have traditionally been seen as synonymous with (modern) methods of language learning in classrooms. Teacher absence, on the other hand, is the very basis of any 'teach yourself' course and these all imply the goal of communicative competence. Conversely it would be perfectly possible for a practitioner to argue that the four beliefs about communicative competence can be achieved by excluding the L1 from the classroom, ignoring all activities which are about the language, concentrating instead on a continuous exchange of information between teacher-learner and then, perhaps, learner-learner.

What gives CLT its strength is the inbuilt flexibility which allows teachers to select that which is most appropriate for the needs of their learners. Its weakness lies in that its very eclecticism is highly dependent on the teacher's integrity and his/her competence, as a reflective practitioner, to deal with its inherent tensions. What makes a practitioner 'reflective' is the willingness and the time to draw on a number of sources in order to make decisions about a classroom strategy or technique rather than on a single source or a subjective reaction to a classroom event. These sources should include relevant studies and their resulting theories, observation of other practitioners and discussions with them, consideration of pedagogic factors at the local level (school, social or ethnic background of the learners) and the on-going evaluation of their own practice. Richards and Lockhart (1994) identify three stages in the teaching process at which decisions have to be taken in a reflective practitioner model: *Planning, Interactive* and *Evaluative*. Given that the evaluative stage alone requires the teacher to ask himself/herself at least 13 questions on how the lesson went, it is not difficult to see the time constraints working against a constant, reflective and principled interpretation of CLT! Figure 2.1 represents the tensions inherent in CLT.

There is very little empirical evidence which can illuminate how teachers bring about (or claim to bring about) communicative competence in their learners. In the FL domain, Mitchell (1988) and Peck (1988) provide some insights but both are set in a period of methodological

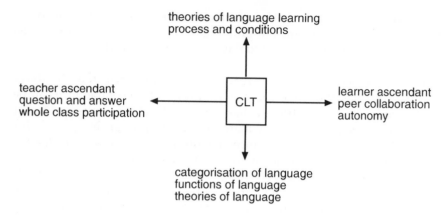

Figure 2.1 Tensions in CLT represented graphically

transition. We do not know what decisions and interpretations teachers make of CLT which are directly linked to bringing about communicative competence. We have observational evidence of teacher classroom behaviour but we do not know why a teacher has chosen to carry out an activity rather than another. As Breen (1991) points out, whilst one teacher will attach a particular set of beliefs and values to an instance of classroom behaviour, another teacher is likely to apply a different set. Secondly, descriptions that we have (for example DES, 1990b) are merely snapshots in a teaching programme or scheme of work. We are not aware of the totality of activities within that teacher's repertoire – does that sort of thing go on all the time or is it counterbalanced by very different activities with a different pedagogical emphasis? Thirdly, we do not know whether the lessons described led to communicative competence *because* of the very activities depicted or because of other factors. Research into second language acquisition and second language pedagogy is nowhere near the stage of being able to link a particular input or activity and increased competence.

If we examine the issue of teacher use of L2 within the international interpretation of CLT we are presented, in fact, with a continuum. At one end is a virtual *bain de langue* or brief total immersion in the target language. At the other we can find examples of teachers appearing to develop learner L2 competence almost entirely through teacher use of L1, the absence of teacher L2 input being compensated by widespread use of tape recorded materials. Within that continuum there are innumerable clutches of activities and variations based on a pick and mix strategy, which amount to a teacher's classroom practice. In

England this pick and mix approach was further influenced by at least three specific developments:

(1) The Technical and Vocational Educational Initiative (TVEI). This introduced into the language teaching vocabulary concepts such as *active learning, process, vocational* and *flexible learning*. Active learning in modern languages was based on the notion that if we wanted learners to do things with words, then they should, wherever possible, be actively engaged in a task which was for a purpose and involved some aspect of problem solving. Thus, if pupils carried out a survey of how many people in their family smoked, this would not stop at the question and answer stage but the data would be collated and represented in some form of pie chart or graph. Flexible learning encouraged the teaching of those skills and processes most likely to be sought by employers of the 1980 and 1990s. It provided a noticeable and welcome boost in making language learning relevant to the world of work, not least because it provided money for INSET training and computer hardware in schools.

(2) The General Certificate of Secondary Education (GCSE). We have already seen in Chapter 1 that the GCSE required candidates to demonstrate comprehension in L1. It also departed, from previous examinations in that it placed enormous importance on authenticity of materials and setting, emphasised communication rather than accuracy and tested discrete skills. Its *backwash effect* on teacher behaviour in the classroom has been considerable.

(3) The Graded Objectives movement (GOML) aimed to take into account the changing nature of the language learning population in the UK in the late 1970s, something which traditional examinations were failing to do (Page & Hewitt, 1987: 1). What characterised GOML was the emphasis on a content syllabus designed in building blocks of language competence. However, language competence was seen, particularly in the early designs, more in terms of horizontal progression across topic areas than in terms of skills development. It was not until the mid 1980s that the 'rising treads of performance' (Hope, 1987: 43) could be discernible. What also characterised GOML syllabuses was that they were designed at the local level by enthusiastic teachers with support from the LEAs. Page and Hewitt report that in 1987, 81 different working-groups of teachers were in existence. Hence changes in methodology, approach and teacher attitudes were brought about through the production of 'home grown' syllabuses and their accompanying materials.

It is not difficult to see why the influence of these three developments (less focus on the teacher, authentic materials and a concern with content) combined with the already described inherent tensions in CLT should undermine the primacy previously bestowed on the teacher as the main source of L2 input.

If these were the influences on the interpretations of CLT in England, are there any guiding principles in the selection of classroom activities that we could propose? In order to do this we need to return to the notion of *communicative competence* as the goal for language learners. In other words, interpretations of CLT can be as varied as the educational contexts in which they are being conceived but they must lead to communicative competence in the learner. Anything else is merely a coping strategy in response to the individual nature of the educational context itself. We might therefore represent the variety of interpretations of CLT by the concept web in Figure 2.2 with the pivotal elements needed for communicative competence at the centre.

Presenting the quasi-totality of themes or activities in this way helps to show how CLT was interpreted internationally. All activities offered to learners in the classroom must contribute to:

(a) developing an internalised rule system of the L2;
(b) the acquisition of vocabulary and idiom;
(c) an awareness of language as a socio-cultural construct;
(d) being able to use language in *real* discourse.

In England, prior to 1992, no one theme or activity was more important than another although, naturally, individual teachers or language departments developed their own hierarchies. Thus teachers, because they felt confident that pupils could sustain 50 minutes of total immersion, might highlight:

- learning through the target language;
- emphasis on oral;
- role play;
- intention to mean;
- pair work.

Teachers who felt their classes would respond with maturity to less teacher-led activities might highlight:

- flexible learning; autonomy;
- collaborative learning;
- carousel of activities;
- learner choice;

- CALL (computer assisted language learning).

With more able or with older learners teachers might highlight:

- problem solving;
- dealing with the unexpected;
- simulations.

Teachers who perhaps had demotivated learners might wish to highlight:

- games;
- authentic materials;

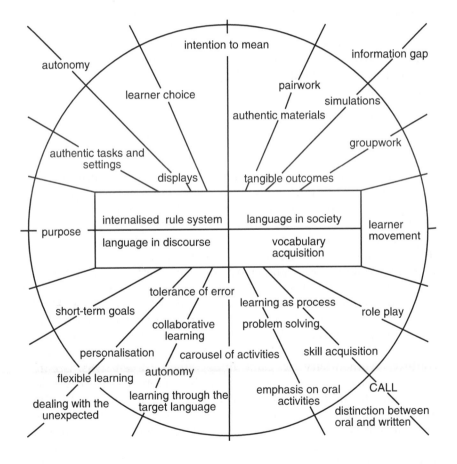

Figure 2.2

- purpose;
- tangible outcomes;
- displays;
- short-term goals.

That is not to say that other themes and elements would be completely neglected, but some would certainly feature more in one communicative classroom than another. For communicative competence to be achieved by learners, however, the four pivotal concepts at the heart of the web (Figure 2.2) would have to be addressed by teachers *in sufficient measure*. A diet of activities which in no respect helped to develop an internalised rule system of the L2 (perhaps for fear of demotivation) would not be leading the learner towards communicative competence.

Another aspect of the interpretation of CLT was the sequencing of activities. Apart from in those classrooms where a learner-centred approach was embarked on in a big way, the sequencing of activities would very likely be:

(a) presentation of new language;
(b) practise of new language in controlled circumstances;
(c) use of language in more communicative tasks.

The first two of these would have much closer ties with a direct method or even an audio-lingual method than any notion of *intention to mean*. Thus, the belief that a communicative classroom (at least in the FL secondary setting) is communicative all the time is a fallacy.

Whether one country's varied interpretation of CLT, and particularly the move away from teacher as the only source of L2 input, brought about increased language competence nationally is impossible to say. Although the number of pupils achieving at GCSE equivalent grades to the former O level exam increased, critics would say that the examination was easier and anyway the tests, particularly those involving productive skills, were not assessing true language competence – an ability to construct creatively language in a variety of contexts. Authenticity too came under attack (Breen, 1985; Grenfell, 1991; Woods & Neather, 1994). What is undeniable is that it did contribute to an increased motivation among learners with much greater numbers opting to continue with learning a foreign language in years 10 and 11 in schools where they still had the option of dropping the subject. A quick scan of the articles contained in practitioner language journals (*Modern Languages, Journal of Language Learning*) shows an evident concern with strategies that worked to improve motivation and pupil attitudes to language learning. It would be more than merely anecdotal to say that teachers in England and Wales felt a lot better about the job they were doing. Confidence about the future of language teaching in the late 1980s was relatively high and government agencies had moved a long way along the road from complacency to a conviction (in the words of Phillips, 1988) that languages were important. But was that confidence no more than the result of a better motivated set of learners? I have argued that motivation alone cannot bring about the goal of communicative competence? We have explored ways by which the reflective practitioner can distinguish between activities which increase motivation and activities which more directly bring about learning. We now need to ask whether, at a theoretical level, increased motivation entails increased learning.

Motivation

We have examined, in Chapter 1, the National Curriculum's intended purposes of learning a foreign language. What are young learners' beliefs of why a foreign language is important as informed by the Tarclindy data? What motivates them to learn French, for example, and to what extent do teachers' interpretations of CLT reflect those motivational forces. Table 2.1 demonstrates fairly conclusively that learners' goals are *instrumental* rather than *integrative* (using the Gardner & Lambert, 1972 terminology). That is, they view the learning of French much more as a tool to further their own goals rather than as a means of satisfying a genuine interest in the target language community or the target language culture. Pupils asserted that it is important to learn French so you can speak it if you go to France on holiday. Their accompanying comments suggest that this was so they could buy things and find accommodation rather than to interact with French people at a social level.

For the learners, at least, there is a hierarchy in the purposes of learning a foreign language. As I argue elsewhere in this book, one of the likely consequences of exclusive use of L2 by teacher and pupils is its contribution to the dominance of instrumental goals over integrative ones. Chambers (1994) reports similar findings in a study involving pupils learning German in a large rural comprehensive. Pupils in year 9 (first year of German) were much more instrumental in their outlook. The results, however, were almost reversed by year 12 (17-year-olds), when learners were much keener to learn about the target language community and enjoy its lifestyle. Chambers speculates that this is because of the emphasis in year 9 on language learning in a conflated

Table 2.1 Percentages of responses of year 8 pupils

It's important to learn French ...	Yes	No	Not sure
So you can speak it if you go there on holiday	80.8	7.0	10.0
So you can get a better job in future	59.0	16.6	22.1
Because you want to get to know French people	24.7	45.4	25.8
Because learning a language improves your brain	28.0	33.9	34.3

N = 271

course rather than giving pupils cultural insights. But cultural insights are not prioritised in the NC, neither at its conception, its implementation, or its delivery. Interestingly, and by contrast to the NC in England, the French National Programme for the learning of English unambiguously places the learning of this language in a context of preparing young people for European Citizenship (BOEN, 1995). Yet French, German and Italian are not international languages in the way that English is. If they were, we would be more justified in promoting their instrumental function in the way that we tend to do in England. The instrumental motivation of going to France on holiday will quickly reach its limitations. The potential that French alone (i.e. the learning of a single foreign language) has to enhance employment prospects is relatively limited compared with perhaps more limited proficiency in a number of foreign languages. Thus language learning in terms of its instrumental motivation needs to be reconsidered. In addition, what learners in England do have is French, German, Italian, and Spanish speakers relatively close at hand offering an expansion to their cultural horizons. These issues will be taken up again in later chapters.

We now have an insight into learners' purposes for learning a foreign language. Is this sufficient to give us a base upon which to construct a teaching approach, or are there other dimensions to motivation which we must take into account? One question we still need to ask is: 'Is motivation primary?' Is there a psychological reality before learning and despite learning. Gardner (1985) would argue that it is. Burstall (1970) reports that the main motivation for FL is success. If success breeds success then motivation is secondary. Ramage (1990) found that intrinsic motivation and attitude were *additional* factors to success (represented in measurable achievement: grade levels and course grades) in having a bearing on whether students carried on with languages. This evidence would be supported by the fact that by 1990, in England and Wales, fewer boys than girls were still opting to continue with languages despite increased success at GCSE. It would appear, therefore, that motivation is both primary and secondary and that motivation research based only on the two goals above are insufficient.

Tarclindy data analysed in later chapters suggests that teacher behaviour is a factor which must be considered in any discussion about motivation and that consequently it must be related to the choices learners make and the persistence in language learning that they show. Chambers (1994) argues that the teacher has a key role to play in motivation. S/he is more important than the methodology, the working environment or the equipment. He lists support, enthusiasm and positive approach as motivation enhancing components in a teacher's strategy. However, without a clearer idea of how that support and positive approach can be translated into observable actions, it is difficult to see how it can be recommended in tangible form.

Oxford (1989) suggests that there may be a link between motivation and whether or not learners are prepared to use certain learner strategies.[4] If the link is high motivation – high strategy use, then the impact of teaching might best be directed at the primary domain, focusing on learners' attitudes and predisposition to language learning. If the link is high strategy use – motivation, then the focus of our teaching might best be directed at the secondary domain, encouraging success through improved learning processes. This would also lead us to understand better whether learners are motivated to persevere by the short-term goal success of content syllabuses (such as GOML) or by the processes implied in the 'learning through language' hypothesis. Does motivation come about as a result of learners achieving successful comprehension of the teacher's L2 input through deduction, use of context and cognates and by negotiating meaning? In other words, does motivation come through a realisation of their growing ability to interact with someone in L2? Alternatively, does motivation result from getting tangible chunks of language, functional exponents and vocabulary, under their belt? A third might be that motivation increases as a result of greater independence from the teacher and in the language. A simple answer would, as always, be 'all of these', and the problem, as always, would be 'in what proportion to each other'. A more powerful solution, if it could be achieved conclusively, would be to discover that it depends on the learner, either in terms of their age, language learning ability or their learning styles – that individual learner differences have an effect on primary and secondary motivation.

We have examined the theme of motivation in some detail because suggestions that it is an unproblematic area are misleading. If motivation is multidimensional, a pedagogic approach which only emphasises motivation in terms of observable classroom behaviour (e.g. are they smiling?; are they on task?) will not be sufficient to bring about improved language learning. The prioritising of motivating activities at the expense of activities which might have a clearer impact on developing language competence (such as teacher L2 input) is just one of the concerns brought about by CLT. As a conclusion to this chapter we will outline some others.

Concerns Related to CLT

Kharma (1989) suggests that CLT lies somewhere in the continuum between the exclusivity of the direct method and the intrinsic value of L1 of the grammar-translation method. We have seen, however, that it does not lie along given points in that continuum by chance. In this chapter we have traced back to the roots of communicative language teaching. I have suggested that CLT emerged as a result of two distinct processes; one about language learning, the other about language. Allwright and Bailey (1991: 7) would suggest that it also emerged at the end of a fight between audiolingual[5] and cognitive methods and that what was discarded was the very notion of 'global methodological prescriptions'. If one disregards prescriptions, however, one is no longer open to criticism on the basis of attacks on theory, but to criticism based on lack of professional integrity. In the period which saw the development of graded objectives and the establishing of the GCSE, a number of issues pertaining to the flexibility of CLT interpretation remained unresolved. These were issues which were essentially linked to course design. However, they became issues, by implication, reflected in teachers' practice such that it was no longer possible to disentangle notions of justified flexibility from notions of lack of professional integrity or simply lack of teaching skills. These pedagogical issues were expressed as a series of concerns:

(1)   That the GCSE was often interpreted as a list of discrete speech acts to be ticked off as they were done, an approach which gave little encouragement to the skills of analysis, problem solving, risk taking and experimentation (Cajkler & Addelman 1992: 65).

(2) That it was unclear when formulaic expressions and pre-formed phrases would become creative language output. In other words, when the internalisation of the language system could be seen to be taking place (Dickson, 1992: 21).

(3) That the emphasis on proficiency through the development of oral skills might be leading to the neglect of other skills, particularly reading (Swarbrick, 1994: 141; Grenfell, 1992: 48; Wringe, 1989: 75).

(4) That a neglect of formal grammar teaching might be contributing to a perceived gap with Advanced Level courses (Clark, 1993).

(5) That there was a lack of understanding of how grammar might be taught within a communicative framework (Mitchell, 1994).

(6) That the authenticity of testing discrete language skills was not tenable (DES, 1990b; Woods & Neather, 1994).

(7) That some teachers were getting away with not using hardly any L2 (Cross, 1985).

(8) That there was a need for a more reflective approach to learning and the development of autonomy (Gathercole, 1990).

(9) That in the graded objectives movement there needed to be a shift of emphasis from syllabus content and testing device to 'clearly defined methodological principles' (Page & Hewett, 1987: 61).

Were these concerns the natural consequence of an eclectic approach? Were these concerns exposed by individual writers and practitioners according to their respective values and beliefs about language teaching? If so, the expression of those concerns merely opened a healthy debate further, allowing individuals to see more clearly the implications of taking one position rather than another. Or was the whole concern greater than the sum of its individual parts? Was there a need for a sudden lurch rather than a gradual process of methodological ripening? The NC (DES, 1990b) was itself caught in the tension as many of the concerns expressed above are reflected in the 'characteristics of good practice' referred to in Chapter 1. In order to resolve this tension the NC proposed a radical prioritising of the 'characteristics' through the virtual exclusion of the mother tongue, thus creating a methodologically prescriptive framework. Is this prioritising able to resolve the tension? It is the purpose of the following chapters to analyse the validity of some of the NC tenets against what we know from studies about SLA and foreign/second language learning.

Notes

1. Montaigne and Comenius being notable exceptions.
2. Not to be confused with the *interlanguage hypothesis* as proposed by Selinker and Corder, see Chapter 4.
3. In the early stages of language acquisition at least, the input hypothesis and a collaborative or student-centred approach seems irreconcilable. The concrete examples given by Krashen and Terrell would support this claim.
4. Wasyl Cajkler, in an as yet unpublished study involving adolescent FL learners in Europe, offers similar conclusions.
5. I have not discussed the implications of the audiolingual approach. For an account, see Richards and Rogers (1986).

3 The Teacher as Input

Part 1: Foreign Language Classrooms

In Chapter 2 we have examined the tension brought about by the flexible nature of Communicative Language Teaching. We will now analyse one aspect of that tension more closely by assessing the impact of teacher L2 input both in terms of quantity and in terms of quality within a model of total classroom input. This model is represented diagrammatically in Figure 3.1. First though, let us take a look inside a FL secondary classroom.

The classroom as a distinct community

If classrooms are in any way strange places, then the Foreign Language classroom must surely get the prize for being the strangest. Let us take a classroom of 30 12-year-olds who have been studying French for a year. It is a place:

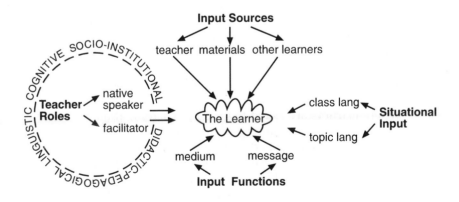

Figure 3.1 Classroom input

- where a learner is asked to operate in a state of almost total linguistic dependence on the teacher;
- where learners know more (at least in terms of content) about every other subject on the curriculum than they know the language they are learning;
- where the subject they are learning can only improve at the same rate as the language they are operating in;
- where the topic of discourse, the linguistic interaction, the pace of delivery, the intensity of language and action, the management of the physical environment, the establishment of social norms and of relationships are all dominated by one member (the teacher) speaking a language both foreign to him/her and to the pupils;
- where, as Cicurel (1989) suggests, learners are involved in a 'discourse performance' where the actors are also the spectators. That is to say a place:
- where a learner is asked to respond to questions and then await confirmation/approval of his/her response, in front of an audience;
- where, in fact, there is a constant running commentary on the linguistic, discursive, theatrical, attitudinal and behavioural achievement of the learners;
- where learners are asked to perform the roles of characters they may never have encountered, in front of an audience;
- where learning the lines has to be done without the script, in front of the audience;
- where a learner has to articulate the language of others (textbook authors), in front of an audience, as if it were his/her own voice;
- where rehearsals turn into performances and then back to rehearsals, in front of the audience;
- where learners have to switch to being themselves, in front of an audience;
- where learners have to give false information about themselves, in front of an audience;
- where learners are asked to give information about themselves the truth of which is unimportant, in front of an audience;
- where learners are asked to give information about themselves the truth of which is *very important,* in front of an audience;
- where if some members of the audience are inattentive to the performance they may not, subsequently, be able to play their own parts;
- where there is often time pressure for the performance to end;

- where the learner's linguistic and *pragmatic* competence is not at a level at which his/her own individuality can pierce through the make-believe. It is also a place
- where learners and the teacher constantly try to repress the knowledge that they share the same L1;
- where (some) teachers try to suppress the learner's use of L1.

The FL classroom then, is a unique social context (Breen, 1985) which teachers go to for the specific purpose of teaching others to speak a language (as well as other educational objectives) and where learners go to with the purpose (hopefully!) of learning a language which, in many cases, they have not chosen to learn. I would therefore argue that the classroom may well constitute a special socio-linguistic domain.

Given the peculiarity of this socio-linguistic domain it is a wonder that the participants 'play the game' at all and abide by the rules (Duff & Polio, 1990: 160) most of the time and that language learning does in fact take place. Or is it really such a wonder? Is 'playing the game' perhaps the *only* way in which learning in such a context could take place? From the teacher's viewpoint it may well appear that pupils will 'play the game' and are prepared to suspend disbelief because: (a) they quite simply like the teacher and want to please him/her; and/or (b) they are, independently of the teacher's efforts, motivated to learn the target language; and/or (c) the teacher can stop them opting out of the game, either through coercion or by keeping their minds off reality for a sufficiently long period of time.

The teacher's roles

In order for a teacher to orchestrate some or all of the activities and role-adoptions that pupils have to undertake in the classroom, s/he will have, in turn, to choose between two discernible roles.

Role 1: teacher as foreigner unable to speak L1

Let us first establish one point. There is no evidence to suggest that native speakers make better teachers. In fact there is some evidence to suggest that a deficient command of L2 in the teacher may actually have advantages over the native speaker teacher in terms of L2 use, particularly in the early stages of learning (Atkinson, 1993b; Medgyes, 1992). By far the majority of teachers working in the FL monolingual classroom today, and all the teachers who contributed to the Tarclindy study were either non-native speakers of L2 (NNST) or native speakers of L2 competent in the learners' L1 (NST). In fact I have never come across a NST working in the UK secondary context who was teaching pupils whose L2 was at a higher level of competence than his/her own L2. Thus, the need for both teachers and pupils to repress the common knowledge of the learners' L1 is as valid for NSTs as NNSTs.

When the teacher uses the FL as the principal means of instruction and as the medium through which directions are given, s/he will in part be adopting a simulated native speaker role, a native speaker who does not speak the L1 of the classroom. A powerful example of this role in action is when a pupil gives an item of information in L1 (I've forgotten my book, miss!) and the teacher pretends not to understand until the item has been given in the L2. Whether this role ever becomes a psychological reality is not known. Whether it is truly accepted and responded to by the learners, for whole lessons, for embedded segments of a lesson or even for short exchanges, has not, to my knowledge, been researched. However, the data obtained from the pupil questionnaires in the Tarclindy project at least gives us some insight into how the teacher's role is perceived.

In the survey, year 8 pupils were asked how they 'thought of' the teacher when s/he *asked them to do something* in French (L2). In other words the question sought to focus on the type of teacher utterance which contained the highest level of communicative content, that of telling/asking a pupil(s) to do something which the pupil(s) was not anticipating and where the teacher was expecting a tangible result from that utterance. Classes for this part of the study were deliberately chosen because they *were not* being taught by NSTs.

As we can see from Table 3.1, in only a small percentage of cases did pupils perceive the teacher to be a real French person. This is not surprising as the teacher would have to use L2 exclusively whenever s/he was in the presence of the pupils. One beginner teacher, in the interview data, did report that she had managed to 'fool a year 7 group' that she was French for about six months. This level of identity suppression is unlikely to be achieved in all but a few extraordinary cases given the administrative complexity of schools as institutions. However, the number of pupils who actually perceived the teacher as someone *trying* to take on a native speaker type role was also surprisingly low given that the researchers knew that the pupils were being taught by teachers committed to teaching, as much as practicable, through the medium of the target language.

The acceptance of the 'foreigner unable to speak L1' role would therefore seem to imply a need for a high level of co-operation from pupils together with an acceptance which might have been accorded in a behavioural response but not necessarily at a deeper, more psycho-

Table 3.1 The teacher is ...

a real French person	10.0
an English person pretending to be French	25.8
an English person helping you understand some French	64.2

N = 271

logical, level. The role needs further examination in a number of domains.

(1) The social-institutional domain.
In order for roles to be maintained effectively they have to be (fairly) constant. Teachers, however, find themselves wearing a number of hats throughout the working week. As well as language providers they are language organisers, classroom educators, heads of department, year heads, administrators, trip organisers, form tutors, counsellors and many other things.
(2) The cognitive domain.
In order for roles to be maintained they have to be understood. To what extent is the 'foreigner unable to speak L1' role understood by pupils? Is it understood implicitly or is it explained and discussed explicitly. As teachers, we often judge the effectiveness of this role by how early on we can introduce it. Thus, many teachers will go into the classroom on the very first day of a new course with the intention of perpetuating this role.
(3) The didactic-pedagogical domain.
In order for roles to be maintained effectively, they have to be seen to be doing things which could not be done as effectively outside the role – for example setting up a group work activity. This issue lies at the interface between what method/approach/strategy the teacher is applying to the job of teaching a foreign language and the learner's perceived benefit to him/her.
(4) The linguistic domain.
In order for roles to be maintained they have to be achievable in terms of the language through which they are expressed. To accept a simulated native speaker role and allow it to succeed, pupils need to acquiesce to the replacement, virtually at all times, of *total communication* with *reduced communication,* of *immediate communication* with *delayed communication,* a communication governed by the linguistic boundaries which reflect the average linguistic competence of the class.

We do not know to what extent they are aware of the potential meanings that the teacher has had to forgo (the totality of what the teacher could have communicated to them if s/he were not in role). We have some understanding of the pupils' reaction to delayed communication and this will be examined in Chapter 4.

Role 2: teacher as mediator/facilitator

When the teacher uses oral and written materials in order to develop receptive skills by exposing learners to the TL, s/he is taking on the role of mediator and facilitator. The teacher acts as a mediator between the complexity or foreignness of texts (authentic or otherwise) and the level of language competence of the pupils. Table 3.1 suggests that pupils in the survey felt that this role was the one they could most readily recognise as being adopted by their teacher. This role would appear to operate less problematically in the four domains described above.

Whether this role or identity is as effective in language learning terms as the simulated native speaker one is impossible to say as most teachers combine the linguistic manifestations of both these roles at some time or other. And yet it lies very much at the heart of the maximising/optimising of the use of L2 debate, and for that matter of the comprehensible input debate, both of which we shall be examining in due course.

At the level of the lesson or segment of a lesson, the effectiveness of role 2 is judged by how accessible a foreign text is made. If the pupils have understood the salient points of a taped weather forecast or a letter from Italy asking for a pen friend, then role 2 has done its job. The effectiveness of role 1, on the other hand, would have to be judged by additional and quite different indicators. One of these would be: how effective is role 1 in enhancing learner output? As I have suggested earlier, the likelihood of being able to measure this causal link scientifically is remote. As a consequence, the effectiveness of role 1 ends up being judged by less powerful indicators. These might include interpersonality and cultural predisposition to language learning rather than language learning itself. Indeed, apparent success of role 1 may not necessarily equate with effectiveness in language *intake* at all but simply by how effective the role has been in contributing to pupil behaviour.

These, then, are some of the questions surrounding the adoption of teacher roles. These roles are important to examine because they do underpin decisions about L2 use made by teachers when planning a lesson or series of lessons. They also underpin the ongoing decisions they make during the course of a lesson and they ultimately have a bearing on the overall teacher's style (e.g. teacher centred or pupil centred).

To complicate matters further, the teacher often needs to be able to handle instantaneous role switching, alternating nimbly between the *text facilitator role* and the *I can't speak L1 role*. The following example was jotted down quickly during one of the observed lessons:

T: alors, il arrive à cinq heures, vrai ou faux ... John? non, Rosie tu lèves la main ... John?

P: Vrai

T: uhm ... non ... c'est ... Rosie tu lèves la main ... un peu de silence là-bas hein ... oui! vous deux, oui, oui vous! Alors il arrive à cinq heures, vrai ou faux? oui ... Amanda ...

P2: Faux

T: oui ... c'est faux. Voilà, maintenant regardez la page ... (taken from Macaro, 1996)

To complicate the overall discourse of a lesson still further, the teacher incorporates other input sources.

Other input sources in the classroom

As we have seen, one of the L2 input sources in the FL classroom is the teacher. A second source of input are the language materials both taped and written. The emphasis and use of one or the other of these two input sources relate (but do not have discrete one-to-one relationships) to the teacher roles and identities which in turn are linked to teacher styles. Macaro (1995) suggests that the communicative lesson rarely flounders as a result of the materials input, provided that the materials are appropriate to the competence level of the learners and/or they are appropriately mediated by the teacher. This means that even if the materials are too hard for the pupil(s) the teacher should be able to provide ways for learners to access (get into) the text. But, as we shall see from the Tarclindy data, however invaluable teacher input may be, there are many more difficulties attached to it which the effective teacher will need to overcome.

Of course it is possible, within a segment of a lesson, to have a mixture of these two inputs. For example, teacher/tape and teacher/written text. Indeed, most FL lessons, particularly at the beginner level, are characterised by the constant stop/start, interweaving and over-laying of teacher's voice and materials. However, as input sources they can be treated quite separately. Interestingly, many teachers have commented that when one substitutes the other, for example if the tape recorder breaks down and the teacher has to read out the dialogue, there is a resulting feeling of unease among the pupils. On the other hand, many teachers have been observed to intersperse a taped dialogue with their own version of the transcript in order to reduce the speed or emphasise key words.

A third source of input is from fellow pupils. As with that of the teacher, this input must presume and necessitate a suspension of disbelief and an acquiescence to play the game by the rules. As we shall see in Chapter 5 not all learners do play the game and abide by the rules. Its value as input might be disregarded because of the low institutional status granted to it both linguistically and socially ('you're not the teacher, why am I listening to you?'). As we shall see in Chapter 5 there is little evidence to suggest that this is happening, although whether its value as input is really being accepted or whether it is merely an opportunity for one of the partners in the discussion to practise his/her own language output in an unthreatening situation is open to question.

A fourth input source might be distinguished and that is the interaction between two teachers in the classroom (e.g. if a foreign language assistant is present). There is not space to analyse the discourse implications of this here and it is omitted from Figure 3.1. A brief account of its motivational value is given in Franklin (1990).

Having outlined the different types of input sources in the classroom we shall now return to teacher input in order to explore it at the level of language function.

Message oriented and medium oriented teacher input

In the above extract from a lesson, the teacher's discourse direction (i.e. the way s/he wanted the discourse to proceed), was hampered by events in the classroom. In natural conversations outside the classroom this also happens, as when the hearer interrupts for clarification. However, outside the classroom, the interruption and subsequent modification is most likely to be about what the speaker was saying (the message s/he was trying to put across). In the extract, however, the teacher was talking about train timetables, where the timetable itself was on an overhead projector. In the phrase 'alors, il arrive à cinq heures, vrai ou faux ... John?', the teacher was therefore asking the pupil to focus both on the teacher's language and the language on the screen. The teacher was asking: 'Is what I have said true or false according to what is on the screen?' We could describe this utterance as being *medium* oriented (about the language) and *message* oriented (demanding an answer). The class management phrases: 'Rosie, tu lèves la main' and 'un peu de silence là-bas' are, on the other hand entirely *message* oriented. They are telling the listener(s) something new (although perhaps in the case of Rosie not that new!), something the hearer did not know. The utterances are not focusing on the language itself, the medium. This distinction is drawn up in Butzkamm and Dodson (1980) quoted in Hakansson and Lindberg (1988) and taken up again in Dodson (1985). Dodson sees areas of overlap between the two orientations. Indeed it seems plausible to suggest, as Hakansson and Lindberg (1988) do, that medium and message oriented communication are actually at two ends of a continuum. For example, by focusing on information about timetables there is some element of new information which is not specifically about the language even though, underlying the teacher's utterance, there is clearly an element of wanting to focus on the language structure *il arrive* and the distinction (if I remember rightly) between the twelve hour clock and the 24 hour one. Similarly, there is a medium focus in the utterance 'Rosie tu lèves la main', given that it is a common classroom phrase and the teacher's underlying purpose may have been both instrumental (I want you to raise your hand) and 'let's remember this phrase everyone', the structure being transferable to other language topics in current syllabi. By contrast, a phrase such as 'remarquez; un chat blanc mais une souris blanche' is right at the medium oriented end of the continuum in the same way that 'demain il n'y aura pas d'examen de français' (said on opening a note just brought into the FL classroom) is right at the message oriented end.

This complexity of teacher language, which might be described as the functional distribution of L2 can, of course, be misconstrued by the learners. Or as Hakansson and Lindberg (1988) point out the teacher may choose language which appears to be message oriented but is in fact medium oriented, as when asking a pupil what colour hair he has. Mitchell (1989) perhaps writing in reaction to a context which was excessively formal and medium oriented draws our attention to the theoretical benefit of message oriented interaction. Whilst this would seem to form the theoretical basis of both the natural approach (Krashen & Terrell, 1988) and an eclectic communicative approach, it is unlikely that it can ever be the only type of input in a formal classroom situation. Even Krashen and Terrell's examples of practice contain medium oriented input. Furthermore, there is no reason why medium oriented dialogue cannot be made interesting by a skilful teacher. Indeed, as we shall see later it seems to cause fewer problems in the FL classroom than does the message oriented dialogue. Nevertheless, this switching between medium and message adds to the complexity of classroom input and discourse.

Classroom language and topic language

We have seen thus far that, in our strange FL classroom, teachers are providing L2 input through at least two roles, through at least two *functional* distributions of L2 and exposing learners to at least three *physical sources* (see Figure 3.1). There is a further distinction which we now need to explore and that is the distinction between what I will call 'classroom language' and 'topic language'. In the Tarclindy interviews a number of other terms were used by teachers and researchers which fell into one or other of these 'situational' categories. That is, the place *where* that type of language discourse occurs. These terms are represented in Table 3.2. Each term may have slightly different shades of meaning but, for the sake of simplicity, I will refer to them by their category names.

As we have seen in Chapter 1 the National Curriculum Programmes of Study Part 2 prescribe that the language of the classroom must be taught and will be assessed. In addition, there are clear references to activities which could not take place without use of classroom language.

Classroom language can be defined as any discourse elements which, due to their particular reference to relationships, status, activities and rules, are normally only found in classrooms and particularly classrooms where the learners are young learners. The following are a number of classroom situations which give rise to classroom language:

Table 3.2 Situational category

Classroom language	Topic language
Terms used by teachers	**Terms used by teachers**
classroom language	content language
peripheral language	topic specific language
management language	external language
internal language	units of work
language for conducting the lesson	situational language
interaction language	

(1)   Calling and answering the register.
(2)   Pupils asking to leave the class or lesson.
(3)   Pupils recording a dialogue on a tape recorder.
(4)   Pupils playing a board game.
(5)   Pupils responding to a teacher checking up on homework.
(6)   Messages or interruptions from other teachers.
(7)   Pupils organising themselves (e.g. preparing a restaurant scene).
(8)   Teacher giving instructions about an activity.
(9)   Teacher making a contract with a class (e.g. let's try to stay in the TL for 20 minutes).
(10) Teacher giving pupils feedback (either on a whole piece of work or on an individual utterance).
(11) Teacher explaining the objectives of a unit of work.
(12) Pupils informing/complaining they can't proceed with the lesson (I can't see the board/hear the tape).
(13) Teacher telling pupil(s) off.
(14) Pupils requesting help with a language problem (medium-oriented).

Readers might point out that some of this language does not only occur in the classroom. This is true. However, some situations are clearly more specific than others. For example, an English youngster could be playing a board game in Germany and using the same language in order to interact. On the other hand, it is difficult to imagine a situation outside the languages classroom where young people would be preparing a restaurant scene in the foreign language and giving each other parts to play and checking that they'd brought the paper plates with food items painted on them!

Topic language, by contrast, is the language that is 'over there'. The language that is specific to situations which the learner might encounter in France or Spain. We are all familiar with the range of topics from buying a bus ticket to asking your correspondent if s/he has a towel to lend you. Of course the language doesn't have to be in a situation over there. The learner could be interacting with a native speaker in England, in which case some of the topics do not apply, or the learner's role might change to one of interpreter. Where this topic language isn't, however, is *in the classroom.* The only merger of the two categories would be asking the teacher permission to go to the toilet whilst sitting next to your *correspondant* in a classroom in France.

Topic language also subdivides into 'situational': learning to function in situations in the target country (at the railway station, staying with a family) and *cultural/informational:* knowing about the target country (French national railways are called SNCF and operate a TGV, information about French family life).

The distinction between classroom language and topic language is an important one as it raises the vexed question of authenticity and real versus unreal communication. For Prabhu (1987), for example, the classroom becomes the only possible reality. In a methodology, such as the one that he promotes, based on task achievement, the language in which the learner needs to perform the language tasks becomes the only valid language. Thus, assumed roles (those of topic language) are subordinated to learner roles. Asher (1993: 63) also takes this line. Pair work and info-gap activities only replicate real language use and *sondage* activities have their communicative force diluted by the fact that they are 'imposed by the teacher and do not spring from individual learners themselves'. For Asher real communication comes in the process of setting up activities, not in their execution. For Breen (1985: 67) the creation of 'other worlds' may be unnecessary; the day-to-day of living in a classroom can provide sufficient authentic potential for communication.

Despite these forceful arguments for 'realness' of classroom language, a paradox exists. All the surveys we will examine later clearly indicate that it is the language that the teacher needs in order to set up complex activities which proves to be the most problematic or difficult to sustain in the L2. And it is pupil initiated language which is most difficult to encourage. Why should this be if classroom language has the impetus of being both authentic and totally communicative? The following are a number of possible answers.

Firstly, the claim that classroom language is authentic needs to be examined if not challenged. It certainly does not meet the criteria of 'produced for native speakers by native speakers'. We have already mentioned that in order for an authentic message oriented dialogue between teacher and pupil to happen they both have to suppress their awareness of each other's L1. One teacher summarised this tension in a Tarclindy interview:

> I think there's a psychological problem as well – in any classroom you are trying to get them to suspend disbelief that there is some realistic communication happening between human being A and human being B who both speak English quite happily anyway and there is no psychological need ... there is definitely an almost insurmountable psychological barrier towards the desire for two native speakers of one language to speak a FL that isn't theirs.

The claim to authenticity is also undermined by the repetitive and artificial nature of classroom language itself, particularly in the early stages of learning when it is routinised to the point of becoming 'iconic' (open your books, listen, etc.) Thus it is not the language which conveys new information but the formalised context and the 'paralinguistic features' which accompany the verbal message. Moreover, a teacher insisting on a pupil using the L2 version of a phrase *after* that pupil has communicated the very same information in L1, is not engaging in authentic dialogue. So the first problem is that classroom language is authentic only in so far as the participants are able to transcend the inauthenticity of the situation in which that language is being used.

Secondly, classroom language contains a lot of verbs. Mitchell (1988: 130) clearly demonstrates this in her study by comparing the number of verbs contained in the teacher input with the number of verbs at the equivalent stage in the coursebook. The total number of verbs recorded, in this Scottish study, as being used by the teacher in year 8 (Scottish S2) was 112 compared to the coursebook's 45. Verbs are more difficult for the learner to acquire because (a) their endings/soundings (*appelle/appelez*) vary much more than nouns and adjectives; (b) because they are much more difficult to topicalise than nouns and adjectives – to put thematic boundaries round them; (c) because they are much more difficult to visualise, being more abstract (e.g. *atteindre, aider, comprendre*); (d) because they can be more difficult to illustrate through body language, realia and use of context; (e) because they have different purposes in different utterances (particularly auxiliary and modal verbs but also verbs like *prendre*); (e) because learners' deviations from L2 norms are more likely to occur in the case of verbs than nouns or adjectives. Classroom language verbs are therefore 'free', unfettered by the constraints of a syllabus or a coursebook. At best this means that pupils are exposed to a language rich environment where the input is roughly tuned but contains i+1 elements (Krashen) for pupils to make the necessary connections. At worst, the teacher becomes a loose cannon firing off verbs at will.

Thirdly, the preponderance of verb use is likely to be made even more salient by the use of the imperative. Classroom language may then become associated with the language of management. In classrooms where challenging behaviour is met with TL, classroom language becomes psychologically associated with the language of control, the teacher's language. This point was raised by teachers in the Tarclindy interviews. The same cannot be said of topic language, which being dissociated from the figure of authority, does not need to meet the challenge of pupil misbehaviour. At worst, topic language can be seen by the pupils as neutral in its direct effect on them.

Fourthly, classroom language, in the course of the Tarclindy project, was observed to be taught differently from topic language. Classroom language was generally taught by one of the sequences in Table 3.3.

In teaching 'topic language' teachers used the full range of activities within the more familiar presentation, practice, use sequence or the pre-communicative and communicative activities sequence (Littlewood, 1984). In other words, the basic methodology for classroom language was much more 'direct', relied on immediate acquisition and put its faith in unconscious learning (at least for the first two sequences in Table 3.3). Moreover, by putting the classroom phrases on the walls made it classroom language in a visual sense of the word! Topic language, in all classrooms observed, retained some element of formal learning, some element of focusing on the language. Above all, topic language did not have the teacher as the only input source and, as Dickson (1992) points out, there are dangers in placing too great a reliance on teacher talk as the sole source of input.

Fifthly, it may well be that classroom language has more of a 'plateau effect' (Mitchell, 1988) than topic language. Within the con-

Table 3.3 Classroom language sequence

listen, look, do	teacher: *ouvrez vos cahiers* and teacher demonstrates this by opening the exercise book at the first desk, then expects pupils to carry out the instruction
listen, repeat, from now on say.	teacher: *je ne comprends pas* when the information has first been offered by the pupil in L1
read, say.	pupil: *j'ai oublié mon stylo* written in a cloud or bubble and pinned to classroom wall or hung from ceiling. This sequence sometimes but not always had been preceded by one of the other sequen- ces. Some pupils wrote a list of these in the back of their books
refer to, say.	pupil: *tu commences* as when pupils were playing a game and a list of support phrases were given (this was observed on very few occasions)

straints of the FL learning environment some pupils may reach a learning limit or at least a drop in the learning curve. This is likely to occur in terms of the complexity of the language they can produce, the number of consecutive exchanges they can cope with and how free/ creative the construction of utterances can be. There is surely less likely to be a learning limit on *the breadth* of their learning. Topic language does offer the possibility of moving horizontally even if the vertical going is getting tough. Topic language also has the extra resource that it can be written input. Classroom language, on the other hand, can only increase in complexity vertically because the number of areas offered by classroom language are finite. It is, moreover, essentially oral (written instructions in the TL tend to be few). It is for this reason that teacher–pupil classroom interaction in year 10 often appears very similar in content and function to classroom interaction in year 7. Unless teachers can help the learners to break through the barrier whereby the interaction becomes negotiated, full of stops, starts, interjections and turn requests (as in L1 dialogue), the motivating force of classroom language will be limited.

Why place so much importance on classroom language then? If the above difficulties really exist why not just teach the topics? The easy answer of course is that the National Curriculum demands it and the inspectorate will be looking for it. Precisely how classroom language will be tested orally is not known at the time of writing. Another answer is that generally all teachers and writers on the issue of teaching through the medium of L2 believe to a lesser or greater extent in its value. What I have tried to indicate above is that we should be wary of succumbing to the same pendulum swings on the issue of its intrinsic value as with other issues in foreign language teaching. In the 1980s teachers and writers focused their attention on functions and notions as encapsulated by topic language. It would be foolish to now brush all that aside with the sudden, illuminating realisation that the only real communicative (and therefore worthwhile) language is classroom language. A clearer criterion for focusing our attention on classroom language is that by doing so it should help both teachers and learners avoid recourse to L1. It seems to me counter-intuitive not to accept the value of using the foreign language as the learning tool with which to learn the subject. The problem is to what extent and how? As we shall see in our discussion on input modification and L2 exclusivity, both quality and quantity of teacher L2 use are problematic.

In the Tarclindy questionnaire year 8 pupils were asked whether classroom language phrases were useful. As we can see from Table 3.4 most thought they were either 'very useful' or 'useful'. However, when

Table 3.4 Pupils' response to questionnaire

Learning a phrase like 'excusez-moi d'être en retard' (sorry I'm late)	*Percentage of responses*
very useful	12.2
useful	63.8
not very useful	19.6
no use at all	4.4

N = 271

we look at the comments the pupils made we have to apply caution as to its transferability to the 'outside world'. Pupils generally referred to its being useful for getting through the lesson. In other words, it may be that its value, as perceived by pupils, is 'classroom bound'.

Teachers interviewed in the Tarclindy project had not, in general, been able to resolve the issue of how to approach classroom language. INSET sessions either before or after the introduction of the NC had not provided a coherent framework to follow. Some teachers said that classroom language was added on *ad hoc* to recognisable units of work or topics. Alternatively, they attempted a slow, drip-feed process of expanding the classroom language. This was particularly the case for 'teacher initiated' classroom language. Others still, 'taught' the language as it came up, usually as a result of pupil inability to express themselves in the TL. The approach was not one of grafting classroom language onto the topic language in a coherent, methodical way, still less was there evidence that classroom language was taught as a series of discrete units, apart from right at the beginning of Keystage 3 when classroom objects and furniture (and their related language bits) were introduced. Some teachers saw this as a definite advantage in that the learners were exposed to these phrases every lesson, the language being reinforced/consolidated whereas the 'vocabulary that you use for the topics' tended to be visited once or twice in a whole scheme of work. Moreover, some teachers agreed with Prabhu (1987) that this was real language, made authentic by the 'necessity to communicate'. It had taken some teachers a long time to stop considering the teaching of this classroom language as a waste of time, time taken away from the topic teaching. Nevertheless, even *these* teachers were aware that they taught classroom language differently from the topic language.

The question remains as to whether classroom language was truly learnt. We need to judge its value according to at least the following two criteria: (a) are the pupils capable of reproducing it over and over again; and (b) are they able to transfer the structures which the phrases contain to other functions and situations? The data collected in the project is not sufficient to give answers to these questions.

How might classroom language be taught differently? Firstly, if our discussion about roles and authority link has some truth in it then teachers should stop projecting the 'let's pretend I'm French' identity. Instead they might try to convince pupils that allowing the teacher to remain in the TL and them saying whatever they can in the TL will help them when they talk to French people in the future. In that way classroom language is not confined to the walls of the classroom but becomes a practice stage for a later activity when the language can be used for truly communicative purposes. Pupils in the Tarclindy project were asked which method they preferred for learning a phrase like 'je n'ai pas mon cahier' (I haven't got my exercise book):

Method 1
You hear French children saying it to a teacher in a taped recording
the whole class practises it with your teacher
you practise it with your friends
your teacher writes it on the wall

Method 2
you say it in English
your teacher says it in French
you repeat it in French
your teacher writes it on the wall

Although the results in Table 3.5 are inconclusive, or indeed show a preference for Method 2, the comments again clarify and enrich the picture. Whilst pupils who opted for Method 2 tended to do so for reasons such as: (a) because it's quick and easier; (b) because I cannot understand people on a tape, those that opted for Method 1 had much more thoughtful and insightful comments to make. For example:

Table 3.5 Pupils' response

Would you find it easier to learn by …	
Method 1	41.3
Method 2	57.9

N = 271

It's better and easier to practise with a friend ... if you both make a mistake you have a laugh ... if you do it with the teacher and make a mistake the whole class laughs at you.
You get more practice with method one.
It's easier to learn when you hear real French people saying it.
It's easier listening to it on tape, in a real situation, than listening to a teacher telling you ...
Method 1 is more fun.

In addition to the way we teach classroom language we might also start to view it as a topic or series of topics which learners experience over a period of time and integrate into their language system. But to teach it as a series of topics it should be accorded all the attention that is accorded to topic language. There is no reason why some or all of the following should not be used to teach classroom language: repetition, taped dialogues with exploitation exercises, question-and-answer technique, games, role play and simulations. A study (White *et al.*, 1991) suggests that when the TL input is enhanced by questioning techniques which focus on the medium as well as the message there is improved learning. Ultimately we may also have to find imaginative ways of assessing it. As one teacher in the Tarclindy interviews said:

I think it's partly because they're not being assessed ... the mentality which drives any of our children to do anything anyway is that they're going to get some positive credit for it – if they say 'tu as un stylo' because they actually need to borrow a pen, they're not going to get a tick and a merit for it.

We also need to categorise classroom language thematically, in the same way that many teachers categorise topic language thematically, in order to avoid the loose cannon effect. Given the short amount of time in the FL classroom the teacher's input may have to be more finely tuned than the natural approach (Krashen & Terrell, 1988) would have us believe.

Finally, teaching classroom language with our eclectic communicative approach may also overcome another problem. It may, paradoxically, help to reduce the focus on the instrumental (Halliday, 1973) nature of its function. This will need a little explanation. Perhaps the relative success that we have had in getting pupils to talk through role plays and simulations is that, whilst on the surface they appear to be using instrumental functions, subsuming the whole is a 'let's pretend' function. It may be that young learners feel less threatened in the world of make believe than in the harsh reality of 'real communication' where words have real consequences. It may be that they are more likely to 'play the game' if it feels like a game. If classroom language is taught in a 'game scenario' it may reduce the impact that it's function is really to 'get the kids to do what the teacher wants'.

We have examined all the different types of L2 input in the languages classroom. We now need to turn to the question of how much teacher L2 use is desirable and practicable.

Part 2: The Teacher's Use of the Target Language

The L1 exclusion debate

As we have seen in Chapter 1, the official documentation which sets about laying down the principles for a national methodology refers to the use of the target language in the classroom by progressing through three different designations of it: *virtual*, *maximal* and *optimal*. The shift from the first to the third designation in the official literature may be a softening of authoritative attitudes in the face of some hostility from teachers. As modern languages teachers, on the other hand, we surely would want to argue that each of these designations reflects different beliefs about what teacher L2 input actually does in relation to learning. *Virtual* and *optimal* would seem to discuss the issue of quantity from an 'is it desirable' point of view? *Maximal* would seem to discuss the issue from an 'is it practicable' perspective. In order to shed light on this distinction let us first look at some theoretical perspectives.

Krashen's (1987) comprehensible input hypothesis implies that there is no place for L1. Krashen and Terrell (1988), in their practical application of the acquisition position, must surely be implying 'virtually all' L2 use in the classroom.

Canale and Swain (1979), in providing theoretical bases for developing approaches to L2 teaching, do not commit themselves to L2 exclusivity. However, the following two conclusions would suggest that high levels of exposure to and involvement in L2 are essential for communicative competence:

(1) That classroom activities should, by and large, reflect the activities eventually to be engaged in by the learner.
(2) That communication involves the continuous negotiation of social meaning (i.e. the meaning of an utterance in its social context) on the part of the participants.

Chambers, F. (1991: 27) sees the 'virtually all' argument as 'theoretically uncontroversial', the problem merely being one of practicalities.

For Skinner (1985) on the other hand, exclusive use of L2, by forming an obstacle to connecting thoughts, is actually detrimental to the process of concept development. Furthermore, he sees a danger in not being able to obtain meaning without contextual clues and, apart from learning at the beginner level, contextual clues, for him, soon reach their limit.

Dickson (1992) in his review, comes to the conclusion that: quantity of teacher L2 input may not be as beneficial as quality of input; L2 input without interaction cannot guarantee intake.

None of these authors can point to evidence which will clinch the argument either way. This lack of theoretical evidence for 100% L2 use, as Atkinson (1993a) points out, should encourage us not to take extreme positions in the debate. Yet some practitioner manuals quite confidently promote virtual use of L2 if not exclusivity:

Halliwell and Jones (1991: 1) refer to maximum L2 desirability in the classroom in terms of learners:

experiencing the foreign language as a **real** (their emphasis) means of communication
experiencing the unpredictability of real language encounters
developing their own in-built language learning system

Macdonald (1993) sees desirability in terms of:

Motivation:
(1) learners seeing language as useful now, not at some vague point in the future;
(2) providing a practical situation and a context for learning (the classroom);
(3) providing enjoyment and immediate success.

And learning:
(1) maximising the time available to promote conscious and subconscious learning;
(2) developing the learner's coping strategies.

We have discussed already the dual nature of reality in the context of the discussion on classroom language as well as the predictability of utterances in ritualised early classroom discourse. Motivation is obviously desirable. The argument of utilising the in-built system (Chomsky, 1965), developing coping strategies and 'working out' what the speaker is saying, is a powerful one and may well be the key to deciding what is optimal use. Yet we are still far away from being able to justify the exclusion of L1. Pattison (1987) would seem to encapsulate the paradox which feeds the L2 debate: 'Although there are good, practical and psychological reasons for using L1 for certain purposes: it undermines the learner regarding the L2 as a means of communication; and it disturbs the natural process of trying to understand from context.'

What few empirical studies there are on quantity of L2 use are also inconclusive. Chaudron (1988), in a general but brief review of research and literature on use of L1 and L2 (in all types of second language classrooms), draws the following conclusions:

(1) teachers apply and expect quite different uses of L2 according to the type of learner/classroom they are teaching;
(2) in all but 2nd language classrooms with mixed L1 learners (EFL1 and ESL1), some use of L1 has been observed to occur;
(3) use of teacher L2 in Canadian classrooms ranges from about 90% in the French immersion to about 70% in the core French (standard FL classroom). (Chaudron describes the latter as 'respectably high levels of TL use in a foreign language educational environment');
(4) the total proportion of L1 to L2 use alone is not the critical variable in determining the degree of ... L2 acquisition.

Lightbown (1991: 204) points to studies where clearly the amount of input does make a difference. However, real differences only show up between different programmes (for example intensive four to five hours per day as opposed to two hours per week) rather than different teacher inputs within the same type of programme.

The above contributions begin to help us with the distinction between *virtual, maximal* and *optimal* use of L2 and it is important to try to arrive at and maintain this distinction. Asher (1993), argues that whilst L2 is difficult to sustain, 'there remain cogent reasons why teachers should extend their methodologies to the boundaries of what is possible'. This argument suggests a confluence of the desirable and the practicable streams. The problem is, however, that linking the two theoretically camouflages the opportunity of shifting the balance towards desirability rather than practicability. As MacArthur (1983: 99) reflects, one of the reasons for the eventual rejection of the Direct Method was that 'it assumed that the student would slowly begin to live the language simply because there was no escape from it'. Thus, if we continue down the *maximal* stream we eventually get to the *virtual* destination but for possibly the wrong reasons. Take the hypothetical example of a class of perfectly behaved, highly motivated 13-year-olds. It would be possible, and it is possible, for the teacher not to utter a single word of L1 and to avoid all overt reference to the learners' knowledge of L1. Can we be sure that those learners are having the best possible learning experience? It may be that they *are* but as yet we have no evidence to prove it. In other words, it remains to be proven that there is nothing that their L1 can offer in terms of helping them to learn L2 – that every second in L1 is a wasted second. It needs to be proven because there is evidence from many sources, including (as we shall see) the Tarclindy project, that teacher L2 exclusivity is maintained at a cost. Do we have any signposts for which route to follow in order to arrive at an optimal designation of teacher L2 use? Is natural code-switching (alternating between L1 and L2) one of those signposts?

Cook (1991: 66) whilst pointing out that there is nothing to prove that codeswitching is inappropriate in a FL classroom, argues that principles should and do exist for codeswitching. The difficulty for the teacher is that these principles lie more at the lexical level (one word in a sentence) than at the segment level or functional level. Moreover, as Cook himself reminds us: 'using the L1 for classroom management and instructions deprives the students of genuine examples of language use and sets a tone for the class', a view echoed by Ellis (1984: 133). On the other hand, Hagen (1992), hints at codeswitching as being a fundamental language skill which (in the context of commercial transaction) needs to be acquired because it is a normal part of the interactive process. Some, like Harbord (1992), see a humanistic need to allow some use of L1. Thus, codeswitching is also a factor which is subjected to social and educational pressures.

We therefore have a paradox of the FL classroom which goes something like this. On the one hand, all the evidence suggests that L2 learning, particularly in the FL context, differs in important ways from L1 learning (we shall return to this theme in Chapter 4). If this is the case there may be ways in which using the in-built knowledge of L1 may actually help teachers and learners to cut corners and learn more quickly. However, each time, as teachers, we use the L1 we are undermining all the beneficial effects of remaining in L2 and probably sending the wrong message to young learners. It is surely this paradox that leads teachers in both the Mitchell (1986) study and to some extent in the Tarclindy study to express feelings of guilt about having recourse to L1. Why do teachers use L1 in the classroom?

Recourse to L1 (RL1)

There have been a number of studies on why and when teachers have RL1. It is necessary to examine these in some detail.

The first study which must be taken into account in any discussion on teacher use of L2 in the FL context is that of Mitchell (1986), a PhD thesis eventually published in Mitchell (1988). The importance of this study, carried out in Scotland, is that it sets the issue of teacher use of L2 squarely in the theoretical context of the acquisition-learning debate and also in the context of a methodological shift prevalent in the early 1980s among the respondents in the survey. In this study teachers reported that the most likely reason for them to have RL1 was when explaining grammar, when disciplining pupils, when giving activity instructions and when teaching 'background' (i.e. the culture of the country).

Another very relevant study, also carried out in Scotland among 201 teachers, was by Franklin (1990). Here, explaining grammar, discussing language objectives and teaching background, were the types of teacher-led activities which appeared to cause most problems. Giving activity instructions was, by now, seen as something which could be done in L2 but with difficulty. Disciplining remained a fairly difficult activity to carry out in L2. An interesting finding (compare to Tarclindy data below) was that 83% of teachers rated 'confidence in speaking L2' as an important factor in RL1.

The problem of RL1 is not exclusive to the UK FL learning context. Prabhu (1987: 26), reporting on the experiences of the Bangalore project (teaching English in Indian classrooms, EFL2) claims that 'when there was an indication of incomprehension, the teacher adopted such strategies as repeating or paraphrasing ... employing non-verbal forms of communication, or providing a gloss in the learners' mother tongue' and 'the teacher normally used it (L1) only for an occasional glossing of words or for some complex procedural instructions, for example: "leave the rest of the page blank in your notebooks and go on to the next page, for the next question"' (Prabhu, 1987: 60).

A small-scale study carried out in Italy (Macaro, 1995), and which served as a pilot for the Tarclindy project, furnished similar reactions from teachers teaching English in upper secondary schools (FL). Teachers alluded to the fact that it was not always possible to set up language activities in L2 and that over-use of L2 in long lessons can become counterproductive. But underlying the whole of the approach to L1 and L2 use seemed to be the need to build up affective relationships with learners and provide a humanism-led environment. Interestingly discipline in L2 was not a problem, or perhaps discipline just wasn't an issue at all!

Kharma and Hajjaj's (1989) very interesting study raises similar issues but also throws light on how course-specific or situation-specific sometimes are the reasons for RL1 in that it produces, in some ortant ways, the opposite of the Tarclindy findings. The study is of ded interest because of its methodological proximity to the Tarclindy roject: questionnaires addressed to 200 teachers (with Arabic L1) of English (FL); questionnaires to learners; observation of teachers and students, etc. Kharma and Hajjaj's summary of the findings includes the indication that:

(1) 93% of teachers used L1 to some degree in the classroom with the most RL1 being for explaining 'new and difficult items' (medium oriented);
(2) that the non-native teacher of the second language inevitably makes use of the L1;
(3) learner competence is a factor in teacher use of L1 (more L1 used at the beginner stage;
(4) teachers use L1 out of their own conviction rather than in response to authority imposed upon them;
(5) the approach of exams at the end of courses makes teachers resort to shortcuts (by using L1);
(6) 75% of learners felt that use of L1 was helpful in facilitating learning;
(7) the small minority of teachers who *did not* use L1 thought that L1 use increased expectations of more L1 use, hindered fluency, destroyed motivation and distracted students.

As we shall see, the Tarclindy data differs radically in results on (1), (2). It partly differs in results on (3), (4) and is the same on items (5), (7). Item (6) is not quantifiable in the Tarclindy data.

It is also helpful to have an insight of the adult (University of California) FL context by reporting observations from a study carried out by Duff and Polio (1990). Here in only two of 13 languages classes did students note that the teacher 'never' used English; students were happy with the amount of L1 used. However, students would not be bothered even if the teacher used the L2 100% of the time. This passivity to methodology is perplexing. Also relevant in the study is that the lesson objective(s) did not appear to determine the amount of L2 use and that for some teachers it 'took too long to get their point across' in L2 (it is unclear whether this was medium or message oriented language).

Returning to the FL context in England, we have what could be described as the crucial consultation exercise carried out collaboratively by the NFER/NCC and summarised in the National Curriculum Council Consultation Report (NCC, May 1991). This asked whether 'you agree with the report's recommendations on the use of the target

Table 3.6

agreed	26%
principle was good, practice less easy	14%
TL not always appropriate in all circumstances	25%
disagreed	7%
Total	72%

language in the classroom' (this referred to the statement 'the natural use of the target language for virtually all communication is a sure sign of a good modern languages course'). It is difficult to gauge the reaction of teachers to this important consultation exercise as the method of data collection and the presentation of the analysis in the Consultation Report are both unclear (NCC, 1991: 12). Were the respondents schools or individuals? Are the figures represented in Table 3.6 the total number of respondents or the respondents to that particular question?

If the former is the case, what did the other 28% think? If the latter is the case, it means that nearly 64% of teachers reported that they had some or a lot of reservations about the 'virtually all' designation of L2 use and that only just over 36% had no reservations. In the same way that the reader was left floundering when confronted with the results of the NCC/NFER survey related to target language testing (see Chapter 1), so is s/he left baffled by the statistics quoted with reference to target language use in the classroom. These figures are important in that they were of 'considerable value in the development of non-statutory guidance and in-service training materials' (NCC, 1991: 8). However, it is useful and encouraging that the distinction between *maximal* and *optimal* may be re-emerging with more teachers appearing to refer to the latter designation than the former one (25% as opposed to 14% in Table 3.6). It is impossible to be certain about this as we have no knowledge as to how the responses were coded and there is no follow up in-depth interview data. In other words do 'circumstances' refer to pedagogic issues (how learners learn) or physical/behavioural issues (I've got 32 of them and in the afternoons they 'tend to lose their concentration!').

The Tarclindy project and L1/L2 use

Work on the Tarclindy project started a year after the publication of the Consultation Report and its aims and method of enquiry are ribed in the Appendix. In analysing the results of this part of the ject it is as well to clarify three matters.

Firstly, were teachers and researchers talking abut the same thing vhen using the term 'Target Language'? In order to gauge whether teachers were clear about the implications of the NC statement on use of the TL, they were asked at the beginning of the interviews what they understood by the term 'Use of the Target Language' as defined by the NC. Most either summarised teacher centred activities through the concept of L2 as the medium of communication (or medium of lesson management) and/or gave examples such as:

presenting materials by using the FL;
explaining an activity;
instructions and commands;
day-to-day business of the classroom.

In other words, teachers were clear that the issue was 'teaching through the target language'. Very few teachers limited their response to 'the language we're supposed to be teaching'.

Secondly, it was clear to both teachers and researchers at the outset that teacher tiredness and stress were factors in use of classroom language by the teacher. As one respondent said:

I tried really hard just now (observed lesson) with year 9 set four and it's really hard work. I have them again last lesson on Friday and I won't try nearly as hard – I won't even probably bother at all!

The physical state of any participant in any activity is bound to make a difference. Whilst not wanting to minimise the importance of teacher tiredness/stress it could be applied to *any* of the categories and responses in the analysis below. For the purposes of the analysis I will therefore exclude tiredness/stress as variables.

Thirdly, teachers' language competence resulted as a *very unimportant* factor in RL1. The questionnaire data (see Table 3.9), the log data (see Table 3.10) and the interviews all confirm this. There is only one mention of teacher lack of confidence in the interview data and this was a teacher's third language! It is useful to be able to exclude this too as a variable from the analysis.

In the Attitude Questionnaire, teachers were asked to react to the following 'global' statement: 'Good language teachers use the TL almost exclusively'.

Table 3.7 shows that only a small number of teachers did not equate good practice in any way with L2 use. This is clearly echoed again and again in all the interview data where there are many references to

Table 3.7 Teachers' global attitude to TL use (%)

agree	34.3
partly agree	48.8
disagree	16.3

reasons for using L2 and teaching through the L2. Nevertheless, here too there is a significant proportion of respondents who have reservations about the 'virtually all' designation.

Before delving deeper into the reasons teachers gave for this reluctance to consider near exclusive use of L2 as the number 1 strategy in the practitioner's overall method, it is worth examining the variables within the questionnaire samples. There was *no significant variance* between the attitudes of the three 'levels of experience' categories of teachers surveyed. There was a slight variance in terms of school location. Teachers working in schools in more challenging catchment areas, where motivation towards a foreign language may be less evident, disagreed more with the proposition than their colleagues in less challenging environments.

This tendency is supported on the one hand by the logs and on the other by the interviews. An overall rough count of the number of times teachers had RL1 during observed lessons provides a much higher figure in the inner city and suburban areas than in the small town or rural areas. In the interview data (and Teacher Comment Data on the questionnaires) there are many examples of teachers citing difficult behaviour, lack of motivation or pupil frustration as reasons for not remaining in the TL:

Some children decide *they will not understand* and this can frustrate the efforts of the keenest teacher.

I don't think it's a bad thing to use English (sometimes) because the kids can get very frustrated if it's like the third time you're explaining.

how do you cope (in L2) with bullies, or boys sexually harassing girls?

When challenging behaviour or poor motivation were not the foremost factors in making a judgement about L2 use, teachers provided a range of attitudes to its perceived usefulness as a learning tool:

positive
the amount of language that is acquired subconsciously by pupils;
the improvement in listening skills;
the exploitation of the medium itself leads to new teaching and learning strategies;
demonstrating to the pupils the importance of learning a foreign language;
demonstrating to the pupils how the language can be used to do things.

negative
L2 for activity instructions can be time consuming;
reaching a point when remaining in L2 becomes counterproductive;
building up the essential teacher–pupil relationship is essential to learning pre-disposition and it cannot really be done in L2.

In general, teachers saw the 'virtually all' designation of L2 use as being unattainable with all but the most motivated classes. Many felt that the task was certainly harder than the NC statement would lead one to believe. Some had felt guilty at first about lapsing into English but, because they were continually redoubling their efforts, had become reconciled to not being able to attain near exclusive use. It was also clear (and encouraging) that teachers recognised the different agendas that they had with their pupils and that each of the pupils had. For the teacher, standing in front of the class, the task was in ensuring that his/her input was comprehensible for the whole group whereas for the pupils the importance was a question of them as individuals. As one teacher said:

> I have to be certain that I am picking up everybody and trying to keep them all moving forward at a pace commensurate with their ability. They're only interested in the pace suiting themselves. I'm teaching and they're learning. They are different things.

It is this dual agenda that needs to be kept in mind when we now examine the different forms of teacher L2 use and the different situations in which difficulties with classroom language arise.

Teacher RL1 (by activity)

The interviewees gave the following as the most prominent reasons for RL1:

giving instructions for pair/group work activities (message oriented);
building up relationships with pupils (message oriented);

dealing with unacceptable behaviour (message oriented);
responding to pupils who seem anxious/uncertain about activity instructions (message or medium oriented);
coping when time is short (message or medium oriented);
giving definition/translation of text when contextual/realia/TPR[1] fails (medium oriented).

Thus, message oriented communication resulted in much greater RL1 than medium oriented communication. The above reasons for RL1, generated by the interviews, were nearly all included in the questions asked in the attitude questionnaire and indeed with the type of areas researchers had used for the observation logs. This was reassuring as the questionnaire and logs had been designed before the interviews (i.e. they did not result from the interviews).

Giving instructions for activities was still causing a fair amount of RL1. As the questionnaire did not try to gauge the complexity of the activity that teachers were referring to, we need to obtain this from the interview and log data. Especially in the context of differentiated teaching and learning, the amount of time used to explain complex instructions in L2, repeating and reformulating them, was not justified by the advantages gained from it. In other words few teachers would agree with Asher's (Asher, C., 1993) statement that the quality of the language input for setting up a task is worth more than the task the pupils are about to engage in. Teachers disagreed with this, especially if it was an oral task. That is not to say that Asher may not have a point. It is possible, for example, that in the ideal classroom, learners would negotiate with the teacher the meaning/information about how to set about the next task. The impression that teachers gave and that observers got was that learners were not at the level of maturity to demonstrate the patience needed for protracted meaning negotiation. Furthermore, the sheer variety of activities and tasks available to the imaginative and creative teacher made insistence on use of L2 for organising the activity counter productive. There was a suggestion also that use of L2 for setting up activities and tasks[2] tended to, in itself, guide the lesson towards a more teacher-centred approach. One teacher expressed it thus:

Inevitably the more complicated and ultimately the more inter-esting an activity is going to be … sometimes if you're going to take half an hour to get it through to them what they've got to do … that's only going to leave them 5 minutes to do what is a really superb activity. I find I can't justify staying in the TL to do that.

In this sense the survey mirrors Peck (1988) in that the greater amount of teacher talk, the less pupil talk is likely to occur. A further refinement here, however, is that the greater amount of teacher L2 talk *to set up* pupil L2 talk, the less time for that pupil talk remains. However, justification for RL1 for these complex activities needs to be set against the background of Table 3.8 where teachers see *virtually no difficulty*, but only *positive value* in remaining in L2 for basic instructions of the 'we're now going to listen to a tape' variety, particularly as this maintained the flow and rhythm of the lesson. Even the more simple and often repeated pair work activities were easy to set up in the L2, according to the interviews and the observations. Similarly, teachers were quite happy with giving ongoing feedback to a pupil or to pupils in L2. Moreover, that they had RL1 for complex activities is not to say that teachers were not aware of the second part of the paradox mentioned earlier, namely that:

> the value of using the L2 is undermined if young learners perceive that L2 is only used for minor and routine forms of class management and not for 'serious' instructions such as giving homework, explaining a test or for crucial disciplinary interventions.

The attitude reaction in Table 3.8 is worth noting. A high proportion of respondents still saw themselves as good teachers even though they

Table 3.8 Teacher attitudes to L2 use by teacher activity

Target Language Activity	Agree	Partly agree	Disagree
TL for organising activities	46.5	44.2	8.7
TL for basic instructions	90.1	8.1	1.2
TL for commenting (giving feedback)	84.3	14.5	0.6
TL for disciplining or controlling	36.4	51.2	12.2
TL for socialising or relations building	7.6	63.4	28.5
Grammar difficult in TL	19.8	51.7	27.9

Table 3.9 Teacher fluency as a factor in TL use

agree	23.3
partly agree	49.4
disagree	26.7

had RL1 in order to maintain discipline. Perhaps the strongest attitude reaction was reserved for the situation which was less teacher-centred, that of building up affective relationships with a pupil or groups of pupils. One teacher who strongly believed in maximising his use of the L2 regretted having to exclude the quips and the banter from his lesson. Another teacher commented:

> Because teaching is a relationship – a relationship of trust, of co-operation, of understanding … it's very difficult sometimes to establish that atmosphere or that relationship with a child if you are trying to use a language which the child doesn't understand.

A difference from the results reported in other studies (Mitchell, Franklin, Kharma and Hajjaj) is that putting over points of grammar was not perceived as a problem. The RL1 as recorded in the observation logs (see Table 3.10) supports this. A cynical reader would say that this is because very little grammar is being taught under the umbrella of the communicative approach, a view shared by Roberts (1994). The answer, of course, is: 'What does one mean by grammar'? Certainly the observers had little evidence of formal grammar being taught (e.g. don't forget the PDO goes …); however, there was a lot of evidence of morphology and syntax being taught implicitly and through the target language. Some teachers (including a teacher of German!) found it easier to teach patterns in language through the target language – for example the subject, verb + direct object.

One feature of RL1, which was picked up through the observations, was the use of 'parroting' which was recorded under the category Translating and Checking Comprehension (Table 3.10). This will need a little explanation. Sinclair and Coulthard (1975) discovered that by far the most common exchange in classrooms (any subject classroom) is the initiation–response–confirmation type. Over the course of the Tarclindy observations it was noticed just how much of the following type of exchange occurred:

T: il y a des maisons et des usines … qu'est-ce que c'est en Anglais, usines?
P: factories
T: oui, factories

Is this RL1 by the teacher really necessary? We probably do it because we want to ensure that all 30 pupils have heard and understood the 'interpreting done by the pupil' and because we want to confirm to the interpreter the fact that the interpretations is correct. However, it does the following things. Firstly it breaks the flow of teacher TL use when there is no real pressure to do so. Secondly, it denies the function of 'interpreting for others' ('you've asked me to interpret, so why are you now doing it as well?'). Thirdly, it denies the importance of collaborative learning, the fact that pupils can learn from each other as well as the teacher, and encourages other pupils to switch off to any input from their peers. Lastly, it encourages the pupil responding to speak quietly and only to the teacher, without the confidence (albeit in this case in L1) to project the voice that, presumably, we would want to see as one of the results of language learning. The search for *optimal* use of L2 has to be taken right down to this micro skill level.

Teacher RL1 (by pupil type)

We now turn to an analysis of the data relating to teacher RL1 by variables other than the teacher's classroom language activity. The

Table 3.10 Factors leading to RL1 as observed and recorded in the logs. Lesson segments or exchanges leading to RL1, calculated in averages per hour of observed lesson. No of teachers = 37

Type	Student teacher	Beginner teacher	Exp. teacher	Average total for segment
Instructions/clarification for activities	8.6	7.1	5.7	7.13
Giving directions and changing focus	3.1	1.0	1.1	1.73
Disciplinary interventions	4.6	1.6	1.7	2.63
Teacher ⇒ pupil (open, class hears)	1.5	1.8	1.7	1.66
Teacher ⇒ pupil (closed, class doesn't hear)	2.0	4.0	2.8	2.93
Feedback to pupil(s)	4.6	4.2	3.8	4.2
Translating and checking comprehension	2.0	3.6	6.0	3.86
Teacher language competence	00	0.07	00	0.02
Teaching target culture	0.4	0.14	0.04	0.19
Teaching language awareness	0.07	00	0.1	0.05
Teaching grammar	0.7	0.07	0.2	0.32
Average total per hour	27.57	23.58	23.14	

following elements resulted from the interviews with regard to age and ability of the pupils:

(1) Ability at *any age* was a variable in the teacher's use of L2.
(2) The greatest variation occurred between low ability older pupils and high ability younger pupils.
(3) Virtually all teachers preferred starting with 'virtually all' use of L2 in year 7 rather than a process of gradually increasing the quantity of L2 use as linguistic competence increased (compare this with the Kharma and Hajjaj study.
(4) Provided that behaviour/low motivation was not a factor, *some* teachers felt they could maintain a large quantity (of time in L2) by reducing the complexity of L2 (a great amount of input modification).
(5) Older pupils tended to reject teacher use of L2 because of social reasons rather than linguistic ones (peer pressure; French isn't cool; anti-European sentiments).
(6) Continuity from younger to older pupils was a factor both intra-departmentally (from one teacher to another) and inter-departmentally (usually between phases: middle school to upper school).

Figure 3.2 displays diagrammatically these age related factors which appear to force teachers to have RL1. However, age related factors interlock with ability related concerns (see Table 3.11). Whilst the socio-situational pressures for RL1 are less in classes of younger pupils (see Figure 3.2), pressures which relate to lack of linguistic competence are nevertheless present. With older learners, not only is the situation reversed, but the interplay between classroom language and topic language is thrown into even greater relief. It is worth looking again at the plateau effect here. Let us take the example of a class of year 10 low attainers. The topic language needs to remain structurally simple because of the ability level and yet it has to reflect the adolescent interests of the group. Skilful teachers using appropriate materials can make the leap from, for example, preferences about pets to preferences about members of the opposite sex. The level of language is still characterised by nouns, adjectives and short phrases in simple communicative functions. With classroom language, however, the leap is much more difficult. A teacher has to relate to a 15-year-old's world through the verb-laden language, dominated by imperatives, which tends to characterise classroom language. As I have argued above, classroom language becomes associated with *management* which then becomes the language of *control* in a situation where, already, socio-cultural

Table 3.11 Teacher attitude questionnaire data

Variables in teacher use of TL	Agree	Partly agree	Disagree
Pupil ability	80.8	15.1	3.5
TL is easier with younger pupils	43.0	32.0	22.7
TL is easier with older pupils	8.7	36.0	52.9

influences may be undermining motivation towards foreign language learning. Classroom language is caught in a catch-22 situation: in order to succeed with less able, older pupils, it cannot remain, for socio-cultural reasons, at the level of simple classroom instructions; it cannot move to a higher level for linguistic reasons. It is possible then that placing a lot of emphasis and faith in classroom language will be fruitful only if pupils can be encouraged to 'appreciate from the outset that they are not learning a language simply for use in school but ... in order to meet people of other countries (DES, 1987: 14). An alternative approach is discussed in Chapters 5 and 6.

We have seen that two significant variables are pupil age and pupil ability. We can now examine a third which is related to the experience level of the teachers.

Features of RL1 related to levels of experience

Although the Tarclindy data suggest that there is no significant variance between teachers at different levels of experience and their 'global' attitude to use of L2, variations do occur in terms of the reasons for which teachers at different levels of experience were observed to have RL1 (Table 3.10). These are not always substantiated by the interview data. There is a suggestion, therefore, that student teachers have more difficulty in being aware of their RL1. Below is a summary of variance by teachers' experience level.

1: Student Teachers (STs)
As one would expect, the type of pressure for RL1 among student teachers is foremost related to the threat or actuality of pupil misbehaviour. STs find it hard to restart use of L2 once an RL1 occurs. In addition, the pressure comes in the form of inability to put across more complex instructions for carrying out an activity. In other words, they find input modification and/or providing additional clues to enhance communication more difficult. This is natural and what one would expect. Moreover, and also quite naturally, STs

RLI

Year 7	Year 11
	greater awareness of ability gap
	individualised learning
	harder texts (sentences, verbs, idioms)
	harder topics (abstract)
	complex functions (embedded clauses)
less language store to cope with input	unlikely to attain native model
fewer decoding skills	peer pressure
inexperience of contextual clues	greater acculturation of LI
Year 7	**Year 11**
initial enthusiasm	exam motivation
behavioural response to school as institution	more language store to cope with input
influence of L1	
inconspicuous amongst peers	
distance from native model seems attainable	
whole group learning	
simpler topics (here and now)	
simpler texts (nouns and lists predominate)	
single functions (expressed in short phrases)	

Figure 3.2 Age related pressure to have RL1

are experimenting with tasks and activities and do not have the hindsight of experienced teachers as to which activities need complex instructions.

When anxiety about indiscipline is evident, pressure for RL1 manifests itself in an urgency to get activities started quickly – hence the strong link between instructions and use of L1 and directing or changing the focus of a lesson. Pressure for RL1 also manifests itself in more general terms, by the school environment (socio-economic catchment area) and by the general motivation of pupils. Student teachers are also affected by the departmental policy on the use of L2 or, to a lesser extent, by the policy of the regular teacher.

Among STs, when the lesson is more pupil-centred, there is less RL1.

Level 2: Beginner teachers (BTs)
BTs have a high rate of RL1 when giving instructions for a complex activity. Simple and often-repeated information gap activities did

not often produce RL1. Giving directions in general also did not pose a problem for BTs. There is a suggestion here (supported by the interviews) that BTs knew the limitations within which they would be successful and were therefore less adventurous than they might otherwise have been (or were before as STs)

At this level of experience teachers are emerging as more individual practitioners (not influenced by practice school and visiting tutors). Consequently, decisions about RL1 are made prior to the lesson beginning and according to the predicted response of the particular class. Thus, at least two BTs used the L2 exclusively with one beginners' group whilst RL1 was almost constant with year 10 group. Also to be noted in Table 3.10 is the relatively high RL1 when BTs are talking to individual pupils quietly without the rest of the class being able to hear. It is possible that this is due to a desire to build relationships with pupils who will be taught by BTs for a number of years.

With BTs there was also the *least* amount of variance between data collected via the observation logs and data collected via questionnaire/interview. In other words at this level there was the least mismatch between the aspiration/ideal of use of TL and the reality in the classroom.

Level 3: Experienced Teachers (ETs)

A significant number of ETs had a lowish rate of RL1 in whole group exchanges (teacher centred situations) and quite high RL1 in one-to-one exchanges both with the rest of the class being able to hear (and intended that they should hear) and in quiet, private conversations.

On the other hand, with *some* ETs there was a high instance of RL1 for giving instructions even though the observer judged that there seemed to be no visible pressure to do so. There was thus a much greater variety of teaching styles among ETs than in either of the other two categories. It is unlikely that this is only a consequence of when and where ETs were trained. More likely local factors have, over the years, influenced the compilation of belief systems. ETs were much more pro-active rather than reactive. Experience would seem to equal divergence rather than convergence of methodology. RL1 may well be both a cause and a consequence of this divergence.

ETs were quite confident that they had sound reasons when they did have RL1. For example, one ET whose lessons were almost exclusively in TL made a definite decision to translate a number of words in order to speed up a comprehension checking activity (see 'Translating' in Table 3.10). Another who rarely had RL1 did so when taking over a new class from a colleague in order to carry out a quick needs analysis of those pupils' language competence. ETs do not experience the difficulty of restarting with L2 after an RL1 as much as STs.

Nystrom (1978) maintains that 'national habits, developed by tradition, influence the choice of language for instruction (L1 or L2) more than differences between individual teachers'. This is not a finding in the Tarclindy data.

We can begin to summarise the L1 exclusion debate. We can talk about:

Total exclusion ('virtually all' L2) – this position equates L2 learning with L1 learning. It equates *caretaker* talk with *teacher talk*. It also equates ESL or EFL learning with FL learning. This position sees no pedagogical value in L1 use by the teacher and in virtually no value in L1 use by the learner. The emphasis is on input with the teacher's input given a very high status. The classroom is little different from the natural language learning environment outside (for ESL learners) except that it is more controlled and enabling. In the FL context it is the *only* place where learning can take place. The focus is therefore on providing a target language model.

Maximal – this position states that there is probably no pedagogical value in learner use of L1 and almost certainly none in teacher use of L1. What distinguishes it from total exclusion is fear of communication breakdown resulting in: pupils being distracted; pupils misbehaving; pupils being demotivated. It is also associated with teacher competence and teacher confidence. It has a more socio-cultural dependence than a linguistic one. Variables are by learner ability and class predisposition. Its potential for increase is halted by the need to build relationships. Teachers may feel guilty if RL1 occurs but may not be able to identify the reasons for that guilt.

Optimal – this position sees *some* value in teacher use of L1 and *some* value in learner use of L1. It relates quantity only to *principles* of codeswitching. It relies on knowing when codeswitching will have a negative impact. Use of L2 is strategic. It searches for a stable and functional distribution of L1 and L2 (Mitchell, 1989: 206). The emphasis is on promoting teacher–pupil and pupil–pupil interaction; it acknowledges that the L2 classroom can operate short-cut strategies through the use of L1. Variables are by age and level of competence. Teachers may feel guilty but can analyse those feelings of guilt against some sort of framework.

We have examined a number of studies relating to L1/L2 use. We have focused almost exclusively on the *quantity* of L2 use. By doing so we have shed light on how we might proceed towards an optimal use of L2. We now need to consider how a teacher can avoid RL1 and whether we can assume that this avoidance is beneficial to the learner. Thus we will examine, briefly, the literature on how teachers use the language differently in class to the way they would use it in normal discourse. This phenomenon in the literature is usually referred to as 'input modification'.

The teacher's input modification

To avoid making too many assumptions perhaps we should start with a series of questions:

How do teachers *know* how to change their language behaviour?
In what *ways* do teachers change their language behaviour in FL classrooms?
Is the input modification for comprehension or for learning purposes or both?
What benefits does input modification have?
Is input modification different from language behaviour modification?

We do know that in normal discourse between NS and NNS the former modifies his/her input (foreigner talk) and that this is achieved intuitively, or at least, without any formal training. Is it possible that teachers have an intuitive ability to modify their input in the classroom? This would seem unlikely given the very few student teachers who are able to achieve effective input from the start. Do teachers learn how to modify input reactively, that is to say, by trial and error when the learners display evidence of not having understood them? This would imply a not very comprehensive list of modification strategies and certainly a list dominated by localised factors, individual learners or groups of learners. Effective, experienced teachers are able to gauge the 'ongoing' comprehension level of a new class very quickly by having built up a whole battery of modification strategies through a process of reflective practice.

Useful reviews of the way teachers modify their input are to be found in Chaudron (1988) and Mitchell (1988). Practical guidance can be found in Atkinson (1993b) Cajkler and Addelman (1992), Macdonald (1993). However, it is important to note that, in these practical guides, verbal modification is mixed in with non-verbal communication aids to learner comprehension. The following are some ways in which teachers modify their L2 input. They do this by:

repeating
speaking more slowly
inserting longer pauses
exaggerating pronunciation of words or phrases
stressing certain words or phrases through intonation change
stressing certain words or phrases by saying them louder than the
rest of the utterance
using a simpler vocabulary
using a certain kind of vocabulary (e.g. cognates)
contrasting the target word with another (demain, ce n'est *pas*
aujourd'hui)
exemplifying (semaine: c'est à dire lundi, mardi, mercredi...)
using marker words to trigger the topic/activity and its associated
vocabulary
using more of the same words (*type-token ratio*)
using a set of key phrases at appropriate moments
substituting one uttered phrase with another (paraphrasing)
modifying syntax through word order (e.g. using *canonical* forms)
modifying syntax through using more commonly used verbs
using the present tense more
modifying syntax through fewer subordinate clauses
shortening the length of utterances

Why do teachers do the above things? Are they modifying their input
in order to achieve comprehensibility? Are they modifying in order to
bring about learning? Their intention, of course, may be to do both. It
is a crucial question, however. Are teachers changing their language
input to maintain one-way communication or to have an effect on the
learner's *language competence*? The Tarclindy Interview Data and
Comment Data in the questionnaires, reveal an enormous preoccupation with comprehension at the expense of a preoccupation with
learning. In the monolingual, young learner context, the fear of
communication breakdown by far outweighs the concern that language input will lead to output. Put crudely, if they're quiet and appear
to be listening, they must be learning. It may be that they *are* learning
through comprehension only, but we cannot be sure. As Chaudron
(1988: 154) points out, there is some evidence that slower speech
improves comprehension. There is fairly conclusive evidence that
simplified syntax helps comprehension. There is some evidence that
frequency of input will lead to better acquisition of vocabulary.
However, there is no evidence, as yet, that comprehensibility alone

helps the learner with *creative construct*, the ability freely to form correct utterances. There is also no evidence, although we might think it's obvious, that frequency of input leads to *creative construct*. In general, then, there is only a tenuous link between comprehensibility and the progress which the learner makes with language competence. The issue becomes even more nebulous if Håkansson (1992) is right and some properties of modification are language specific, the implication for teachers who teach two foreign languages being that they should be using different modifications for each language they teach.

If teacher input modification is not providing us with many answers about learning, is there any mileage in looking at the way that teachers check for comprehension? *Teacher talk* cannot be the same as *foreigner talk* as Krashen and Terrell (1988: 34) argue. In a FL classroom of some 30 learners the comprehension checking device operates in vastly different ways. In one-to-one (or even small group) NS-NNS discourse there is the opportunity for fairly immediate comprehension checks on both sides. In the 1:30 situation teachers have three choices: (1) they can take Halliwell and Jones' advice (1991: 14) and *not* ask pupils if they understand 'because they will nearly always have understood **enough** (their emphasis)', in which case the action taken here is to see if they understand by scanning the way they react; or (2) they can teach pupils appropriate forms of interruption (Cajkler and Addelman, 1992: 89); or (3) they can do both.

Whichever strategy is emphasised will determine whether a teacher's concern is primarily *comprehensibility* of input or learning *through* input. I am, it will be noticed, steering clear of non-verbal communication, not because I do not consider it useful for aiding comprehension but because it can only be useful in aiding *comprehension* and not learning to produce language.[3] However, the ongoing process of checking for comprehension, if the focus is as it were, both on the message *and* on the message as medium, may provide the occasions for learner mental processes to occur. Müller (1988: 91) identifies four forms of tuned input: the right amount of information; adapting speech to what the learner can understand; making generalisations about the language; communication of meaning. If the teacher's comprehension checking strategies could include all of these it is possible that they would be ensuring both comprehension and learning.

Thus, we may have to look beyond comprehension of input towards a broader notion of teacher language behaviour modification. By this I mean looking at discourse and interaction rather than one-way modification. It may be that it is in the process of confirmation and comprehension checks that learners make progress in language learning, that unless meaning is 'negotiated', in a way vaguely akin to the negotiation in real discourse, comprehensibility will remain just that. But how can we do that in a class of 30 pupils working at different levels of both comprehensibility and *interlanguage*? How do we give learners the opportunity to stop the teacher and demand meaning negotiation, whilst maintaining the flow of the lesson? I hope to make an attempt at a way forward in the remaining chapters.

Summary

In this chapter we have examined the various ways in which the teacher's use of language operates as an input in the classroom.

The FL classroom is not a natural, unproblematic place for language learning. Within the make-believe world generated by the participants it becomes futile to stake a claim as to the authenticity of one language input over another. Whilst we can see a situational distinction between classroom language and topic language, the claim for 'real communication' of the former is undermined by the shared L1 of the participants in the discourse. The 'real communication' claim can only be supported if the learners perceive the teacher to be the native speaker unable to communicate in L1, and the evidence, although limited, would suggest that this is not the case. In this context, sustaining L2 use is the result not only of comprehensibility achieved through modification of verbal input but also of pupils agreeing to 'play the game'. This agreement is not always readily and freely given.

We have traced a distinction between teacher utterances which contain a message and utterances which refer to the language itself, the medium. A classroom discourse, based on an eclectic communicative approach, which relies entirely on message for promoting language learning is unrealistic and unachievable.

We have discussed other input sources such as materials and input from fellow pupils and noted that these need to be examined for the implications they have for teaching and learning styles and for the beliefs they reflect about language learning. We will return to this theme in Chapters 5 and 6.

We have attempted to break down the language of the classroom into its constituent parts and tried to give answers as to why many teachers find it a problematic area. We have noted reasons why we should, nevertheless, persevere with using it. We have put forward the notion that we cannot expect the pupils to use classroom language unless we teach it, and suggested an approach we might adopt. This approach is proposed as a 'Practical idea to try out' at the end of Chapter 4.

Only by understanding the nature of classroom discourse can we begin to contextualise the debate on how much L1 should be used in the FL classroom. The empirical studies examined have indicated how much L1/L2 is used and the reasons for and functions of L1/L2 use. We have observed that, internationally, the 'virtually all' designation of L2 use is rarely encountered in any learning context apart from EFL1. In any case there is no evidence that exclusive L2 use leads to more effective language learning. That does not mean we need say nothing about L2 use and leave it all up to individual teachers to decide. It is important to distinguish between the pessimism of the *maximal* approach which relies on teacher failure to sustain L2 and the *optimal* approach which relies on the teacher's informed beliefs about the value of L2 use as well as the recognition that L1 can have its own, albeit limited, part to play.

Practical ideas to try out

(1) Try one lesson in which you never 'parrot the learner'. You may need to explain this at the beginning of the lesson. What is the effect on the rest of the class? What is the effect on the pupil answering your question? What is the effect on the flow of the lesson? What is the effect on you/your role as a teacher?

(2) Get a colleague to observe you trying to put across a difficult message (achieve comprehensibility). How did you modify your input? Were you successful in making the pupils understand? Did you have to resort to non-verbal communication to assist you in putting the message across? To what extent, would you judge, did the pupils learn new language from your efforts. To what extent did they consolidate previously learnt language?

(3) Using an observation log like the one proposed in the Appendix (Figure A.1), get a colleague to monitor your recourse to L1. Were you aware of your RL1s (if there were any, of course!)?

Notes

1.   Total Physical Response. See Asher, 1969.
2.   If there is a distinction between the two in the literature I have not yet come across it. A useful, but still weak, distinction might be that activities would tend to be general and whole class (a listening comprehension, a worksheet, simple pair work) whereas a task might be more pupil or group centred and defined by an end product (design a poster, carry out a survey).
3.   It may, of course, help learners with putting across their own message through non-verbal communication.

4 The Pupil as Learner

In Chapter 3 we explored teachers' views on L2 use and analysed observation data of teaching through the target language. The exploration was set against an international background of L2 use and against a national policy on target language use in England as stated in official documentation. This exploration has illuminated only one perspective of the issue: that of the educators. Historically the aim of second language pedagogy has been to discover how best to teach with scant attention being paid to how learners learn or say they learn. Whenever teachers or educators of foreign languages have been faced with individual or collective failure on the part of their learners the reaction has been to change the teaching approach. Indeed, even across a spectrum of 'modernist' authors and practitioners, Littlewood (1984), Hawkins (1987), Krashen and Terrell (1988), we read of theoretical predictions about what might best be a collective response to data which has exposed that which learners have in common. In addition, institutionalised rituals and practices have meant, at least in UK schools, that the way language learners may operate is often subordinated to traditional preconceptions of what is 'proper' procedure in a school. Examples of this are the struggles language departments have had in convincing senior management and parents that homework need not be written work and that not all written work need be corrected by the teacher. This tendency to focus on teaching and subordinating the individual to the collective has begun to be challenged in the past 15 years. On the one hand there has been an attempt to identify the characteristics of effective learners and the implications this has for all learners, Naiman *et al.* (1978), Wenden and Rubin (1987), Oxford (1989), O'Malley and Chamot (1990). On the other there has been an investigation into the ways in which learners differ from one another or groups of learners differ from other groups of learners, Gardner (1985), Skehan (1991), Little (1994). What has characterised both the approaches and the resulting implications for teaching is that the methods of enquiry have involved asking learners to reflect about themselves as learners and to then relate this data to observable language learning behaviour in the classroom. Of course, as in teaching methodology, so in research approaches, it would be dangerous to be influenced by massive pendulum swings. This chapter therefore examines a selection of collective learner and individualised learner research in order to arrive at a more multidimensional perspective of target language use and its relationship to pupil centred learning.

What can second language learning research tell us about learners in the FL classroom? Most discoveries, discussions and controversies about approaches to second language learning and teaching tend to find their origin in the debate about to what extent L2 acquisition is like L1 acquisition. It would be so simple if it were all one way or the other. Unfortunately nothing is ever that simple where something as psychologically and sociologically complex as language is concerned. Moreover, writers on L2 acquisition have tended to oversimplify the issues in L1 acquisition or, at least, to give an impression of a consensus which in reality does not exist. Despite this caveat, if we could establish to what extent L2 learning is like L1 learning, it might place us in a better position to draw up principles of L2 use in the classroom.

L1/L2: Some Similarities and Differences

When a child learns its first language some sort of language processing system is in operation. Although Chomsky's Language Acquisition Device (1965) (or later his concept of Universal Grammar) is contested, there is still a consensus among authors in general that a mechanism for processing language input exists inside the brain. It is something we are born with. This system is the mechanism for the construction of the language system in all humans. The mechanism appears to be at least partly functioning with L2 learning as well. Certainly it would appear to be being utilised by very young L2 learners. However, the older the L2 learner, the more his/her cognitive skills play an active part in learning and supersede the innate processing system. Nevertheless, both L1 and L2 learning incorporate similar abilities to acquire *subconsciously* aspects of language or patterns in language.

The belief that all L1 learners have 'natural sequences' in the way they acquire language structures in L1 has been shown to be only partly true. The language environment *can* effect the acquisition. But some discernible 'stages' of learning remain. Development of L2 learning resembles L1 in that it too is 'staged' (Towell & Hawkins, 1994: 10). However, L2 learners are particularly influenced by factors (depending on their learning environment) which affect a natural or staged sequence. L2 learners *individually* develop their deep-seated under-standing of language through a process of trial and error, hypothesis testing and experimentation. This process and the stages at which it is measured is called 'interlanguage' by some researchers. Although L2 learners probably develop an 'interlanguage' based on L2, they also inevitably make use of L1. They *do* transfer rules and patterns from their L1. This aspect of language study is referred to as 'contrastive analysis'. Transfer of rules from L1 is a learner strategy in making sense of L2 facilitated by a more highly developed cognitive ability than can be found in a young child.

There is no equivalence in the L1 and L2 psychological developmental stages: A child at the age of 11 explores and tests the world in a very different way to the way a child explores and tests the reality of the world at the age of 3. The L2 learner at the age of 11 would have to backtrack to the most basic developmental stage in order to simulate L1 learning (Skinner, 1985). As an example, for adolescent L2 learners, the concept of 'one word' and 'two word' stages of development are meaningless (Sharwood-Smith, 1994: 46).

'Teacher talk', with conscious reference to language patterns, makes more impact in L2 learning than 'Child Directed Speech' does in L1 learning.

Both L1 and L2 learners need exposure to language in order to be able to acquire language. In L1, however, even at a conservative estimate, children receive as much as 3,650 hours of linguistic interaction between the emergence of the first word and a recognisable language proficiency[1] (Richards, B., 1994). By contrast, FL learners in an English classroom receive only 300 to 400 hours of instruction in the five years of the National Curriculum.

L1 learners and L2 learners have similar powers of vocabulary acquisition. The notion that L1 learners are like 'sponges' more than L2 learners has been challenged even though at 18 months L1 learners are said to make vocabulary 'spurts'. Whilst the capacity to acquire vocabulary may be similar, the process by which we are exposed to vocabulary (for example) in natural L1 settings and unnatural (even communicative) L2 settings is inevitably very different. The different way L2 learners categorise and store vocabulary may be a consequence of this. It may also be a consequence of a highly developed cognitive ability.

In L1 and L2, the same four language skills (in able-bodied people) are available for development. This is obvious. Moreover, whereas oral skills development does not seem to be greatly affected by 'intelligence', both in L1 and L2, writing and reading skills (and other *conscious* analytical aptitudes) are. The same speech organs are available to both L1 learners and L2 learners. There is no reason why an able-bodied L2 learner should not, mechanically, be able to utter a target language sound. Although the speech organs are the same, in practice, L2 learners no longer have the range of sounds available to them that a baby has. L1 learning has produced a continuous process of 'specialisation' of sounds. Thus with L1 the learner proceeds from a wide range to a narrower one, whereas with L2 learning the learner is trying to proceed from a narrow range to a wider range (i.e. to incorporate the L2 sound system).

Both L1 and L2 learners use strategies to compensate for not knowing how to say something. The opportunity to communicate a reply to a question using resources other than the verbal medium is available more to the L2 learner than the L1 learner. The former has, after all, had more practice.

Some L1 learners also have to go through a process of learning a kind of L2 when they adapt to standard forms (e.g. Standard English) from their language community 'dialect'. In this situation *codeswitching* happens frequently and naturally.

The vast majority of L1 learners learn to speak a language to a degree comparable to other proficient adults. The vast majority of older (certainly past the age of around 15) L2 learners do not reach native speaker oral proficiency.

L1 learners receive feedback from parents and siblings. L2 learners in classrooms receive feedback from teachers. Their progress is evaluated by teachers. Their output is likely to be commented on by their peers. The security of the former environment is likely to be more conducive to acquisition than the environment of the latter.

The written form is immediately available in L2 but not in L1.

Some Implications of L1/L2 Similarities and Differences

Let us now consider some implication of the above. We will not deal with all of them here; some will emerge as issues in later chapters.

(1) L2 learning resembles L1 learning in a number of ways but the ways it differs are very strong and influential. FL learners (as opposed to other L2 learners) are more learners than they are acquirers. It is perhaps this more than any other factor which actually makes FL learning in a classroom possible.

(2) L2 learning is both conscious and unconscious. Learners need to be exposed to a lot of message oriented language in order to trigger natural processes. They should also be drawn into interaction with a focus on medium oriented[2] language in order to 'speed up'

interlanguage development. L2 language syllabuses based on linear progression of developing competence (e.g. short phrase to multiple exchange) are artificial.

(3) Vocabulary meaning *can* be understood from the context in which it is received. However, because L2 learners are able to categorise vocabulary, they *can and need to understand* meaning in much more detail than the acquisition hypothesis would tend to suggest.[3] We should therefore allow *some* codeswitching in class.

(4) Exposure to an L2-rich classroom environment is going to be essential for any inbuilt processes to be activated and for the acquisition of vocabulary in context. In addition, the learner, as a more adept cognitive-performer, is going to need the opportunity to manipulate and to have a say in the language of that environment. Early production of language for the FL learner may be a necessary condition for hypothesis testing given both the time constraints and the sophisticated learning strategies that s/he can deploy. Learner errors are a clear indication that learning is going on. Non-threatening error feedback therefore becomes useful because it helps to confirm the pattern the learner is developing for a particular language element.

(5) We should always be working with the L2 learner's attributes and not against them. If these attributes are age-related, we should take them into account. For example, we should not insist too much on pronunciation with older learners. If these attributes are individualistic, we should try to provide opportunities for individual development. If learners maintain that writing phrases down immediately helps with memorisation, we should allow it.

(6) L2 learners need to spend some time consciously *learning to learn* as well as learning a foreign language.

The above discussion throws into a more focused perspective the NC's claim that FL learning is 'natural'. We will now relate these few insights into how natural L2 learning actually is, to learning through the medium of the target language as that process is perceived by pupils.

Tarclindy Project Data

The interviews carried out with pupils in the Tarclindy project generated a number of categories about the way FL learners said they learned languages or reacted to language teaching in the secondary school context. There were two underlying themes which emerged from the interview data:

(1) The pupils' understanding of their teacher's methodology approach or style. Pupils often made references to the way the teacher taught as part of a recognisable pattern rather than a random set of operations. (See later section: Informing Learners about Pedagogy, p. 127).

(2) There were many examples of individual differences and different learning styles. This was thrown into greater relief by the group response on best-fit system which was used for data collection (see Appendix). As many of the groups disagreed (i.e. individual respondents within the groups) as agreed. This evidence is interspersed within the analysis of the specific themes.

There were at least seven specific themes resulting from the data:

(a) Comprehension of the teacher's TL, frustration and negotiation.
(b) Being forced to speak (in answer to questions) in the TL: making mistakes; embarrassment; peer pressure.
(c) Pupil initiated questions: classroom language; transferability.
(d) Learner strategies – classroom oriented; reaction to teacher.
(e) Learner strategies – home oriented.
(f) What language content should learners be learning through? Transferability.
(g) Collaboration in and also out of the classroom.

Apart from themes (e) and (g),which will be dealt with in later chapters, I shall try to relate these themes to the issues about L2 learning discussed above.

Comprehension of the teacher's TL, frustration and negotiation

Burstall (1970) found that many children soon became bewildered when French was used indiscriminately in class to give instructions without ascertaining that they were clearly understood. Clearly a comparison with the present day is only partly valid because the circumstances in which the Burstall study was conducted were quite different. Burstall was gathering evidence in a period when the principles of learning a language for the purposes of communicative competence were not established and when the importance of learning a foreign language in the European context was not fully appreciated. Moreover, the study was being carried out on pupils of primary school age involving teachers who had not necessarily undergone a substantial period of training in language teaching and yet were pioneering a new methodology. We would hope and expect therefore that the pupils' reaction 25 years later, to teacher use of L2 for the purposes of giving instructions for a task, would be almost entirely positive.

The first important indication from the Tarclindy interview data is that learners were split into two groups. There were those, a minority but a considerable one, who did not get flustered when the teacher used large quantities of L2 and who believed that they did not need, in any case, to understand everything . They believed that, as the words were wafting over them, they were learning anyway. This group welcomed the teacher's attempts to paraphrase or give other context enhancing clues. This group tended to be made up of girls rather than boys (although not exclusively) and were likely to consist of more able pupils. Even this group, however, forcefully adhered to the proposition that teachers should give important information (e.g. homework or test instructions) in English (L1) after they had first done so in L2.

> I think that's quite important (important information in L1), although to a certain extent it's good to try and work out what they're saying, because I mean, if you're in France or if you're in Germany, then not everyone's going to be able to say, 'That's this and this' in English.

> It would be easier (in L1) probably but probably we wouldn't learn as much.
> It would be pretty pointless being in a German lesson.

> It would be easier if the teacher told you what to do in English but better in the long run if she used French.

> You can ask the teacher to repeat.

> You get used to the words after a while.

> You can say I don't know what the word means and they (teacher) can explain it to you in another way, then you can use the word in other sentences.

The other group of children had quite strong reactions to the idea that you could learn more if the teacher spoke in L2 even though they couldn't always understand. One respondent echoed the views of several that: 'If you don't understand you can't learn anything'.

This negative reaction was the result of two sources of unease. The first was that these pupils wanted the exact meaning of words and phrases. They were hinting at two levels of knowledge and under-standing, a functional level and a literal level. Or they might know the L2 word or phrase, in the sense of recognising it but did not know its actual meaning in L1. An example of this might be the activity title: *On prend rendez-vous* (Briggs *et al.*, 1992: 97) where pupils had an idea that it might be to do with meeting people (perhaps from the pictures on the page) but were not aware that *rendez-vous* was an appointment and *prend* was the verb used for making an appointment. Another more extreme example (but a recorded one) would be not knowing the real meaning of 'elle' even though they knew the meaning of *elle a douze ans*.The second source of unease were the 'consequences' of not understanding the teacher's input. For many, including some in the positive reaction group, this meant a whole series of frustrations and subsequent failures to achieve tasks set by the teacher. Homework needed to be understood, otherwise the teacher told them off. Written instructions needed to be clearly understood otherwise: 'if you get the instructions wrong you've ruined the whole thing'.

If the teacher carried on for too long in L2 then pupils said they might 'shut off' and then when they were asked to do a task they thought, 'Oh dear what am I supposed to be doing?' Some pupils admitted nodding and pretending that they had understood when they in fact had not. This *appearance* of comprehension may have led OFSTED inspectors to report (1995: 4) that in KS3 pupils were able to follow without difficulty lessons carried out in L2.

What advice then might teachers glean from the above? To a certain extent this learner acceptance or rejection of extensive use of L2 was related to specific teachers but not conclusively. Differences within classes and within interview groups indicated that the link was not a direct causal link. It was not, moreover, departmental/school specific even though the department may have had a clearly stated policy on use of the TL. It is probable that individual learner differences were more powerful in producing a reaction one way or the other than differences in teachers' methods even though the latter should not be discounted. As teachers we should note this and try to find out more about our learners as well as developing our ability to put across meaning. Moreover, although different reactions to teacher use of L2 have come to light through an analysis of the Tarclindy data, it is important to note that the interview data continually reminds us that all learners wish to go deeper into words and their meanings (Chambers, G., 1994: 16). Whilst we should not confuse this tendency with the bi-lingual approach advocated by some authors, (e.g. Dodson, 1985), it is relevant to ask the question as to whether the comprehensible input hypothesis holds less well in large classes of young FL learners (as opposed to smaller classes of older ESL learners) precisely because the trawling effect is harder to achieve with bigger numbers all having different needs and learning styles. Teacher input directed at 30 learners has inevitably fewer points of firm contact. There is, yet again, an indication that the lock-step paradigm needs to be challenged.

There was a strong consensus, particularly among the more able learners, that the teacher ought to attempt to put over the message in L2 at least twice before resorting to English. Pupils were aware, furthermore, that waiting for the teacher to go into English eventually might be an easy way out for some. They had no answer to this problem yet none admitted doing this on purpose. Some pupils actually mentioned that they liked the teacher to stay in L2 as a sort of test for him/her, forcing the teacher to come up with alternatives. One teacher used an 'English square' which he would jump into if he really couldn't put it over in L2. Another said the word *sous-titres* (subtitles) before going into L1. Explaining in L2 could therefore be made into a game. Clearly creating the right atmosphere of trust is essential if clarification, confirmation and negotiated understanding is to take place. The right atmosphere can only be present if the pupils feel it is their right to ask for clarification. As one put it: 'We should be extremely free to ask'.

It is salutary and positive that we can discern learner feedback to the teacher amongst young learners in the same way that it has been explored amongst adult learners. What is also encouraging is that some learners reported being aware of the strategies the teacher used in order to achieve comprehensibility. Among these were:

- teacher talks more slowly (than in normal speech);
- teacher breaks up long sentences into small bits;
- teacher says it in a different way;
- teacher uses mime;
- teacher demonstrates things or points to things (e.g. pictures);
- teacher writes (difficult things) on board;
- teacher shows pupils in the book (where there are contextual clues or translations);
- teacher asks someone to explain.

If the pupils gave evidence of having observed the types of strategies the teachers used in order to help them understand, they also gave evidence of strategies they used in order to signal lack of comprehension and request for clarification. They did this by:

- simply saying they didn't understand (in L1 or L2);
- giving each other puzzled looks going round the class (almost as a chain reaction);

- making a sound such as 'errrrr';
- asking a friend 'overtly' so that the teacher can spot lack of comprehension and amend or intervene (but without being asked directly to repeat).

This dual awareness of the learning process (ways of requesting and satisfying that request) is very encouraging and should be further explored and promoted in our classrooms.

An important piece of evidence to emerge was that the more successful learners were the ones who claimed they were prepared to negotiate meaning with the teacher, who were actively involved in ensuring that they understood rather than passively hoping that the teacher would come through in the end. [4]

The value of interaction as a causal factor in promoting language proficiency is unresolved. Chaudron (1988: 97) cites a number of studies Naiman *et al.*, (1978); Strong, (1983); Swain, (1985) which show some correlation between the amount of interaction/participation learners involved themselves in and language proficiency. Equally, however, there are studies which show little or no correlation (Sato, 1982 and Slimani, 1987, quoted in Allwright & Bailey 1991: 131). Chaudron concurs with Allwright and Bailey, therefore, that it is probably self-evident that successful learners will perform more in language classrooms on the basis of self-esteem and confidence rather than as an aggressive learning strategy. Swain (1985) claims, on the other hand, that what occurs when listening to teacher input is *selective listening*. Selective listening means that learners can focus on vague meaning without considering form or more in-depth meaning. Selective listening means that the learners are not processing input or are not able to process their own output. Simplified teacher input is not sufficient or as optimal as the input which comes from negotiated work in interaction. In other words, it is at the level of interaction that modification may be more important - dialogue modification rather than monologue modification. Varonis and Gass (1985) have demonstrated how conversations differ between native speakers (NS–NS), non-native speakers (NNS–NNS) and NNS–NS. They differ particularly with respect to the amount of negotiated meaning through the use of L2 (e.g. do you mean A or B? ah, A is like C?, I didn't know!). Because NNS have a shared incompetence in L2 there is no embarrassment about committing errors and therefore greater opportunity for negotiated meaning. We shall return to this theme in Chapter 5. Negotiated meaning also leads to greater attentiveness and involvement in the discourse. Chaudron (1988: 106) defines negotiated meaning thus:

Speech acts that are contingent on previous utterances and that in some way negotiate meaning or maintain conversation by reacting to the preceding discourse: clarifying, modifying, repeating, asking for clarification ... linguistic, semantic and pragmatic rules of the learner's interlanguage are put to the test ... as opposed to simply responding or initiating.

The following three hypotheses, whilst not in themselves being proven, would appear to be interrelated and, in combination, their presence seems to correlate with successful language learning:

(1)   If you make the teacher ask you more questions you learn more.
(2)   If you speak more you learn more.
(3)   If you negotiate meaning more you learn more.

Failure in the languages classroom according to these criteria is seen to occur when learners do not call upon their right to draw on the teacher as a resource (Prabhu, 1987: 59) or do not deploy constructive strategies for making the teacher help them learn. Thus teacher–pupil interaction can be communicative if it is the result of attempts to negotiate meaning. In so doing it also avoids frustration. However, negotiating meaning in this way involves learners having to speak when they might not feel ready to. To what extent can it be justified and can embarrassment be overcome?

Early production versus silent period

There are a number of methods which have advocated that learners should not be required to speak in L2 until they are ready. Extreme forms of the Silent Way (Gattegno, 1972) have been demonstrated (Nunan, 1991) to be nothing more than audiolingual behaviourist techniques dressed up as mystical processes. Total Physical Response (Asher, 1969) and Natural Approach (Krashen & Terrell, 1988) draw on notions of a silent period but again incorporate as a result, elements of behaviourism. However, they do all stake one claim which must be taken seriously and that is that they do care for the feelings of the learner by not forcing him or her to speak 'until they are ready'. Activities which spring from a desire to put the learner at ease whilst making him/her the focus of the language can be said to be humanism-led as opposed to institution-led or society-led or National Curriculum-led. However, a dilemma occurs the moment one of these strategies is seen to be producing long periods of silence on the part of the learner. Krashen and Terrell (1988) would seem to be contradicting themselves in that they are claiming on the one hand 'not speaking until ready' as a vital ingredient in lowerng the *affective filter* and on the other hand that adolescents get more comprehensible input directed at them because they negotiate more meaning, ask for help and negotiate the topic more than younger learners. If this is the case, then any silent period or extended teacher monologue is reducing the opportunity for learners to understand and learn language. This is apart from the fact that they may just switch off through boredom. As we have seen, there is little evidence that learning can take place without interaction or that progressing from a 'not prepared to speak stage' to a 'being prepared to speak' is a natural process which should be replicated in the unnatural classroom.

Nevertheless the question of readiness to speak is an important one. In a class of 30 11-year-old FL learners we are confronted with the following complex issues:

- How does the learner know that s/he is ready to speak?
- How does the learner signal that s/he is ready to speak?
- How does the teacher satisfy many learners who are ready to speak?
- How does the teacher know that the learner is *not* ready to speak?
- In terms of language learning progression, is readiness to speak horizontal, vertical or spiral?

Readiness to speak seems to be fraught with problems. The Tarclindy teacher interviews provide little evidence that the readiness to speak criteria was something that teachers were considering.[5] Yet only a minority of pupils chose the 'no problem' card (see Appendix), where the suggestion was that 'this was what language learning was all about'. Not many, it is true, adamantly opposed themselves to the teacher strategy of requiring them to speak immediately, perhaps because questioning/eliciting techniques are so widespread or, as Wringe (1989: 87) claims 'it has long been recognised that questioning is one of the most central and effective of all pedagogic techniques'. Nevertheless, there were severe reservations about the impact this had on them as learners and as individuals. These reactions and reservations were that being expected to answer questions was:

(a) Embarrassing, people laughed at you, there was an audience (which could later comment on you):

> You could be confident in what you're going to say and then you say it wrong and everyone laughs at you.

Sometimes when the teacher asks you, your mind just goes off, even if you know it, it goes, and you can just feel your heart beat, and that's all you can hear, you can't hear you voice. (NB This was in a girls-only school!)

(b) To do with knowing or not knowing the answer.

It depends whether you know the answer definitely or not. If you don't know the answer, if you haven't made any attempt to say sort of say, yeah I can answer this question, and if the teacher picks on you, it is embarrassing.

If everyone else has got their hand up (and you haven't) then it's embarrassing.

I think in our class, the rest of the class are relieved that the question hasn't been asked to them, that it's been asked to someone else.

(c) To do with not understanding the question, the fact they hadn't been listening or the teacher's selection procedure and the reasons behind it.

It's *not* no problem basically (strong reaction to card 7 – see Appendix). It can be extremely hard. If you're not sure what she's talking about, and she says, 'Answer this question'.

People put their hands up, then she picks somebody who hasn't put their hand up to answer it.

(She picks them) if she thinks that someone's not paying attention. Or someone who's just quiet and needs bringing out of their shell almost. And when they do put their hand up, then she doesn't pick them.

(d) To do with being in a no-win situation regarding peer pressure: being a square, a keeno, a swot, smart or teacher's pet.

Sometimes it's embarrassing if you do know the answer because the others think you're square. Embarrassing if you don't know 'cos the others go 'neerrr ... *I* knew that!'.

On the other hand there were many encouraging signs that pupils were coping with the embarrassment and the pressures. What helped them to cope was one or more of the following: the teacher, their friends, the atmosphere established in the class and the desire to succeed despite the embarrassment.

We usually just whisper it to each other, especially if one person knows it. I usually sit next to Emma, and she usually helps me a lot, she just whispers it to me.

As long as she (the teacher) doesn't wait for too long waiting for you to say it when you know you can't.

She'll ask someone to help you. Ask the class to help. I don't mind that, 'cos then you've got some back-up.

Nobody minds really. Whole class laughs and you find it funny yourself. You realise what mistake you've done and think 'whoops' and laugh as well.

People making fun of you are losing out – they won't learn anything.

In Yr 7 I felt nervous about speaking French in front of the class. I'm more confident now. No one takes the mickey.

We can sympathise with the pupils who find speaking when they are not ready or answering questions difficult. Yet do we not have to go along with the notion that precisely those learners who are most eager to provide responses are those who would also initiate interactions (Chaudron, 1988: 100)?

To return to the topic of being forced to speak and some of the pupil comments above. We cannot ignore the enormous influence of peer pressure on language learner's attitudes towards use of the target language. Allwright & Bailey (1991: 176) reviewing diary studies on the subject, confirms this anxiety resulting from being either the best *or* the worst in the class, an anxiety which can have a debilitating effect on language learning. Furthermore, self-esteem may well correlate positively with oral performance and low self-esteem may be further influenced by the teacher's reaction to error.

It looks, therefore, as if we need teacher-pupil input and interaction at an early stage in schemes of work given the limited amount of FL teaching and the developmental stage of the learner. At the same time we need to be wary of its effect on the self-esteem and motivation of the learner. These two learner needs would appear to be irreconcilable and there is plenty of scope for further research into ways of reducing the impact of peer pressure. In doing this it may be that we shall come to question the unchallenged belief that *question and anwer technique* is indispensable for language learning. Moreover, it is unlikely that these two learner needs will be reconciled in protracted use of lock-step, 1:30 classroom approaches.

So far, we have focused on teacher initiated discourse and interaction and its effect on the learner. Our experience tells us that this is by far the most common form of discourse in all types of classrooms. Does research back up this intuition? We will now look in some detail at interaction which is initiated by the learner.

Learner initiated dialogue (LID)

There was little evidence of learner initiated dialogues (LID) in the observation of the classes during the Tarclindy project. Initialisation of topic was virtually non-existent (e.g. Madame, je suis allé voir Nicola à l'hôpital hier soir). The most common form of LID was the single phrase to which the teacher responded with a yes/no or with simply an acknowledgement that the LID had been achieved by the learner. There were very few cases of LIDs with the teacher involving two or more exchanges. We could, mischievously, conclude that teachers kept the lid on this aspect of classroom discourse. This would concur with the evidence from the INSET questionnaire sent to LEA advisers that much more work needs to be done on developing the learner's use of the target language in the classroom.

There is clearly a need to develop the ability and the desire in pupils to ask a lot more questions in class, a need to bring in a lot more questioning functions. Some teachers in the Tarclindy study promoted learner initiated dialogue by refusing to accept questions or request in L1. However, this was limited to questions relating to not under-standing the teacher input or requests which assisted the continuance of a teacher initiated activity or discourse. In other words, the teacher was still totally in control of the discourse and the pupil interjections were mere minor deviations along the intended route. Mitchell reports (1988: 161) that, in one school, incidents rejecting pupil use of L1 happened only when the teacher felt the 'appropriate FL exponent had previously been taught'. The operative word here presumably is 'taught' rather than 'learnt' (see below). She concludes that without active pressure from the teacher pupils will not spontaneously adopt L2 as the language of self-expression even when teachers have done so to a considerable extent. There is an urgent need to find out why this is the case. Are learners refusing to initiate in L2 because of the psychological barrier existing between two speakers of the same L1? Alternatively, does the traditional lock-step classroom with its over-whelming emphasis on teacher control of the discourse discourage L2 LIDs? It may be that learners so rarely have the opportunity to practise self-expression that, when they do, they try to ensure 'immediate communication' in L1. It may also be that teachers are sending out a number of signals regarding LIDs in a pressurised secondary class-room. Hakansson and Lindberg (1988) in a study on adult immigrants to Sweden learning Swedish, report that some learner questions were simply ignored and some had to ask permission to speak through some form of pre-utterance or other. Learner questions were not perceived by the teacher as fitting into the traditional pedagogical interaction pattern as when the authors noted that 'some of the learner questions were received with an embarrassed laugh from the teacher, which indicates that something quite unusual and unexpected was taking place'. If this is happening in a less formal adult classroom, it is even more likely to occur in a pressurised secondary one.

A number of variables in learner initiated dialogue may well exist and these need to be explored.. Among those that concern us here are the ethnic origin of the learner (Asian learners are less likely to initiate, for cultural reasons); the age, role and status of the learner vis-à-vis the teacher; the number of participants in the discourse. Intuition would also suggest the following as variables: teacher–pupil relationships; classroom atmosphere; departmental or individual teacher 'stated' policy; gender; ability or previous language learning success.

The Tarclindy interviews tried to ascertain whether LID felt awk-ward, was OK as long you knew what to say or made the learner feel good (see Appendix). Most interviewees felt that the 'OK, so long as you knew what to say' was the one they could most identify with. The few that chose 'awkward' felt this very strongly. The few choosers of 'makes you feel good' articulated this opinion with less enthusiasm, but this is understandable given that pupils in England don't like to sound as if they're really enjoying language learning in front of their peers.

The following issues emerged from an analysis of the pupil inter-view data regarding LIDs:

(1) Whether the teacher insisted on use of L2 for LIDs in the case of already learnt elements.
(2) Whether the teacher continued to insist on the use of L2 for LIDs from one year to the next.
(3) Whether the teacher insisted on use of L2 for LIDs in the case of elements not learnt (by teaching them on the spot and then requiring pupils to say them in L2.

Teachers say, if you want to ask the person sitting next to you for a rubber, then you have to say it in German or French, but we don't actually do that. We just say, 'Give us your rubber'. I don't think the teacher actually takes it seriously, what they're asking us to do.

Ros: Does your teacher insist on you asking for things in French?

P1: She doesn't does she?

P2: No. She tells us in French what we should say and we just repeat it, so we know for next time.

Ros: And would you say it in French the next time?

P1: Some of it. Not all of it.

P2: Last year we had to do that. We weren't allowed to do anything if we didn't say it in French, but this year, normally you can just say it in English.

The type and length of LID

P: You can say to the T 'comment dit-on x en français' and T will repeat it. It is 'awkward' because if you don't know it exactly, e.g. if it's a long word, and you get it a bit wrong you have to keep repeating it.

P: Simple things are OK like 'can I have some paper' 'cos everyone says that every day. But one-off things – personal things – are more difficult.

The method, situation and frequency of teaching, the types of language elements likely to be needed for LIDs

P: In the old French room, they had pictures of them up on the wall. It said 'I have forgotten' and then it had it in French 'J'ai oublié' (i.e. this wasn't *learnt* language).

P: Or they'll just prompt you – say if you get stuck half way through the sentence, they'll give you the next word and you'll probably know what to do.

P: If we said 'Can I have a new book?', she'd teach it to us in German. get us to repeat it. Bit by bit, slowly build it up. Then put pictures on the wall to remind us.

The perceived usefulness of LIDs and pupil questions: The perceived transferability of LIDs and asking questions

P: Yeah, because otherwise we don't usually get a chance to ask questions in French.

P: You can't just learn the answers, you've got to learn the questions. The question words and stuff, you've got to know how to use them. Like 'qu'est-ce que tu' and all that.

P: Because if you're on a street in France, somebody's not going to come and ask you where to go, you're going to have to ask somebody else 'cos you won't know, and so that's when you're going to need the questions.

The effect LIDs had on the pace of the lesson

P: We tend to want to get on with work and therefore we ask in English.

The feeling of embarrassment, of being spotlit and of peer pressure when attempting or being called upon (surely a contradiction in terms!) to carry out a LID

P: Yeah. Especially if you don't know what to say. If you ask it in English they want you to say it in the language and they say it really slowly to you while everyone else is watching you so that you can repeat it .

Whether LIDs and pupil questions should be tested and rewarded

Ros: Do you think that sort of thing ought to come into your exam?
P1: Could be useful. It's not as if you're going to be living at the station all night. Don't want it on the higher paper. Basic (paper) maybe.
P2: (We) used to get a merit for asking questions in French, so they (fellow pupils) would keep asking silly questions like 'What's the time?'

We can now compare some of the above data with what the teachers said regarding LIDs. In doing so we find some articulation of pedagogical considerations but above all of practical difficulties:

(1) *Time* to insist on pupil use of LIDs. This was particularly problematic at the beginning of a lesson when pupils had a lot of business and problems to sort out. However, it also occurred at changeovers of activities when, again, practical problems all arose at once (no pen, no worksheet, don't understand!).

(2) *The energy* to insist on use of L2 for LIDs. What particularly sapped teachers' strength was the continuity of LIDs and remembering to insist on elements already taught 'on the hoof', as it were, whilst they were probably trying to sort out something else connected with the lesson.

(3) A feeling that it was *unfair/unreasonable* to always expect learners to use L2 for LIDs.
(4) The difficulty of actually setting time aside to teach it. *Planning* for LIDs was difficult. There was a feeling that this body of language was less 'graspable'. You could tick it off in your mind as something that had been done but if the opportunity for its use cropped up again, teachers would have to reactivate that in the pupils' minds. It then raised the question of how to get them to see the link with something they had done some time in the past, to formally reactivate the language and for pupils to seize the opportunity to re-use that language in a different language context or with structural modifications.

Also mentioned, but with less frequency, were:

(5) The influence of *peer pressure* hampering the promotion of LIDs.
(6) Lack of *training* to teach LIDs.
(7) *Age* – the fact that it was easier with younger pupils.

Virtually all teachers saw value in LIDs not only for developing learner spontaneity but also to demonstrate survival techniques (communication strategies) in the foreign language. Teachers were aware they were not doing enough to promote them. Moreover, teachers claimed that reluctance on the pupils' part to use LIDs was more attitude related than ability related (see below the discussion on learner strategy training).

There are two important indications emerging from an analysis of the data on LIDs. Firstly, it is quite clear that learners themselves see great value in initiating a dialogue with the teacher instead of always waiting to be asked things. The fact that they limit LIDs to questions requesting permission on clarification/how to say things, is a reflection of the fact that we have not moved that far away from the traditional classroom in terms of who controls the topic, the turn taking and the feedback. Of course it may be argued with some justification that (a) in classes of 30 it is impractical to relinquish those areas of control to individuals (therefore it's the 1:30 that has to be tackled); and (b) the interviewees were in the early years of learning with only a few hours of lessons accorded weekly and were consequently incapable of sustaining anything but the most basic and short dialogue which they had initiated. My own experience would suggest that the answer lies in (a) rather than (b). It would seem therefore that our patterns of interaction will have to change quite significantly in order that learner initiated dialogue can be actively encouraged. For this to happen further progress needs to be made away from the up-front lock-step teaching towards more flexible groupings of learners[6] – (see Chapters 5 and 6).

Secondly, as indicated in Chapter 3, we need to change our approach to the way we teach the classroom language topic, making it much more akin to the communicative methodology we use to teach other topic areas. Waiting for the phrases to arise will never be totally avoided; we could never pre-teach all the possible things that the topic of classroom language throws up, but we could teach a sizeable amount, thus avoiding some of the anxieties caused by spotlighting which we have reported above. More importantly, perhaps, we need to categorise it in manageable chunks. Figure A.4 gives a possible list of classroom language topics of which many could be, or result in, learner initiated dialogues. (See also 'Practical ideas to try out' at the end of this chapter.)

Changing our approach to teaching classroom language and categorising it as a topic are, yet again, teacher-led decisions. What can the learners themselves do which might facilitate aspects of learning such as interaction and initiation? In order to try to answer this question we need to take a look at the area of *learner strategies*.

Learner Strategies

We have identified a number of strategies during the course of the analysis of the pupil data which the pupils have indicated they use in order to signal to the teacher that they have not understood his/her input. These form only a small part of the total number of strategies and categories of strategies identified by researchers. There is indeed a wealth of literature on learner strategies, much of it of an accessible and practical nature. Rubin (1981) makes a useful distinction between direct strategies (use now, in the classroom) and indirect strategies (use later, at home or in later life). Naturally there will be considerable overlap between these two categories. However, for the purposes of this book I will examine the former in the current chapter and the latter in the chapter on autonomy. The question we must also not fail to ask is: in the context of optimal use of L2 by teachers (and learners) in the classroom, how can learner strategy *training* most effectively be done?

Why should we concern ourselves with learner strategies? Firstly, if we wish to accelerate the shift of focus from teaching to learning we need to look at other strategies which learners might deploy in order to assist them in that learning process. Secondly, a number of differences in attitudes to language learning, self-evaluation of success and reaction to teacher methods have been identified in the interviews. Is it possible that they are the result of successful learners being able to deploy a number of strategies which less successful learners are not aware of? Is it possible that strategy training could bring about a change in some low-achievers' self-esteem by attributing their lack of achievement to lack of effective strategies rather than laziness or lack of ability. O'Malley and Chamot (1990) report that in one study of FL learners, more effective students were using more learner strategies than the less effective students but that the latter *were using some*. A final reason is that we would wish to give greater responsibility to learners for their learning.

At this point I would like to signal a difference between a learning strategy and a communicative strategy even if this distinction is not emphasised in the literature. I would want to propose that the former helps you learn, the latter helps you speak and keep a conversation going. In order to illustrate I will use a personal example. I was on holiday in Italy and speaking to my uncle about the English education system. He asked me why I didn't send my children to a private school. I replied that, apart from other reasons, in the sort of job I did, I would be crucified! As I was speaking I realised I wasn't totally confident about the verb 'to crucify'. I had a choice of course. I could avoid the use of the unsure verb and opt for something like: 'they'd put me on a cross'. This would have kept the conversation going without any problem. Instead, I risked 'crucificare' overgeneralising from the English plus the common Italian 'are-ending' verbs. With a certain amount of facial glee my uncle reminded me that the correct form was 'crocifiggere' and that I had not done enough to maintain my native language. However, by attempting an overgeneralisation of the verb I was using a learning strategy to test and hypothesise about the verb ending and, as it turned out, the root as well. If I had used the noun phrase, which I was sure of, I would have been using a communication strategy by substituting something I knew for something I didn't know, thus keeping the *message* discourse going. By using the overgeneralisation I made the discourse less efficient but I learnt something.

The following is a selection of quotes from the Tarclindy pupil interviews when asked what helped them learn and what helped them remember language.[7] They illustrate the diversity and (if previous comments about embarrassment at speaking are taken into account) the individual differences which young learners bring to the classroom:

I think homework does ... you really go through all the dictionaries and everything and you really try to look for it, and once you've looked for it, it stays in your mind.

I can remember the first French song we ever had and that was quite a few years ago.[8]

If you can't pronounce something right and the teacher is telling *you* that it's wrong, then you are more likely to remember it than hearing her tell someone else.

Cover up the German (L2) and look at the English (L1) and try to remember it.

Writing things down ... numbers in German ... couldn't remember them until I wrote them down.

(Acting things out) we had to act ... thunder storms we were under the tables ... when it was hot we were on top.

and the following from one group of interviewees which serves as a reminder that individual differences are sometimes not psychological but social or circumstantial differences:

P1: I normally do it (homework) with my mum and dad.
P2: I just read it through myself – my parents come home from work too late to help me really. Half the time I can't really remember it so it's horrible when the teacher has a go at you.
P3: It's easy for me in French 'cos my mum's French so she can help me at weekends.

Lists and categories of learner strategies

There are many taxonomies of learning strategies in the literature cited above and it is not the purpose of this chapter to add to those lists or refine them. However, I offer below a selection which seems particularly appropriate to the secondary FL classroom. The selection is adapted from a very useful study by Grenfell and Harris (1994) of pupils aged between 11–14. Another relevant study is Chamot *et al.,* 1987 (reported in O'Malley & Chamot, 1990: 123), a study of FL learners in high school. Most studies have otherwise been carried out with advanced adult learners.

(1) Making sense of the L2 input.
   (a) Use a number of strategies to guess what words mean.
   (b) Think if words which look like English words (or other L2 words? Spanish? Italian?).
   (c) Ask for clarification or repetition/more slowly/ individual words.

    (d) Play tape recorder again to listen to what you haven't under-
        stood.
    (e) Scan and skim text.
    (b) Tackle narrative text with a who/where/when/how approach.
(2) Pre-communicative.
    (a) Practise saying new words out loud.
    (b) Practice saying new words under my breath (or answering
        questions directed at other people in your head).
    (c) Turn language into songs, rhymes, raps and mnemonics.
    (d) Act out language (either physically or in your head).
    (e) Look for other opportunities to use a new word or phrase.
    (f) Learn by making mistakes which the teacher corrects.
(3) Study/revision/redrafting skills.
    (a) Look up words in dictionary or coursebook.
    (b) Make a note of new words; write language down.
    (c) Make word links in a text (e.g. animal – dog) or a word web.
    (d) Make a mental association of difficult words (perhaps with
        something funny).
    (e) Learn vocabulary via a technique, e.g. through look/hide/say/
        write.
    (f) Enlist the help of others, e.g. parents or older siblings.
    (g) Use a computer/word processor to help redraft some written
        work.

It is interesting that pupils in the Grenfell and Harris study made most progress with the strategies related to collaborative learning (see Chapter 5 of this book) rather than personal learning or learning related to teacher activity. For example *don't just copy somebody's answer but ask them why /practise saying new words out loud* got a low score. This may not be possible within the framework of current teaching styles. For example, teachers in the study may not have given pupils the opportunities to activate those learner strategies. How many teachers would tolerate that background of chatter (positively useful though it may be) whilst they were helping pupils understand some new text? Note also that the Grenfell and Harris data provide us with an indication of what the pupils *said* were the areas of most and least progress in strategy use. This is one of the strengths and weaknesses of learner strategy research. As Cohen (1991) points out, researchers will not find out what strategies learners use by simply observing them.[9] Moreover, there is no evidence as yet of a link between increased strategy use and increased language competence. The rationale for strategy training, which Grenfell and Harris (1993: 24) outline, needs further consolidation. They suggest that 'pupils learn more language when they learn how to analyse and control their linguistic systems and how to process linguistic information in an efficient manner'. As the authors admit, this is an area which is crying out for more high quality research. There is some evidence (O'Malley & Chamot, 1990) that it improves language learning, but it is tentative.

Issues related to learner strategies

There are a number of other issues related to learner strategies which still need to be resolved. The lists of strategies are not definitive nor are the categories or individual strategies sufficiently carefully refined or reliable (Chaudron, 1988: 116) to be confidently applicable across a number of learning situations. Indeed, no single research instrument has yet been found which can provide a definitive taxonomy. Thus, we do not know *all* the things that learners do to help them learn. As we can see from contrasting the above list for young learners with one for 'educated adults' it is unlikely that a single list would apply to all learner types. Furthermore, we do not know why some learners don't use any/some of these strategies. The learning process includes both conscious and unconscious learning and therefore learners will be aware of some strategies but not of others. In *The Good Language Learner*, Naiman *et al.* (1978) listed a number of strategies. However, these are not all the same for everybody. Different things work for different people, possibly because of their different learning styles, possibly because they have developed that skill elsewhere (e.g. note-taking, ordering a series of items coherently). Learners *can* adopt strategies or be taught to use strategies and can make decisions about which strategies best suit them from a list once they have been made aware of their existence. However, as Skehan (1991: 288) points out, it may be that all learners use strategies. What good learners do is to choose the right strategy for the right occasion. He goes on to argue that, 'There is still the worrying possibility that good learners are ones for whom the use of effective strategies are possible, while for poorer learners they are not.' This seems an unnecessarily pessimistic anxiety given the evidence of the Grenfell and Harris study which suggests learners can increase their strategy use. A more optimistic hypothesis is put forward by O'Malley and Chamot (1990). Individuals with a special aptitude for learning foreign languages may simply be learners who have found *on their own* the strategies which are effective for efficient language learning. What the Grenfell and Harris study does not make clear is whether *all* learners managed to increase at least some strategy use. Cook (1991) suggests that we have no proof as yet that strategy training is actually teachable. As many strategies are not observable by the teacher, you can make pupils aware of their existence and constantly try to remind them but whether they will use them is another matter.

Learner strategy training in the FL classroom

Should strategy training be carried out as part and parcel of the language learning scheme of work or should it be part of a separate short course taught at the beginning or at some appropriate stage during the scheme of work? Indeed, there is some argument for learner training to be carried out on a whole school basis, as part of a personal and social educational programme (PSE) or study skills programme, given that many strategies such as deduction and inferencing apply to other subject learning as well. However, it would seem that the immediate applicability of strategy training being carried out by language teachers in languages classrooms would outweigh the advantages of a whole school approach (such as not encroaching on language lesson time and avoiding recourse to L1). A short separate course allows the strategies to be more definable by the teacher for the learners and possibly leads to greater generalisability of strategy use by the latter. If taught early, moreover, there is greater likelihood of helping those learners who would otherwise be deploying strategies less. Should the training be explicit or implicit? In other words, should the students be aware they are being taught these strategies or not? Certainly one would expect advantages in language materials which were structured to both elicit the use of strategies and demonstrate the effectiveness of strategy use. In any case teachers teach strategy use already. Through stress and intonation when reading through a text, the teacher is implying the skill of scanning. However, it could also be argued that the awareness of the value of using strategies is best brought about through explicit training in strategy use.

These questions on implementation of strategy training have, of course, a direct bearing on the amount of L1 use teachers should allow themselves in the classroom. Clearly an integrated/implicit approach would help avoid recourse to L1. It is less likely, however, that such an approach would assist those very learners who would benefit most from strategy training, and it is also unlikely that it would be as effective in developing learner autonomy, especially out of the classroom. We do not know as yet how much strategy training can be carried out in L2. Atkinson (1993b: 72) suggests two occasions when it is justified to use L1 for strategy training: (1) when the learners do not have enough L2 to do the activity in L2; and (2) when the learners actually need the training in L1 anyway – i.e. they couldn't do it as part of a mother tongue exercise. Both these criteria (as I am sure Atkinson would agree) are not watertight. They do not stand up to all the circumstances in which training might occur. In the case of (1) teachers could use the development of one strategy (e.g. looking words up in dictionaries) to put across the awareness of another. For example, teachers could do a *sondage* (survey) in L2 about what pupils do when they don't understand the teacher input. Preparation for the *survey* could be a worksheet where pupils have to look up words and phrases they don't understand like: je lève la main, je dis 'répetez, svp'. In the case of (2) it is surely possible to learn some strategies in L2 without first having learnt them in L1. However, there will be times when the complexity of the strategy (or the technicality of the language needed) and the importance of making pupils aware quickly, overrides considerations of recourse to L1. In which case it fits better with the notion of not undermining future L2 use to plan part of a lesson for the purpose of strategy training as a separate chunk and to do it all in L1. Hopefully it will be possible to return to and remind/reinforce the strategy successively by remaining in L2 and doing so through the use of language materials themselves.

Little systematic work has been done to identify which strategies are most susceptible to training or what lengths of training time are needed to give results which justify the time taken away from language learning itself. Research in this field is urgently needed as well as the development of FL materials which teachers could use for strategy training. The one course of action for which most proponents of strategy training would find least justification is postponing any training until the learners have enough L2 to do the training in L2. Chamot (1987) in the study of high school learners of Spanish found that intermediate/advance learners were not using many more strategies than beginner learners (16.9 and 12.4 respectively). This indicates the possibility that not much progress is made by the learners alone in strategy use and therefore training from the outset would help. The following sequence for strategy training might be followed:

(1) Providing activities which develop learner awareness of the existence of learner strategies. These might include finding out from a class (and other classes) which ones they use and helping them to identify which ones they use.
(2) Providing learners with a further range of strategies they have not

identified and demonstrating the use of strategies in an active language learning context.

(3) Providing opportunities to implement the strategies in everyday language learning situations.

(4) Asking the learners to evaluate (is the strategy right for me? is it helping me learn?).

(5) Transferring the strategies to different or new tasks.

An alternative, more teacher-led approach might focus on early and late categories of strategies. For example, using the O'Malley and Chamot model: *cognitive* would be developed early (note taking, using dictionaries, categorising and memorising vocabulary, ensuring they can hear the tape recorder, ensuring comprehension of teacher input), as would *social* (interacting with other students or with the teacher) whilst later bringing in the *metacognitive* ones (planning and thinking about learning, monitoring one's own learning, evaluating progress).

It may also be the case that a questionnaire is first administered to the learners to test their assumptions about language learning and then a programme of training devised according to their responses. The questionnaire itself should generate discussion and awareness. As Grenfell and Harris (1994) suggest, it may be that a developmental sequence in learner strategies has to be related to the learners' social and emotional stage of development.

As well as the social and emotional stages of an adolescent learner's development, we would do well to consider his/her attitudes to foreign cultures. We have looked at this briefly under the heading of motivation in Chapter 2. If attitudes to foreign cultures are important in motivating learners to learn the target language we need to investigate how curriculum time can be attributed to raising awareness of the target culture. This *predisposition* to learning a language needs to be broadened to a predisposition to language learning in general and an awareness of the diversity of languages in the world. We have to consider preparing the pupil as learner.

Learner Predisposition and Target Language

Atkinson (1993a) argues that radically monolingual 'approaches' (exclusive use of L2) in the classroom run the risk of being mis-construed by British learners, particularly adolescents, as an attempt to impose a form of cultural imperialism which threatens their own cultural identity and thus, paradoxically, causes them to retreat further into xenophobic monoculturalism. Even if the threat of French or

Spanish 'cultural imperialism' over the all powerful English language in an English classroom seems something of an overstatement, the point needs to be taken seriously. In some classrooms learners need to be reassured that the teacher is aware that they do have a language of their own and a measure of control over what they say and how they say it. Moreover, we must not forget that in order to promote a positive disposition to tackling a topic or text we must first awaken curiosity by establishing prior knowledge (Chambers, G., 1992). Rather than denying pupils the opportunity to express their own ideas, it may be desirable and appropriate to allow brief introductions to topics and texts in L1.

Pomphrey (1994) argues, as Hawkins (1987) does more extensively, that there is a need for space in the curriculum to explore and reflect on language in a wider sense. Indeed Hawkins, Donmall and others argued through the NCLE publications (1985) that a single language learnt could never be an end in itself. Pomphrey summarises the types of activities carried out under the now ragged banner of Language Awareness (LA)[10] as: knowledge about languages; knowledge about language structure and knowledge about learning languages. There is not space here to explore in detail reasons for its virtual demise but these can be summarised as follows:

(1) An unenthusiastic report compiled by inspectors (DES 1990c).
(2) The limited introduction of Knowledge about Language (KAL) in the mother tongue (English) National Curriculum. KAL addresses only in part the shortcomings left by the demise of the Language Awareness initiative.[11] Yet, as James and Garrett (1992: 15) point out, there is support among mother tongue educators for an analytic dimension to LA.
(3) Twenty years after the Bullock Report (1975) argued strongly for whole-school language policies there is little evidence of their implementation in schools.
(4) The National Curriculum in MFL, whilst appearing to adopt a commitment to an *Awareness of Language and of the Learning Process* (DES, 1990b: 35) in reality defines it in terms of an awareness of *the language being learnt* rather than (or even as well as) an awareness of languages in general. This restricting tendency is given added impetus by the *virtually* all insistence of the use of the target language. Teachers wanting to teach pupils that the English language owes a debt to a number of other linguistic sources, not all of them European, may have balked at the prospect of trying to do so in L2.

Without an intrinsic predisposition to language coupled to an understanding of the instrumental necessity of learning a language, some of our 11-year-old learners will quickly lose their initial enthusiasm.

Can anything be salvaged from the old Language Awareness wreck? To start with, we have to admit that some of the programmes of the 1980s *were* too *ad hoc* and perhaps took too much time away from learning an actual language. From that position we can begin to extract, from those programmes, themes and activities which really did change attitudes and broadened learners' world view of languages. We could then identify where those activities could be carried out partly or wholly in L2 and materials redesigned and updated for that purpose. More importantly, it should be possible to embed the language learning skills (e.g. learner strategies) into an *Awareness of Languages and the Language Learning Process* programme which itself runs along side the 'content' of the Areas of Experience.

Foreign language learning needs to take place in the framework of an awareness of the multilingual context as well as an awareness of the learner's own cultural identity, what Byram (1992) calls needing to 'know how others see me as well as how I see others'. He adds that this awareness is essential if we are to communicate *with* each other and not just communicate messages *to* each other. We are in an era where the question of single identities is being challenged. Mass migrations have brought about the establishment of language communities at a historically unprecedented pace. The European Union is an inescapable fact which entails membership and identity at the local, regional, national and European levels. Yet, as Convery *et al.* (1996) demonstrate in a study involving 1300 European teenagers, a sense of European identity amongst English school children is probably the lowest in Europe and the European Dimension in Education, an initiative agreed upon by the education ministers of all member states, is neither actively promoted by UK government agencies nor adequately financed.

As FL teachers we must take care not to reinforce this situation, linguistically or through the choice of materials and content – for example, by repeatedly emphasising the diversity of cultures rather than what they have in common. It is unwise, moreover, for teachers to assume that the celebration of other cultures and the development of tolerance through multiple identities will come about merely through developing communication skills. But is it realistic that we can ask learners just starting with a language to confront, in L2, the complex ideas embodied in an ethnographic or social anthropological approach to the study of target cultures? If we did, we would be deluding ourselves that anything but a superficial understanding would result with possibly negative outcomes in terms of pupil attitudes. A mixture of L1 and L2 might be possible where certain facts were processed in L2 but ideas and opinions expressed in L1. Later, as the language competence grows, more and more work of this type can be carried out in L2. It is the same dilemma as with learner strategies: it is desirable for these foundations skills and attitudes to be addressed in the early stages of a language learning programme, but in so doing we are also restricting the time available for learning the language itself.

Another related and also controversial question is what areas of language should our learners be learning through? Is the content of language learning specific to a particular country? Can we separate content from process? Table 2.1 in Chapter 2 indicates the purposes of language learning that the pupil questionnaire data provided in the Tarclindy project. As was suggested in Chapter 1, the purposes of FL learning can compete with one another and, as it were, jostle for the limelight. They should never be mutually exclusive. To form a sound base of the skills required for work and leisure should not be so overemphasised as to neglect or exclude the encouraging of positive attitudes to speakers of foreign languages or to offer insights into the culture of the target country. In other words, we should aim for a balance between satisfying and promoting instrumental and integrative motivation for language learning. It may be that it is precisely the GCSE's overemphasis on leisure in the target countries that has brought about the attitudes to language learning suggested in Table 2.1. Work needs to be done in increasing the aspects of schools' schemes of work which involve practical communication with foreign people as real people not as stereotyped providers of goods or information. Readers should note that Table 2.1 refers to information about France. There may be some cultural stereotypes, supported by pronouncements in the British media and reflecting the opinion of senior politicians (see Convery *et al.*, 1996), that pertain especially to this European country rather than another.

There is the opportunity too for pupils in language classes to arrive at a greater understanding of themselves and examine their own culture as a backcloth to the understanding of the cultures of the target countries. Grenfell (1991) proposes a radical revaluation of the content of our programmes of study. He argues that a vital additional component to transactional language and the insights into language is a 'sense of self-identity' in the language because psycholinguistic research suggests that 'language is the very blueprint of our identities as social beings'. He argues for 'processes' which bring out the energy in language learning rather than, 'materials'. There is value in this assertion. However, mitigating against this type of 'process learning' is not only lack of appropriate training for teachers but the refusal of linguistic development in L2 to mesh with the adolescent's psychological development. As I have argued, by the age of 12 learners have already used their L1 to make quite a lot of sense of the world. To require them to perform the same mental activities in L2 would meet with resistance. Moreover, as we have shown earlier, the FL classroom is an artificial, sometimes bewildering, place. Can we really expect learners to work through their teenage crises in such an environment in a language they can only tentatively relate to thought? Again, this is a peculiarity of the FL classroom. An ESL classroom can more easily accommodate topics related to the anxieties and issues pertaining to being a foreigner in the country the language of which you are learning. Being in a classroom with fellow learners in the same circumstances, is an added facilitator.

In this chapter we have so far developed two broad categories of implications of L2/L1 use by pupils. The first category is the ongoing teaching/learning process with its unplanned recourse to L1. Within this category developing the internal rule system seems best served by L2. Satisfying a desire for 'in-depth' meaning may sometimes best be served by short cuts using L1. The second category is a sort of 'preparation' of the learner for learning. This is more likely to occur in a pre-planned 'time out from L2' approach. Within this category come themes such as Learner Strategies and Predisposition to Culture. A third theme within this category is involving the students in the teaching/learning process and we shall take a look at this now.

Informing Learners about Pedagogy

It is one of the disadvantages of first becoming a language teacher and then a parent of a language learner, that you find out too late just how aware learners are of their teacher's approach or method. Young learners may not be able to express it as a coherent set of principles or as recognisable logical sequences but they are aware of teachers' styles and they love to make comparisons. The interviews with pupils in the Tarclindy project underwrite this impression. Pupils talked about teachers who did lots of group work and those who didn't[12]; teachers who insisted on L2 for learner initiated dialogue and those who allowed English; teachers who believed in ensuring total understanding and those who liked to 'gabble on'; those who encouraged requests for clarification and those who, more or less, forbade it; teachers who waited for answers and those who supplied them almost immediately or asked someone else. The list of pupil observations of this sort could easily be much longer. There were times, of course, that from what the pupils said, it was clear they were not aware why the teacher was doing something and a study which adopted the approach of observing the teacher, asking the teacher then asking the learners, all focusing on the same lesson would be in a better position to document this theme.

Researchers and practitioners seem united in the belief that it is desirable to inform learners and perhaps even negotiate with learners why one is going about something in a particular way. But in what language do we do it in? If my answer here is L1 then the reader is justified in totting up all the instances over the past two chapters when I have suggested L1 might be acceptable and start getting a little anxious. And yet if we look at the way Krashen and Terrell (1988: 74) advocate informing not only about goals but also how the teacher intends to get there it is difficult to see how this could be done in L2 at the beginning of a course of study:

> your teacher will speak in French exclusively;
> you are free to use English until you yourself feel ready to try speaking French;
> you should not try to use French until you are completely comfortable doing so.

Perhaps to avoid using L1 in class pupils could be given this sort of information to take home and digest although this strategy would prevent any form of clarification or negotiation. Macdonald (1993: 21) seems to suggests getting it all over and done with before starting and in L1. This may well be the best course of action although it would need to be evaluated. Subsequently, teachers could have short bursts of time-out in L1 where the teaching approach is restated, refined or negotiated. The important criteria for time out in L1 is that it is *put to a purpose*.

Summary and Optimal Use of L2

One of the overarching themes of this chapter, and indeed the book, is that the FL classroom cannot provide the total language learning experience. Undoubtedly it is the place where, for many learners, it is going to be virtually the only place they experience a foreign language. That is one reason, and certainly not the only one, why we must reaffirm a complete belief that L2 should be the main medium of communication in the classroom. The view is an intuitive one as there is as yet little research which documents the effect of teachers L1/L2 use on language acquisition and learner competence. It is, however, an intuition which is in line with the views of the vast majority of teachers and learners in the project. Dickson (1992: 22) suggests:

> The challenge for teachers is to arrive at a judicious mix .. this perspective underlines the fact that target language use is only one of the variables governing classroom learning. In specifying principles for target language use it would be necessary, therefore, to allow for variables which apply in individual classrooms.

I believe we have to be a little more explicit than this. Over the course of the past two chapters I have tried to qualify, therefore, my use of the phrase 'optimal use of L2', that is to say for those moments and for those activities when L2 is *clearly* or *more likely* to be the most linguistically beneficial way of proceeding. In order to explore the limitations of L2 it seems that I have had to approach the issue in a negative way, by highlighting instances when it is *not likely to be* beneficial. I hope that this is because the instances when L1 is appropriate are in the minority and not for any other reason. They are, however, an important minority of instances and activities which, because we want learners to become better learners and less dependent on teaching, we have to address in FL contact time – that is unless curriculum managers and designers can be persuaded otherwise.

Summaries of recommendations for L1/L2 use can be found in Atkinson (1993b: 15); Cajkler and Addelman (1992: 94); Pattison (1987: 15); Duff and Polio (1990: 163), as well as the contributions from Macdonald (1993) and Halliwell and Jones (1991) examined in Chapter 3. The following are my own. As I have said, these fall into two broad categories which I will refer to as: Pre-planned Time-Out in L1; and Unplanned Recourse to L1.

This chapter has dealt with those aspects of classroom activities which I have considered essential from the point of view of the learner if the learner is going to be able to take some responsibility for his/her own learning, acquire autonomy transferable to other situations, and contribute to the way the learning proceeds. These were:

- learner strategies;
- predisposing learners to language learning;
- informing students about pedagogy.

We have also, in Chapter 3, touched on these:

- explaining and negotiating objectives;
- reviewing progress and tutoring;
- building up personal relationships with individuals.

Justification for carrying out these activities in L1 *can* be made by teachers. It will be noticed that I stress the word 'can'. In all cases of recourse to L1 teachers should try to reflect on whether it was absolutely necessary to do so. Having come to that decision, teachers should feel confident and not guilty. Even so they should still ask themselves whether it might be possible the next time to carry out some or the whole of the activity in L2. As a general principle, I would suggest that these types of activities are pre-planned rather than on the hoof and presented in such a way (Time-out from L2) as to demonstrate to the learners the value of the activity and the value of L2 time.

In Chapters 3 and 4 we have also examined occasions when teachers have recourse to L1 because of some unforeseen classroom event. Of course careful planning and input modification minimises these events, but no amount of planning can pre-empt all classroom events! The most justifiable of these unplanned RL1s are:

- when the L2 instructions for an L2 activity are actually postponing that activity from taking place;
- when teachers judge it beneficial to put over the exact meaning of a word, phrase or idiom and are unable to do so by other means;
- when the teacher wants to signal danger to the pupils.

In this chapter we have also examined the views of young learners on a number of issues, many of which relate to the dichotomy between *natural* L2 learning and taught L2 *learning*. Whether pupils are made to speak straight away; whether they should understand most of what the teacher says; whether they should engage in negotiated meaning – all these relate to what extent learning a foreign language after, say, the age of 10 is still like learning a language in the first few years of a child's life.

I have argued for much greater learner initiated dialogue and suggested alternative approaches for the teaching of the more common categories of classroom language (see also 'Practical ideas to try out' below). I have hinted at a methodological threshold which we must step over if we are to give learners the opportunity for much greater control of what they say, how they say it and if we are to accord the time for them to say it in. This will take up much of the discussion in Chapters 5 and 6.

Practical Ideas To Try Out

(1) Cut up the statement squares in the Appendix (Figure A2). With a teacher colleague identify all the ones which you would *always* carry out in L2 and put them to one side. Identify those which you would occasionally explain in L1. Make sure you can justify this in terms of 'pupil learning.' For example, 'It might be stopping pupils from speaking'; 'It might be postponing a highly valid active task'. On the other hand, could meaning negotiation have been deployed? Could you prepare for it, thus avoiding recourse to L1? For each of these pieces of paper give a *variable*. For example, 'I would always use L2 with year 7 for this'. Were there any that you would never use L2 for? How can you justify this?

(2) Cut up the statement squares in the Appendix (Figure A3). Apply the same procedure as in (1) above. You might also like to ask a group of learners what they think.

(3) Choose a category from the list of topics for classroom language (see Appendix Figure A4). Define what vocabulary and structures you wish the pupils to have acquired by the end of this topic. Devise a way of teaching it along the same lines as a normal topic. An example (exemplified in English but applicable to many languages) might be:

Vocabulary and structures:
(a) Can I leave the room?
(b) Can I go and see Mrs Taylor?
(c) Can I go to the toilet?
(d) Can I go to the library?
(e) I've got to go to the doctor's.
(f) I've got to go to the dentist's.
(g) I have a music lesson.
(h) I've got to meet my mum.
(i) I've got a note (of excuse).

Activities:
(a) Listen to a cassette where (for example) Italian pupils are asking for permission, etc.
(b) Question-and-answer of phrases using OHT symbols.
(c) Do a matching activity between symbols and written phrases.
(d) In 'open pairs' pupils ask and give permission (perhaps throwing a soft ball as a 'trigger').
(e) In pairs, pupils do dialogues involving asking for and giving permission.

(f) In groups of nine pupils do a 'mental accumulator' activity with the phrases.

(g) Pupils listen to a cassette where a teacher gives reasons for denying permission.

(4) Decide that you are going to explain your objectives for a topic or unit of work to your class. However, do it as a listening comprehension in L2. You might be able, if you have a foreign language assistant, to record it as a simulated dialogue between a teacher and a pupil. Devise some activities which will help learners to understand what you (or the recording) are saying about what they are going to learn. An example would be true or false statements.

(5) Ask pupils to make a list of all the things that they do that help then understand your input in the 1:30 situation. Compile the whole list and then do it as a survey of the class or another class. Can this part be done in L2?

(6) Ask pupils to make a list of all the things that they do that help them learn vocabulary or short phrases. Then proceed as with (5). See also Appendix Figure A.8.

Remember that if you have student teachers in school they will, no doubt, be happy to help you to prepare and carry out some of these activities!

Notes

1. For example, through the use of tag questions in English speakers.
2. As with our discussion (Chapter 2) of developing the internalised rule system of L2, medium oriented language input is not to be understood as being synonymous with explicit teaching of grammar rules.
3. There is evidence, for example, that the *type* of practice more than the *frequency* is important in vocabulary learning (Cook, 1991).
4. Other studies lend support to this notion. Seliger (1983) found that high input generators (those that actively used language to get more exposure to language for themselves – to have more input directed at them) outperformed low input generators by simply achieving higher levels of competence even though they produced more errors. Seliger's methodology has been attacked on the grounds of validity and reliability, however.
5. Admittedly there were few year 7 interviewees (mostly year 8 and year 9). However, my own experience of teaching and observing others makes me feel reasonably confident that the criteria of 'don't speak until ready' was *not* in operation even at the absolute beginner level.
6. Even though, in the UK at least, this may seem politically unfashionable!
7. This data was not collected using the best-fit system described in the Appendix although it was collected during the course of the same semi-structured group interviews.

8. It could be argued with some justification that songs/raps, etc. only become learning strategies when they are undertaken independently of the teacher, i.e. 'I think I'll try and remember this bit of language by making up a rap about it'.

9. See Cohen (1991: 110) for a list of alternative research methods related to learner strategies.

10. The very low scores regarding recourse to L1 when teachers were teaching Language Awareness type activities was due to the absence of those activities from the lessons observed, not to the fact that they were unproblematically carried out in L2!

11. For readers unfamiliar with the English context, it may be useful to know that during the 1980s a substantial number of schools taught courses on the awareness of language before, or alongside the language teaching. Some of these courses were entirely school-specific. Others drew on published materials.

12. Even those who did some one year and not the next!

5 Collaborative Learning

If we were to start all over again, planning our education systems from scratch, what would our language classrooms look like? Would we actually have people called 'teachers' with the primary function of transmitting to learners knowledge and skills that they themselves had acquired? Would we indeed have language classrooms with rows of desks facing a single source of language input such as a teacher or tape recorder or screen or blackboard? Would there be fixed times for language learning and a pre-determined curriculum? Would teachers want to inculcate in learners, through their actions and their assessment system, the concept that only an individual learner in competition with other learners can acquire that body of knowledge and skills, that elusive language, that the teacher possesses?

In our 'fresh start' language learning environment we might at least question many of the assumptions, belief systems and values about learning. Hopefully, a radical (and unlikely) 'fresh start' will be unnecessary. Hopefully, the above notions are not too fixed in our educational psyche and they are not too underpinned by the structural cohesion and coercion of school as a managed institution for gradual change to occur. The question remains as to how learners can be empowered through more responsibility and control of their learning and through a greater awareness of the learning process itself. One of the contexts in which this empowerment can be achieved and is being achieved is through collaborative learning.

A definition of collaborative learning is when learners are encouraged to achieve common learning goals by working together rather than with the teacher and when they demonstrate that they value and respect each other's language input. Then, the teacher's role becomes one of facilitating these goals.

Tarclindy Data

Let us keep within the spirit of this and the previous chapter and start with what the learners had to say about working collaboratively (pupil interviews).

The most favoured rank ordering for the focus group cards (see Appendix Figure A.5, pp. 215–17) is as follows:

(1) It makes you feel comfortable and confident.
(2) You learn a lot and remember a lot.
(3) It's OK but you do tend to chat in English.
(4) Sometimes my partner doesn't want to work with me.
(5) It's not good, I prefer talking to the teacher.
(6) It's a waste of time.

Those groups which did not have this type of ranking tended to come from the same school or were taught by the same teacher. We could venture, therefore, that the teacher's attitude to collaborative learning makes a considerable difference to pupils' attitudes. Pupils who differed from the above rank order chose 'tended to chat in English' as being the card they most associated with, or as being much more the characteristic they identified with collaborative work. Even these groups, however, then put 'comfortable and confident' and 'learn a lot' high in the ranking. In fact, only two pupils came out strongly that it was a complete waste of time and there was only one instance of a pupil actually preferring to answer the teacher. In other words, by far the vast majority of pupils reacted favourably to pair work and group work, the only fly in the ointment being an acknowledged tendency to go off task and chat in L1.

Pupils elaborated on their choices by affirming that working collaboratively made you feel comfortable and confident because it was much easier to work at the same level and pace than in the whole group situation. They felt that it was less threatening when the teacher was not in opposition to the learner, firing awkward questions. The teacher could come round and offer individual or small group support and feedback. In pairs they could work out answers and work through dialogues together and they could take joint responsibility for their work. Lastly, they said, it gave them an opportunity to talk to different people in the class.

But did they feel that it actually helped them to learn? Generally pupils agreed that it helped the learning process by helping them to remember. Collaborative learning also helped because it led to a better understanding of language, getting more ideas from the small group situation than a whole class. Moreover, they saw value in getting another go at saying something. Finally, as one said: 'Helping your partner helps you to learn.'

So pupils generally responded favourably to the language learning value of collaboration as well as its social contribution. But here too they were realistic. They recognised that they did, some more than others, lapse into English. Some of this was still in a positive light as when they did not know how to proceed with a task and had to resort to L1. Other instances were self-confessed poor attitudes: 'wandered off' task, 'finished task off early and couldn't be bothered to do it again', were typical of the responses in this category. The remedy most saw was in the teacher patrolling and monitoring their on-task L2 rather than self-control. They pointed out that this need not always be done in an authoritarian way. For example, one group suggested the teacher could stand in the middle of the room with his/her eyes shut and point in the direction of where (English) L1 was coming from. Their teacher did this.

They were also reflective and realistic about the social side of collaboration. Although the vast majority reported working constructively with their partner(s), this wasn't always the case. It was, for example, annoying when 'your partner is mucking about, or annoying if you've just said a long sentence and people aren't listening.'

Most pupils said they preferred working with their friends even though a number recognised the value of working with different people. However, it was generally felt that you were 'less fluent' with people you didn't get on with. There were no instances of pupils claiming that they deliberately, if given the choice, paired themselves with someone they perceived as more proficient than themselves.

How do Young Learners Collaborate?

Collaboration in the secondary classroom takes a variety of forms but I will distinguish three main categories: *Teacher directed collaboration, Learner directed collaboration,* and *Learner generated collaboration.* There is substantial overlap within these categories but I will keep the distinction (Table 5.1) in order to facilitate the discussion.

Teacher directed collaboration is distinguished by the teacher's premeditated intention for a particular type of class behaviour or group behaviour. The collaborative behaviour results directly (if the learners are compliant) from the teacher's instructions. This is probably the category of collaboration most commonly found in current classrooms. That it is common practice is evidenced by the fact that when practitioners talk to one another they do not need to explain the procedure for these types of activities (8L did a really good *sondage* today!). Collaborative activities which are teacher directed are generally well documented in CLT practitioner manuals and FL coursebooks.

Table 5.1 An audit of collaborative activities[1]

Activity description	Teacher directed collaboration	Learner directed collaboration	Learner generated collaboration
Dialogue reading	☯		
Reading to each other	☯		
Open pairs			☯
Role-play	☯		
Simulations	☯		
Surveys	☯		
Making a video		☯	
Playlets		☯	
Games	☯		
Revising together	☯		
Peer testing	☯		
Making materials for games	☯		
Quizzes in teams	☯		
Compiling (e.g. brochures or poetry books)		☯	
Composing songs, raps		☯	
Jigsaw stories	☯		
Listening to a tape (as a group)		☯	
Assisting listening (whole class)			☯
Learner Initiated Dialogue			☯
Pupil interpretation teacher confirmation	☯		
Symbiotic			☯
Reporting back to teacher as a pair	☯		
Reporting back to each other	☯		
Processing and passing on information	☯		
Collective clarification request			☯

Table 5.1 (*continued*)

Activity description	Teacher directed collaboration	Learner directed collaboration	Learner generated collaboration
Collective feedback to teacher			☺
IT: two to a keyboard		☺	
Whispering answers			☺
Asking a friend to ask the teacher			☺
Asking a friend to explain			☺

Learner directed collaboration occurs less often, probably because it is considered as an end-product activity rather than a means to an end (see the discussion on *Interaction* below). Typical of this form of collaboration is when learners are required to form groups and prepare, for example, a scene from a restaurant before performing it in front of the rest of the class. Although the initial directive or global instruction comes from the teacher the preparation stage is carried out, for the most part, independently of the teacher. The details of the collaboration are then achieved by one learner directing operations, or, better still (especially if in L2), by negotiation within the whole group of learners.

Learner generated collaboration is probably the category which occurs most often but which we know least about, it is referred to less in the literature and seems to be least valued by practitioners and researchers alike. It has this low status because it is usually covert or semi-covert behaviour, because it is fleeting and because, by its very nature, it is *learner* generated. Learner generated collaboration is not necessarily synonymous with learner initiated collaboration although it includes it. Rather than giving a precise definition, let us examine the examples of *Learner generated collaboration* identified in Table 5.1.

Learner Initiated Dialogue (LID)

Just as with open pairs the LIDs, which were discussed in Chapter 4, can become a form of collaborative learning whereby the other 'listeners' see value in listening to the phrase or dialogue. There is some evidence (Slimani, 1987, cited in Allwright and Bailey, 1991) to suggest that for some learners, listening to the participation of other learners is at least as profitable as participating themselves.

Asking a friend to ask the teacher

When the teacher is insisting on use of L2 for a LID, pupils sometimes ask their friends to do so on their behalf (interpreting). This is a high level of peer collaboration!

Pupil interpretation and teacher confirmation

We have already mentioned the observed teacher technique of parroting (Chapter 3). I wasn't aware of how much I did it myself until I observed it in others! Let us remind ourselves through another example:

T: Va bene ... adesso ... lavoriamo in gruppi di quattro. Spiega cosa ho detto, Nathalie.
Nathalie: We're going to work in groups of four.
T: Groups of four (with a downward stress).

As I have suggested, this form of repetition in L1 of a pupils' translation/interpretation occurs very frequently in monolingual classrooms. What is the hidden message being put over, however? (a) I have asked Nathalie to interpret what I said for you but I don't trust you to have listened; (b) Nathalie, I have asked you to interpret for those who may not have understood but I don't value your interpretation or your effort; (c) I have asked Nathalie to interpret but you needn't listen to her because I'm going to tell you anyway.

Is this not a negation of the type of collaborative learning that we are trying to nurture in the class as a whole? If the pupils are assured that I'm *not* going to 'parrot' Nathalie, they are much more likely to listen to her attentively.

Assisting with listening

When listening, as a whole class, to a tape recording (but even more so when listening to the teacher), pupils will whisper, murmur or say out loud bits of language they have understood. This is only partly a demonstration of individual comprehension. It is also a collaborative act, helping learners who are struggling with comprehension, usually close friends. It may be as an answer to a friend's request for help or it might be given spontaneously. One teacher reported: 'If we're listening to a tape they'll all be talking to each other saying, "What's *fraise*? Oh yes, it's strawberry ... course it is". I often see pairs pausing and helping each other.'

When asking pupils to listen to a taped recording I, like most teachers, strive for the perfect listening atmosphere and tend to discourage this sort of learner reaction. In so doing I am stifling collaborative potential and nurturing individual achievement. This is a problem, as both strategies would appear to be conducive to good learning. A balance has to be struck, perhaps by allowing limited whispering in taped listening situations and encouraging more overt collaboration in comprehension when the teacher is talking. It is, of course, important in the latter case to distinguish between pupils interjecting 'benignly' for the purpose of moving forward collaboratively and those who are doing so merely to be disruptive. Experienced teachers who know their pupils well are more able to make this distinction.

Collective clarification request

I have discussed evidence of this already in Chapter 4. It is when by some process, probably very much manifested through fellow learners' body language (for example fidgeting), a class lets the teacher know that a sufficient number have not understood his/her input or the recorded input. Again, there is here the positive element of moving forward collaboratively. It is as though learning the target language is not accomplished until it has been learnt by the collective rather than by individuals who, as it were, learn on your behalf. One of the antitheses of collaborative learning is the attitude: 'We've done that bit because Becky's answered the question/understood the language item, even though I haven't'. The motive for this type of collaborative behaviour is not necessarily altruistic. It is helping to ensure that the right conditions for effective learning are extant. It would be fruitful to discover through research to what extent pupils are aware, as teachers are, that unless the whole class or group have understood a particular stage in the learning sequence, procedural difficulties will arise for the next stage.

Collective feedback to the teacher

This is similar to the preceding item but it is to do with learners collaboratively letting the teacher know how, in their opinion, the lesson is progressing – by smiling perhaps!

Open pairs

Open pairs (Peck, 1988) is when a teacher asks pupil A to ask a question. The teacher then either selects pupil B to give an answer (Technique 1) or asks pupil A to select pupil B to give an answer (Technique 2). The first observation to be made here is between the two techniques:

Technique 2 is clearly the more collaborative, according to my definition above. Technique 2 is the only *learner generated collaboration* of the two even though it is still not learner initiated.

Within Technique 2, Dialogue X is more natural than Dialogue Y:

Dialogue X
Pupil A: James, Qu'est-ce que tu as fait dimanche?
Pupil B (James): Je suis allé chez ma grand-mère

Dialogue Y
Pupil A: Qu'est-ce que tu as fait dimanche … er … James?
Pupil B (James): Je suis allé chez ma grand-mère.

In Dialogue Y, the teacher directs the question first to the whole class and then selects or gives the turn to James. Whether Dialogue X is more collaborative or not depends on a number of factors, many of which will be unknown to outside observers, and possibly unknown to the teacher. It is likely, however, that they are known to pupil A. The pupil interviews in the Tarclindy project (indeed as everyone knows who has asked young learners systematically about their learning) reveal a whole series of undercurrents, trends, anxiety-induced behaviours, shared knowledge and beliefs that pupils hold. Is James known by his peers to enjoy answering questions in front of the class? Does he like to be the first or does he prefer to repeat a reply already formulated by someone else? Does James like to take risks? Does pupil A know that James is listening? How collaborative is pupil A being? Does s/he say the question loud enough or clearly enough?

In the case of Dialogue Y more time is available for all the class to formulate the answer and then wait to be 'called'? To what extent is the rest of the class being collaborative in the learning activity by, for example, being as quiet as possible? To what extent are they listening to their peers' questions and answers in order to learn themselves? These questions need to be separated from the general notion of class management, from the notion of social behaviour. Instead, they need to be answered in the context of collaborative language learning behaviour.

Open pairs activities may seem to lie at a very teacher-centred end of a collaborative continuum, but in fact Technique 2 requires a very high degree of implicit collaboration between learners.

Symbiotic collaboration

During one of the observation visits I was particularly struck by the amount of collaboration between two boys in a year 10 Spanish lesson. In whole class activities, they worked together, demonstrating many of the collaborative aspects described above. In pair work they openly shunned (in a polite way) the teacher's help. The following is an extract from the subsequent interview with the teacher:

T: Ramon and Danny didn't want me at all – they wanted to work it out together. They like to share ideas. I think it's to do with confidence.

Author: Danny is very good isn't he? So what is it that makes those two collaborate with one another?

T: They both want to succeed. Ramon wants to speak impeccable Spanish because his dad's Spanish and he'd feel humiliated if he didn't ... Danny too ... Danny respects Ramon's feel for Spanish whereas Ramon respects Danny's ability just to learn it and remember things.

Learners can, by collaboration, succeed though a process of complementary attributes, perhaps even by temporary interdependence.

Individual examples of *Learner generated collaboration* might seem trivial to some readers and all too obvious to others. I would want to argue, however, that collectively it is an extremely powerful force in bringing about not only the conditions for effective learning but learning itself. It is also the social and psychological framework which needs to be in place before more transparent and tangible forms of collaborative learning can be proposed to learners. It is part of what teachers mean when they say a class is 'beginning to gel'. If the gelling process could be analysed and described it might prove a powerful tool in teacher training, teacher in-service training and practitioner self-development. Further research may indicate that the above examples have only scratched at the surface of the collaboration and potential collaboration available in a languages classroom. Moreover the phenomenon, although different in nature, is present in any formal second language learning context, whether with very young learners, adolescents or adults.

The psychological benefits of collaborative learning have been documented at a theoretical level by a number of authors. For a summary of the psychological theories connected with collaborative and experiential learning see Kohonen (1992). These authors submit that an individual's self-concept is shaped through the interaction with his/her environment. In the case of FL learning the environment is the classroom and thus the learner's self-concept as related to the language being learnt will be shaped by the organisation and processes prevalent in that environment. Collaborative learning gives learners a sense of importance and individual worth. Learners with high self-esteem are less likely to feel threatened (Kohonen 1992: 23). It would seem logical therefore that learners with low self-esteem would experience relatively higher self-esteem in small groups. At a social level collaborative learning in the classroom mirrors the outside world and the world of work. Whilst there is clearly a need for every learner to achieve his/her maximum potential as an individual s/he must also develop the awareness and the skills needed to operate as a member of a team. Collaborative learning therefore provides the very skills needed both in adolescence and adulthood.

The advantages of group work for language teachers are numerous and well documented. They range from TEFL to secondary FL teaching (Ur 1981; Prabhu, 1987; Cajkler & Addelman, 1992). Its theoretical contribution to language acquisition, however, goes well beyond organisational and management considerations. It goes even beyond its didactic value as giving alternative opportunities to *reinforce* or *fix* language already presented and practised (Brumfit, 1984: 76). It is a natural environment for linguistic behaviour, a behaviour rich in the functions which are also to be found in everyday social discourse. It plays a part in the indispensable processes of language acquisition itself. Before examining the rest of the Tarclindy project data we will take a brief look at some of these processes.

Input and Interaction

To move beyond Krashen's (early) position that *comprehensible input* is sufficient for language acquisition, we will need to prove that *interaction*, learner's language *output* in a real discourse context, is a necessary requirement of second language development. This is the position among others, of Long (1983) and Swain (1985). The difficulty with studies on *interaction*, is that it is impossible to make confident statements about causal relationships. Do learners who interact more make faster progress or do they interact more because they are more proficient in the first place? Do they achieve prominence in the eyes of the teacher merely because they interact more? As has been already indicated it may be that *interaction* need not always involve actual verbal participation but just attentive listening to others' *interaction* and some kind of mental formulation of L2 output. The problem for the teacher is that it is not always possible to distinguish active (but silent) attention from inattention. To reduce individual learners' *interaction* to 'voluntary contributions' is therefore just not an option for the conscientious teacher. However, rather than insist on equal participation from reluctant contributors in the whole class situation, teachers can, through collaborative work ensure the conditions in which *interaction* can take place. A number of studies, summarised in Chaudron (1988) and in Allwright and Bailey (1991), suggest that small group work not only produces more general interaction (in the sense of more dialogue) but also a much wider range of communicative functions.

We have examined in Chapter 4 a study by Varonis and Gass (1985). In this ESL study comparing NS–NNS exchanges and NNS–NNS exchanges there was strong evidence of more *negotiated meaning* in the latter than the former. This would seem, at a theoretical level, to be applicable for the FL secondary classroom too. Given the right attitudes, motivation and determination to stay in L2, we would expect the pupil–pupil situation to negotiate more meaning than even the one-to-one teacher–pupil situation, where the teacher is going to find ways of quickly putting over meaning and then moving on, a strategy which may perhaps increase the speed of comprehension (and probably classroom management!) but will not elicit very much interaction both in terms of quantity or variety of communicative functions. Thus, even if we are not sure that interaction *directly* affects acquisition we can be sure that collaborative learning using oral skills *has the potential* to produce a range of output which in its variety of language function deployment entails a number of linguistic processes. It is these processes which, even at a basic level of competence, allow learners to begin to move away from formulaic expressions. Whilst formulaic speech is an important factor in early second language acquisition, it may be that it is the process of comparing, choosing and modifying these utterances that trigger the start of a more independent and creative rule system (Ellis, 1985).

In collaborative learning situations, however, learners are exchanging language which may well be incorrect. Does this matter?

Interlanguage

I have indicated that one of the features of collaborative learning which is specific to second language learning is the trust that the participants have to have and the value that they place in each other's language even though that language is obviously (apart from at very advanced levels) far from perfectly acquired. The term 'interlanguage' was coined by Selinker (1972) and taken on by Pit Corder, eventually published in book form in Corder (1981). Interlanguage gives what we might call a value label to the various staging posts of the L2 learner's language whilst it is still not like that of the native speaker. It is also a value label because it stresses not the comparison with the native speaker by describing it as an inadequate version of the target language, but a sort of transitional dialect, a system in its own right which the learner has internalised in his/her attempts to make sense of all the L2 input. The process of inferencing and hypothesis testing would suggest that the input has to be perfect all the time in order to move towards acquisition of correct forms of the L2. However, if the 'interlanguage hypothesis' is correct, then learners of L1 and L2 do not share the same developmental processes. Nor do different learners of the same L2 share the same development, the emphasis still being placed on *individual* mental processes. Their internal processes, like their surface manifestations of language competence, are not lock-step. Moreover, the influence of L1 on the processes involved in L2 acquisition (for example positive and negative transfer of rules from L1 to L2) is limited. Consequently the correctness of the language environment in which L2 acquisition is occurring is probably also of only partial importance. Logically then, provided this is not the *only* language learners hear, it should not be detrimental to the learning process if a learner is interacting with another learner. We do not have space here to go into the arguments and counter-arguments centred around the *interlanguage hypothesis*. It is no doubt this line of thought as well as teaching experience which leads many practitioners and theorists alike to speculate, as Krashen and Terrell do (1988: 97), that interlanguage talk does a great deal more good than harm as long as it is not the only input that learners are exposed to. In order to give further substance to this suggestion we can examine briefly how teachers in fact give feedback to learners.

Error and feedback

Teachers can react to error[2] in four ways:

(1) They can ignore it.
(2) They can inform the learner (verbally or non-verbally) that s/he has made an error.
(3) They can elicit an 'immediate'correct response from the learner.
(4) They can pursue a course of 'treatment' (repetition, focused exercises, post activity evaluation, etc.) which may eradicate the error from the learner's rule system (Chaudron, 1988).

It is unlikely that peer learners, especially in the secondary FL classroom, adopt more than reactions (1) and (2). It is just possible that with older learners reaction (3) occurs. We might therefore conclude that, if there is any value in feedback, we must ensure that there are many opportunities for the teacher to provide that feedback. There are three factors, however, which might lead us to question this assertion. Firstly, the interlanguage hypothesis would suggest that a learner would have to hear another learner utter the same ungrammatical phrase, 'uncontested' by other correct utterances, many times before it became part of the hearer's internal system.

Secondly, we would naturally want to move towards a situation where the learner is able to self-correct – something akin to Krashen's 'monitor hypothesis' and what Allwright and Bailey (1991: 107) call self-initiated self-repairs. In order for learners to do this they will need the time and the opportunity to undertake a self-repair process. It is unlikely that these conditions will exist in the teacher up-front situation, with all the pressures of multiple learner demands.

Thirdly, there is no evidence to suggest that teacher-fronted activities produce fewer errors than collaborative activities (Pica & Doughty, 1985). Porter (1986) found that in peer-group interaction, NNS did not often take the initiative in correcting other NNS. However, when they did, they gave correct feedback. In other words, if the results of this study can be replicated in the secondary FL classroom, teachers should not be concerned that in collaborative learning situations learners are getting incorrect feedback from their peers. Indeed, in the Porter study there is more than just a 'there's no harm being done' suggestion. There is also a very pedagogically challenging possibility that learners *will* correct peers *when* they feel confident of their own accuracy. If this were found to be the case, and given the notion that each learner's interlanguage state is different (i.e. different learners have got a hold of different bits of the target language rule system at any one time), it would be a powerful argument for an increase in collaborative learning in the classroom.

Communicative strategies

In Chapter 4 I made a distinction between 'learner strategies' and 'communicative strategies' by suggesting that 'learner strategies' were more to do with learners maximising the learning environment for themselves (for example by ensuring feedback on their hypothesis of the correctness of a word or phrase), whereas 'communicative strategies' were about maximising the chances of keeping communication going by avoiding problems, pitfalls or at least getting round them if problems occurred. In a sense we could classify communicative strategies as common collaborative goals between speakers – in our case, learners. What is basically happening when learners try to maintain communication is that they are utilising some of the list of modification strategies that we saw teachers using in Chapter 3. The difference here is that the complex discourse interaction is happening in pairs or small groups of learners working independently of the teacher. Participants will have to therefore *want* to collaborate in this process. What is going on in this discourse that will keep the conversation going?

(a) the hearer has to signal if a message has not been understood;
(b) the speaker has to be on the lookout for these signals;
(c) the speaker has then to find ways of making the hearer 'get the message';
(d) the hearer has to signal that the message has now been understood.

These are all communication strategies which were involved in the teacher input discussed in Chapter 3. In addition, however, the learner in the collaborative situation will have to compensate for not having (in many cases) very much language to communicate with and, therefore, not able always to say exactly what s/he wanted to say. It seems logical to call this subset of communication strategies, 'compensation strategies'. The speaker will then have to resort to such things as:

(a) thinking of another word which is approximate to the unknown word;
(b) thinking of a phrase which describes the word (*où j'achète un ticket de métro*);
(c) contrasting the word with another;
(d) using mimes or pointing to an object or picture;
(e) coining new words or using L2 versions of the L1 form (*il faut jumper* [instead of *sauter!*] accompanied by an action);
(f) using a different tense;
(g) reducing the complexity of the language (e.g. lots of short phrases instead of subordinate clauses);
(h) using a noun instead of a verb;
(i) using an L1 word as a last resort.

Some NNS may of course take the easy way out and employ reductive strategies (Faerch *et al* 1984: 161).That is, they decide to reduce what they say compared to what they might have said in L1. Now this is all well and good and we would obviously want pupils to keep the conversation going as much as possible because (a) success is motivating; (b) it stops them reverting to L1; (c) it stops them getting off task. However, as I have often suggested in this book, it is also necessary to ask the question: is it actually helping language learning? (That is of course unless we are content that motivation, success and class management are synonymous with language learning). We therefore have to ask what kind of interaction should secondary FL learners be engaged in during collaborative learning activities?

What kind of interaction?

As a consequence of the tentative conclusion on the different aspects of 'interaction' above, it would be reasonable to claim that if there seems to be some process value in interaction, then there is obviously some value in keeping that interaction going. However, what sort of interaction should we be aiming for? This strikes at the heart of the debate resulting from the Tarclindy data below. Should we be aiming for 'controlled interaction' or 'free interaction'? Should the tasks be highly structured or loosely structured? Should there be a lot of input *before* the collaborative work (thus ensuring that the right phrases and vocabulary are used) or should we put the emphasis on learners dredging up their own communicative solutions and 'getting by'? Particularly for the purpose of this part of the discussion, we need to ask the question: Is the deployment of compensation strategies themselves the key to communicative competence, or is it the quality (not grammatical accuracy but rather fluency and range) and quantity of the language with which the collaborators are interacting which is important? These interlocking themes are crucial in the teacher's methodology decisions. Should the teacher arrive at collaborative oral work after much careful and controlled language input, thereby possibly pre-empting the use of compensation strategies, as in Teaching sequence A (Table 5.2)? Alternatively should the collaborative work come early, with learners employing a wide range of strategies to keep the discourse going, but with little language advance, in content terms, as in Teaching sequence B (Table 5.2)? I shall return to this in a moment. What do we know of the effect of communication strategies on learning? Freeman (1992) in his description of one teacher's classroom practice attributes language learning progress to 'the language evolving through the students themselves', in a classroom where there is no textbook but where language is brainstormed by the teacher and learners. Unfortunately it would be difficult to prove that this has

Table 5.2 Steps to collaborative learning

Sequence A	Sequence B
Teacher informs class of the objective for a unit: discussing where to go for the evening.	Teacher proposes end product: two learners to discuss where to go for the evening.
Teacher exposes learners to a body of vocabulary and language through repetition, etc.	Teacher gives pairs some limited preparation time: pairs think through some vocabulary and structures.
Teacher practises language through question and answer, gradually building in more language items.	Volunteer pair performs the dialogue 'as best they can' using compensation strategies.
Pupils hear tape recording of native speakers discussing where to go for the evening. Feedback on this listening exercise.	Teacher praises the 'maintenance' of commuication then writes on board or elicits a few additional vocab/structures.
Teacher demonstrates what an eventual dialogue might look like, perhaps written, perhaps through two learners (not in real time) teacher supervised and controlled.	Second volunteer pair perform 'as best they can' using compensation strategies.
Teacher invites two learners to model a discussion in front of the class (in real time but teacher supervised and controlled); teacher praises, comments, makes fine tuned adjustments to language performance.	At this point either (a) teacher writes additional language on board and a third pair have a go or (b) there is an evaluation of progress.
Learners perform the discussion (in real time); no teacher control apart from 'dropping in'.	
Evaluation of progress.	

anything other than a purely motivational effect on the learners or at the very most the effect of improving their powers of language recall.

In the study by Grenfell and Harris (1994) compensation strategies appear on the checklist of strategies given to 100 pupils for awareness and possible adoption. Unfortunately in the analysis there is no reference to whether and to what extent pupils adopted any of these strategies. For Kohonen (1992: 26) the language learning value is in what the learner does to the input, turning it into real, personal output – involvement in the task being one of the requirements for effective learning. Again though, he would seem to be referring more to a behavioural or attitudinal domain rather than a psycholinguistic one. If it were in the psycholinguistic domain it would raise the very useful question of what input should the learner be working on through the communication strategies in order to personalise it (by which we could at least be moving towards the notion of an internalised linguistic system). Should it be recent input and specific to a lesson (more like teaching sequence A) or should it be the cumulative store of language acquired in the past (more like Teaching sequence B)?

Clearly sequence B is going to develop compensation strategies more than sequence A. However pupils in sequence A are going to use more appropriate language much earlier. Which approach best furthers the goal of communicative competence? Di Pietro (1987), from whose Strategic Interaction techniques Sequence B is adapted, would claim that the latter does. Di Pietro advocates: strive for interaction first, then for meaning, and finally for structure (Di Pietro: 125). Many teachers, however, would opt for sequence A. Kellerman (1991) dismisses the value of focusing on compensation strategies altogether (as a skill to develop) because, he argues, they exist in L1 anyway. If this is the case, he continues, what is the point of training the learners to use them at all? If they are not using them it is because they do not possess the linguistic means to use the strategy. Teachers should therefore concentrate on teaching the language. This dismissal, confining itself to a theoretical construct based on native/non-native and proficient/less-proficient comparisons, would seem to be ignoring a number of important points. Firstly, many L2 learner strategies also exist in L1. If training in one type of strategy is pointless, the same should go for all strategy training which is interlingual. Part of training for any skill is creating the conditions wherein a latent skill can be externalised or a little used skill encouraged. An ability to perform an action in L1 does not necessarily transfer to an ability to do so in L2 – inhibition being only one factor among many. Secondly, communicative competence is not only a final goal (native speaker competence) but an intermediate means by which one communicates meaning successfully. Learners may need explicit personal demonstration that communication can be achieved other than by L1/L2 lexical or structural equivalence.

Sequences A and B above are, of course not the only possible sequences in oral collaborative learning tasks. They are meant, in opposition, to inform our discussion on compensation strategies. Two further sequences might be illustrated:

Sequence C, where the teacher informs the learners of the end product as in Sequence B but this time there isn't an immediate performance based on limited language. In this sequence learners prepare the performance by gathering language items from various sources, including the teacher, and then performing. This is probably the type of sequence which is most common in more advanced FL classrooms. An example might be a dialogue involving four learners discussing the advantages of flying over car or rail travel.

Sequence D, where the teacher explains that the objective is one of problem solving or data gathering in L2, where the language inter-action between learners becomes an end in itself rather than an end-performance in front of the rest of the class. This type of activity is also more likely to be found in classrooms of older, more advanced learners. An example might be where one group of learners (the residents) have to convince another group of learners (the developers) not to build a by-pass.

We have looked at the implications of interlanguage development in collaborative learning. We have also considered the issues of error feedback, communicative strategies and the quality of interaction within the same context. We will now examine these collaborative learning-related issues via other data collected in the Tarclindy project.

Tarclindy Project Data

A starting point for the analysis of the teacher data related to collaborative learning is the observation logs. It will be remembered that the observers made approximate recordings for each lesson observed as to whether the lesson was more teacher centred, more learner centred or about half and half (see Appendix 'Target Language Logs'). This decision was made on an approximation based on lesson *segments*. These lesson segments were related to types of activities such as: oral presentation, pair work, writing and reading in groups, etc. It was found that the lessons were overwhelmingly more teacher centred than learner centred. Crudely put, the teachers spent much more time at the front of the class than amongst the learners. Teacher centredness was also a tendency across all independent variables, the experience level of the teachers, the age of the pupils (bearing in mind however that the majority of lessons observed were years 7, 8, 9) and the socio-economic situation of the school. So we are not looking at a sample of practice in which collaborative learning is in any way prevalent. Some development, but not an enormous amount, has occurred in the past 10 years if, for example, we compare the observations to Mitchell's early/mid-1980s study reported in Mitchell (1988). Mitchell found that: teachers generally used role play for practice rather than real communication (Mitchel, 1988: 65) teachers demonstrated a preference for pair work over group work (Mitchell, 1988: 39); pupils said they found substantial face value in group work (Mitchell, 1988: 72). If the Tarclindy data shows any pedagogical development it is in the area of increased information gap activities. That is, more real communication is occurring. Possibly as a consequence of this, the group type most found in the classes observed was the pair rather than larger numbers, it being easier to organise a two-way information exchange than a three or four-way exchange.[3] We will therefore start by examining pair work activities. Readers may find it helpful to refer to the full questionnaire statements on page 191 of Chapter 7, whilst examining the data in this section.

Pair work activities

The project aimed to identify what were the teacher's beliefs about this form of learning in terms of:

- its contribution to increased use of L2;
- its contribution to real communication;
- the need to control or pre-determine the learners' discourse;
- the need to pre-structure the learners' discourse;
- the need to monitor the learners' discourse;
- the effect of age as a variable;
- the effect of task as a variable;
- learners' errors in the discourse;
- the possibility of habit formation;

An overall indication of teachers' conviction that pair work encourages L2 use is reasonably optimistic (Table 5.3).

Whilst we evidently have to explore further why there are reservations about the likelihood of pair work encouraging L2 use only in *some*

Table 5.3

	Agree	*Partly agree*	*Disagree*
Pair work encourages TL	37.8	51.2	9.9
Pair work encourages TL in some pupils only	69.2	26.7	3.5
Pair work encourages real communication	43.0	50.0	6.4
Pair work yes – only if monitored	50.6	41.9	7.0
Pair work yes – if not monitored	7.0	61.6	30.8
Pair work yes – Independence for some pupils	58.1	38.4	2.9
Pair work yes – but structured	70.9	27.3	1.2
Pair work yes – but unstructured	7.6	45.9	46.5
Structuring depends on ability	75.6	16.3	7.6
Structuring depends on task	73.8	19.2	6.4
Pair work and error	25.0	61.0	13.4
Pair work error $\Rightarrow$ habit	19.8	50.6	29.1

pupils, the number of teachers actually not reporting a positive link is small. What then were the reservations? Was it to do with the individual (or class) responses of the learners to the collaborative opportunities being offered to them? The interviews and questionnaire comments would, again, put heavy emphasis on ability and motivation as factors contributing to successful pair work:

> Depends on the class, whether they can actually sit and do pair work together … some of them are fairly low on social skills anyway.

> One of the things we've inherited from the middle school is a task based culture which the children come with … what is critically important (for the pupils) is to get the thing done. It doesn't matter how you get it done, but you get it done … so if you can short cut the whole thing by showing each other the piece of paper or a few words in English you get the task done.[4]

Not surprisingly, therefore, teachers saw the need to monitor (check, remind, encourage, bully!) pair work as a vital prerequisite of getting value out of collaborative work. If we examine the results in Table 5.3 we can easily detect a conviction that the teacher has a vital role in ensuring on-task behaviour in L2 through monitoring. This conviction is qualified by the fact that some learners, usually the more successful, can be allowed to work more independently. One student teacher, in the questionnaire comments, echoes the views of many more experienced colleagues:

> Getting pupils to talk in pairs must be one of the most effective ways of encouraging communicative exchanges, if closely monitored, without pupils feeling intimidated by the teacher. I have found that only the most able pupils are prepared to use the target language without supervision.

> They need a clearly defined task. You can't just say: 'Talk about your family' not unless they are in Year 10 or 11 and in good, top sets.

Control of collaborative learning does not, of course, only occur once the task is under way. Control can be achieved by careful structuring of the task and of the language beforehand. The teaching sequence A (Table 5.2) above demonstrates this tight control of both aspects of the discourse. The extensive oral presentation controls the language whereas the build-up through the demonstration and modelling controls the sequencing of the participants' discourse. As a result, pair work activities often take on this unnatural 'I speak then you speak then I speak then you speak' appearance. In addition, each pair of learners is using almost identical language to get the intended communicative message across. Teachers, however, were fairly unanimous (Table 5.3) that L2 use could not be guaranteed without this quite rigid control from them. They firmly defended their assertion, apart from with able pupils, that learning would take place only if the controlled ('structured') processes and conditions were applied. The fact that the amount of structuring also depended on the task only serves to underline this belief. That is to say that simple and often repeated tasks needed less structuring in that they contained *within them* those very elements of control:

> Even if they want to express themselves they will arrive quickly at a point where they can't do so or they'll go off at a tangent ... they can't cope with it unless it's structured in a fairly formalised way.

Some teachers (with experience again not a variable) *were* beginning to grapple with the more subtle distinctions and contradictions resulting from control of collaborative learning:

> Instructions need to be clear and the limits defined but not necessarily highly structured.

Structured to start with, but more creative pair work activities are more stimulating.

Pupils are more prepared to use the TL in pair work if they are sure of what they are doing. However, the whole point of pair work is to give the pupils the opportunity to communicate with each other with minimal intervention from the teacher.

Thus, whilst teachers had developed, in the main, a high opinion of the value (and especially the potential value) of pair work, they were as yet sceptical about being able to let go sufficiently so as to develop learner independence on the one hand and promote extended and unfettered communication on the other. Table 5.3 demonstrates a strong reservation about the limited function of pair work.

Interestingly, teachers' attitude to error in collaborative work was not an important factor leading to the tight control of activities. We can divide this structuring under three headings:

(1) Structural (the way the dialogue should proceed: turn taking; number of exchanges).
(2) Linguistic (the language used: structures; vocabulary).
(3) Behavioural (on task monitoring).

Whilst most teachers agreed that pair work did not, by and large, offer many opportunities for correction of error by the teacher, it did not raise major anxieties. This was probably because there was not a strong link in their minds between pair work and habit formation (Table 5.3). However, we would be justified in speculating as to the chances of error fossilisation being a consequence of the (still relatively scarce) collaborative learning given that collaborative work was seen as

- an end product;
- a highly controlled activity;
- essentially a reinforcement of language already extensively practised.

The majority of errors could be eliminated before the collaborative learning would take place. What would be most teachers' conclusion, we might therefore ask, about error fossilisation if they observed lesson after lesson of the types described in teaching sequences B and D above? Thus control of collaborative learning could in part also be due to a concern about the recurring errors that learners might make. In any case teachers reported carrying out the type of error evaluation and remedy found in Sequence B *in addition* to deploying a tightly controlled sequence A-type sequence. They pointed out that there was always the possibility of 'check sessions' immediately following pair work and that the teacher could identify certain consistent errors, stop the activity, explain and then allow the activity to continue.

Two further points arise from this aspect of the discussion. The first is that the issue of class size was mentioned several times in relation to how effective monitoring could be. The second is that within the theme of error habit formation there seems to be some variation in teacher response according to experience level, more experienced teachers displaying greater anxiety about error. The following were all from experienced teachers:

> Damage liability can be reduced with careful and effective technique from the teacher.

> I feel strongly about this ... both risks (uncorrected error and habit formation) are very important.

> I set myself targets. I will aim to hear 10 pupils (pairs) for example in one lesson so that I can correct error and also praise and encourage.

> There is a danger that pupils will not know if they are making fundamental errors unless they are monitored.

That is not to say that others did not take the more 'interlanguage' position:

> Changing partners helps as a new partner won't be making the same errors.

> Making errors is part of language learning.

> An error not corrected in one session will be tackled at another time.

Group work activities

The project, whilst including some of the lines of enquiry relating to pair work, also attempted to get a picture of teachers' attitudes to the different implications of group work, defined as exchanges involving at least three learners. Was group work:

- a worthwhile activity?
- difficult to set up in L2?
- possible to assess collectively?
- an activity which generated a lot of TL use?

Defining group work is much more difficult to achieve than pair work, again perhaps because teachers are less familiar with it. There is something which is FL specific about group work which adds an extra dimension, especially in the oral mode. It is also much more closely connected in teachers' minds with notions about pedagogy in general (whereas pair work seems more an opportunity to practice language). For example, group work for some teachers is more to do with social seating arrangements – clusters rather than rows or horseshoe shapes. For others it is an opportunity for differentiated learning – either (a) grouping by apparent ability or (b) grouping with more able/confident learners taking lead roles.[5]There are issues related to permanent groups and temporary groups, the way they are selected or negotiated. Groups can be grouped randomly, in friendship groups or according to ability. Whilst some pupils may prefer to work with friends, some are themselves less convinced that working just with friends is actually better for their learning (Harris & Noyau, 1990: 57) . For some teachers, group work tends to be associated more with activities (usually carried out in L1) leading to a tangible product such as a poster or a brochure. Other teachers consider it an opportunity for oral negotiation in L2, but here there is a tendency to restrict this activity to more advanced learners. For this reason, questions 30 and 32 in the questionnaire were exemplified for the respondents (see pages 192–3 in Chapter 7). Table 5.4 gives an indication of teachers' attitudes to group work.

Respondents saw no difference in terms of face value between *oral group work* and *general group work* the latter being exemplified by 'composing a poster collaboratively'. This is surprising if we take the results of Table 5.4 which strongly suggest significant concern with the limited amount of L2 output in the general group work activities. There seems to be a contradiction in reporting little target language output by

Table 5.4

	Agree	*Partly agree*	*Disagree*
Group work (oral) is worthwhile	59.9	34.3	5.2
Group work difficult to set up in L2	30.2	53.5	15.7
General group work (as in poster) worthwhile	59.9	34.3	5.2
Group work worthwhile activity to assess	34.3	48.8	16.3
Group work produces L2 output	3.5	51.2	44.8

pupils and simultaneously giving that activity equal value as an activity involving pupil use of L2. There are two possible explanations for this:

(1) The questionnaire as a data collection instrument is not sufficient to give the whole picture with regard to this topic. A question about whether oral group work brought about lots of L2 use might have been responded to negatively, even though many teachers still regarded it as worthwhile.

(2) Teachers really did see both activities (group work as an oral activity and group work as a collaborative task) as completely different: one using L2, the other a lot of L1, but found them both valid, the latter perhaps when pupils needed a rest from the oral mode of the target language. So do the interviews and questionnaire comments shed any light on this puzzling result?

Responses to group work provided a very revealing picture of the internal debate that teachers were engaging in. This was much more so than in the case of pair work where there was greater consensus on its function as largely limited to practising language and re-enforcing language already practised. Moreover, the experience level of teachers was, again, not an issue in differentiating attitudes to its value. Most teachers saw a clear divergence of function for group work in that:

Group work in writing and designing is OK but group discussion in TL is less effective.

General group work is worthwhile but not if the TL is the main objective.

Pupils love group work and work well but its usefulness in generating TL is doubtful.

Its PSE (Personal and Social Education) potential, particularly for the less able, is high and should be exploited.

It provides a welcome change from regimented lessons but not so much in the TL.

One of the main problems of the communicative approach is that many pupils do not know how to interact socially, thus to communicate. Group work is my main method of encouraging this.

It involves so many other skills such as listening to each other and this is definitely what my pupils have difficulty in doing.

Harris and Noyau (1990: 58) in their observation study also indicate

an 'impression that the top sets adapted most quickly to this (collaborative) way of working'. They also point to the fact that girls approach
group work much more in the spirit of true collaboration than boys
who tend to look on set tasks as an excuse for a race to see who can
finish first.

Perhaps as a consequence, in terms of *assessment,* no respondent in
the Tarclindy project qualified the medium rating given for group
work (Table 49) by confirming its value in TL interaction. Most
commented on its function as providing opportunities to assess
abilities other than 'academic' ones.

Other teachers expressed a concern at the lack of direct involvement
that group work encourages as opposed to the more easily observable
involvement in pair work. There was little evidence, moreover, of
learners in a group work situation interacting in L2 (in the classroom
language sense) as well as carrying out the task 'the content' in L2.

To summarise then, the teachers surveyed and the classrooms
observed gave few instances of group work being a major vehicle for
the development of language competence. The activity itself did not
have intrinsic value as a device for language acquisition through
learner interaction. Whilst collaboration of this kind was generally held
in high esteem by teachers, it had either to be closely structured and
monitored for any worthwhile L2 output to occur or it was seen as
having a socialising function which might lead to a better predisposition to language learning.

Target Language Implications

The above data begins to shed some light on the balance, in terms
of input and interaction and in terms of quality and quantity of L2,
between teacher centred and learner centred classrooms. The observation log data (Table 3.10, Chapter 3) would tend to emphasise even
more than other surveys the amount of teacher talk at the expense
of pupil talk. Chaudron (1988: 51) reports that even in bilingual
education programmes proportions as low as 11% of student talk have
been recorded. We have already indicated, in our discussions on RL1
(Chapter 3), a concern among teachers that *setting up* collaborative
activities in L2 (except for the most simple and often repeated) is
problematic and that perhaps the more creative activities are possibly
being avoided in order to defer RL1. Table 5.4 would again support
this finding. Di Pietro (1987), with his emphasis on the primary
importance of interaction is one of the few authors to tackle this issue
head on:

The functions of language in the strategic interaction classroom fall into two categories: pedagogical and performance. The pedagogical category ... includes explaining, describing, critiquing and evaluating and typifies language use in rehearsal and debriefing. Either the native language or the target language may be used to execute these functions. The performance category includes all strategic functions and requires the use of the target language. At the outset of instruction, the target language is restricted to the performance phase ... as time passes and the class develops greater proficiency in the target language this language can take over some of the pedagogical functions. Ideally the final stages of the course of instruction will find students using the target language for both pedagogical and performance functions (Di Pietro, 1987: 123)

Whilst some may want to argue against this developmental sequence, it is at least clear and refreshingly unequivocal. It is also in direct contrast to the overall concept of L2 use as advocated by the National Curriculum and as understood by teachers surveyed in the Tarclindy project. For the NC the target language is seen as an essential tool *from the outset* for both the pedagogical category as well as the performance category. The progression is then inverted when many learners demonstrate an inability to sustain and operate in a context of teacher exclusive use of L2. As OFSTED (1995) points out, the pedagogic category of target language use (again using Di Pietro's distinction) *decreases* as the course proceeds from its initial stages in year 7 to its termination in year 11.

The arguments given against Di Pietro's sequence are not linguistic ones but social and behavioural ones. Proponents of L1 exclusion would argue that learners exposed to L1 for explanations would become entrenched in a position where if explanations for collaborative learning activities were then not *continued* in L1, they would be rejected. Once young learners adapt to one teaching style they cannot, even gradually, progress to learning through another. The evidence for this is anecdotal. Furthermore, it does seem a very pessimistic behaviourist position to adopt as we have not explored the potential of making the progression itself part of the stepping stones in the learning and, if necessary, in the assessment process. What would be particularly depressing is for this position to bring about a state of affairs where collaborative activities were eschewed. Collaborative activities from the simple pair work to the complexities of producing a town brochure are held in high esteem by a consensus of teachers, learners and theoreticians. They are one of the few, real winning tickets in language learning. Discussions should therefore centre on how to maximise collaboration and interaction.

Prompting interaction

One tangible area for discussion is the current issue of prompt cards. These are the tools given to learners in order to carry out collaborative activities in general but role-plays and information gap activities in particular. What should be on these prompt cards? Should it be tasks set in L2, tasks set in L1 or tasks set via an assortment of symbols? Teachers interviewed reported the whole range of preferences. Some preferred these to be in L1 because it was the quickest way of getting on with the task. They, however, saw a disadvantage here in that the process was not far removed from a process of translation. A particular problem was where some pupils asked the teacher: 'How do you say: *tell the policeman?*' where the italicised phrase was on the prompt card. Other teachers used symbols but recognised that firstly the teacher had to be a good artist and that, even given that skill, a lot of work had to be done with the pupils in establishing the precise meaning of the symbols. It would seem that there is also a problem with the language limiting nature of symbols. It is reasonably easy to portray a generic symbol, such as a bird, but how does one differentiate between canary, budgie, duck and goose? Verbs are notoriously difficult to convey precisely through a symbol. Is the symbol of a man walking referring to the verb 'to walk' or the verb 'to go' and in what tense? Teachers who have had to go through the process of excessively stereotyping large small, fat and thin people will also recognise a problem with adjectives. Apart from at the advanced level, use of tasks in L2 is as yet untested. The same debate pertaining to rubric and comprehension tasks in exams that we saw in Chapter 1 is appropriate here. Firstly, will the learner know what to do from the instructions? Secondly, will s/he understand clearly the kinds of things s/he is expected to be saying? Thirdly, will s/he be able simply to lift from the text chunks of language which are then regurgitated as supposed communication. In Figure 5.1 I offer alternatives for readers to reflect upon in the light of the above discussion.

Clearly in terms of input alone the L2 version has the advantage. The learner is required to understand the prompt card before interaction can take place. This focus on both message and meaning will undoubtedly provide an extra opportunity for comprehensible input and intake. In addition, the L2 version will not require as much teacher prior input given that the essential vocabulary and structures are

L1 version	L2 version
you are in a chemist shop.	Tu es dans une pharmacie
Tell the chemist:	Dis au pharmacien que:
your brother has had a tummy ache since this morning.	ton frère a mal au ventre depuis ce matin
you are worried.	tu es très inquiet(e)
ask if you should go to a doctor	demande si tu devrais aller chez un médecin
tell the chemist you have an E111	dis au pharmacien que vous avez le E111

Symbols version	L2 trigger prompts
I invite readers to make an attempt at representing the above (or some of the above) in symbol form.	tu es dans une (✚) frère – mal au ventre tu es inquiet(e) médecin? voilà E111

Figure 5.1

already there. The L1 version, on the other hand, should lead more quickly to interaction because the learner will not have to understand the scene setting nor will s/he have to think of how to manipulate the language from the second person singular to the first. In the L1 version the learner will have to rely on acquired language plus communicative strategies, in the L2 version the learner will have to rely on his/her understanding of language rules plus a reduced number of communicative strategies. The last possibility, that of a series of what we might call 'L2 trigger prompts' might serve the purpose of avoiding use of L1 and at the same time require a deployment both of *some* acquired language *and* the use of communication strategies. This option, however, is open to learner misinterpretation and possible frustration. Underpinning these issues is the constant nagging concern that the more L1 there is around the class the less learners will get used to operating through L2. The backwash effect from exams will be an important element in arriving at a decision.

A further implication is: In what language are learners to interact with one another in collaborative learning situations? Can we at least encourage if not expect L2? How might we do this?

Classroom language interaction between learners

We have already discussed the value of developing pupil–pupil interaction language (one element in classroom language). As a bi-product of the Tarclindy project a limited number of what we might mischievously call *interaction research cycles* were attempted. As is shown in Figure 5.2 a topic was taught to pupils in the usual way using a basic presentation, practice and use sequence. The focus of interest then occurred either at the practice stage (if this was learner centred) or at the use stage. Let us take as an example a group of year 9 pupils who had worked on the topic of 'means of transport' according to 'departure point and destination'. One of the learner centred practice stages was a game of pelmanism (matching pairs) where the match was, for example, the phrases:

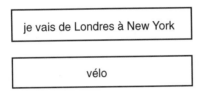

(i.e. the phrases did not match!)

Stage 1

Four different groups of pupils were recorded, with their permission, as they played the game in groups of twos or threes.

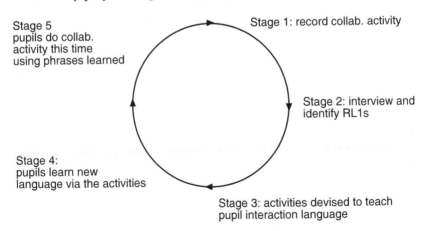

Figure 5.2 Interaction research cycle

Stage 2

Subsequent to the game, at the end of the lesson, these pupils were asked when and for what reasons they had had recourse to L1. Language related reasons were noted, whilst social-behavioural reasons ('I got fed up', 'We just wanted to talk about something else') were ignored. This was to raise their awareness of the interaction language they had used in L1. The tape recordings were listened to and the same procedure adopted: language related RL1s were noted, social-behavioural related RL1s (and foul language!) were ignored. There was a high degree of correlation between what pupils said about the RL1 and what was found in the recordings.

Stage 3

Activities were devised for teaching the language that would be needed to avoid in future the same RL1s in the same situation (e.g. it's your turn; hurry up; no, that's impossible!)

Stage 4

Pupils went through the activities to learn the new words/phrases.

Stage 5

Pupils played the pelmanism game again after having been encouraged (in L1!) to use the new L2 interaction language that they previously had not had. Groups had a list of the phrases to refer to just in case they forgot. The game was recorded again.

The results were encouraging. The groups used the interaction language frequently as part of the game. Some groups used it more than others. This seemed to be due to 'good old motivation' and prior learning success. Generally it was felt that the groups used the language in a communicative way. That is to say, not just for the sake of using it but when the need actually arose.

We cannot draw anything but the most tentative conclusions from the limited number of interaction cycles carried out. The results so far, however, are too exciting to ignore.

Summary

Underpinning all our discussions in this chapter has been the belief that collaborative learning can bring about increased interactive output from learners. Moreover, it can be argued that given the constraints and pressures of teacher-fronted activities, it is the logical place to develop extended output: longer, open-ended and more complex utterances; longer and more complex exchanges. That is not to say that in all classrooms collaborative learning is bringing about these desired ends. Indeed, the project data draws a very limited picture of the time allocated to pair work and group work and its perceived pedagogical purposes.

We have seen both in this chapter and earlier that there are times when the exclusion of L1 by the teacher is conflicting with the promotion of collaborative activities and in so doing may be preventing the generation of learner L2 output. A few teachers in the project also alluded to the lack of time available for collaborative work due to the pressures of the National Curriculum. If this feeling were to spread, and the advances in communication and interaction halted, the consequences for language learning motivation could be disastrous. The situation has not been helped by the revised National Curriculum document's diminished emphasis on collaborative learning through the removal of the section on 'developing the ability to work with others' (DES November, 1991: 26) itself only a recognition of the social-behavioural benefits of collaborative work rather than a confirmation of the linguistic benefits.

We have seen that teachers too are limiting their support for collaborative learning to its social function (they need to get on with one another) its behavioural function (if they don't get a break from me up front, they'll become disruptive) and its pedagogic function (otherwise they'll never get to practise the language very much). Whilst these are all very desirable reasons for collaborative learning, it would be hoped that we could move on to a recognition of its linguistic function (there are processes going on here which actually help them to learn). Within this domain, should be included the need to develop a greater awareness in learners of the way that natural discourse operates – something which highly structured and controlled dialogues fail to do. It is salutary that in the more limited and less well-articulated comments of the pupil interviews, there are proportionally more references to these learning processes than in the teacher interviews.

I have discussed briefly a number of aspects of this process: interaction, interlanguage development, communicative strategies, feedback to learner error. I have attempted in each case to analyse their relationship and implications for collaborative learning and vice-versa. I have suggested that whilst research evidence is not conclusive, there are strong indications that these aspects of learning find a fertile soil in a collaborative environment.

Practical Ideas to Try Out

(1) Departmental activity: cut up the statement squares (Appendix, Figure A.6) relating to collaborative learning. Put to one side all the

ones you all agree with. Discuss the ones (if any!) which are left. What are the *variables*?

(2) Choose a collaborative activity and carry out the five stages of the interaction research cycle as described on page 163. You will find that either *games* or more *complex collaborative activities* produce more interaction language (classroom language) and therefore more pupils' recourse to L1, than simple pair work activities. There are some likely candidates for such activities in the Appendix, Figure A.4.

(3) Look at your Scheme of Work and see how you might develop a programme of training learners to use communication strategies in general and compensation strategies in particular.

Notes

1. Obviously this is not meant to be an exhaustive list.
2. There is not enough space here to discuss the conceptual difference between *errors* and *mistakes* although the distinction is an important one in any discussion of the interlanguage hypothesis.
3. Under pair work I am therefore including all types of two-way exchange activities: individuals moving freely round the class, lines of pupils 'snaking' round the class, etc.
4. This comment has made me realise that older pupils whilst not wishing to 'play the game' in the 1:30 situation are much better even than the younger learners at playing the game in small groups. There is something in the psychology of 14/15-year-olds, as many parents know, that prefers to draw a cloak round their activities and those of their friends.
5. I came across the difficulty of definition even more in Italian schools (Macaro, 1995).

6 Learner Autonomy

In the previous chapter we have explored in some detail both the theoretical and practical benefits of moving towards a less teacher centred approach as well as the implications for target language use. Through interactive and collaborative activities, we have placed the concept of the 'pupil as learner', much higher in our pedagogical list of priorities. We will now examine a further dimension to that concept, that of developing the pupil as a more *autonomous* learner.

Learner autonomy, in the context of foreign language teaching and learning, is not a new phenomenon. Just as in the study of the classics there was an element of inductive learning through memorisation of large chunks of poetry so was there also the development of autonomous language learning skills, a 'knowing where to look' for knowledge (Evans, 1993: 17). An accomplished learner, according to Comenius, was one who could work independently (quoted in Evans, 1993).

Communicative Language Teaching in the monolingual classroom, in its inception, emphasising as it did purposeful oral communication, perhaps marginalised the contribution that learner autonomy could make to the process of language acquisition. As the maturing process in CLT has progressed so has there been in recent years something of an international revival of interest in learner autonomy.

Like CLT, the roots of autonomy lie in a number of cultures and, as a consequence, it has been subjected to a number of different interpretations and definitions. It has been both labelled and described through such concepts as *independent learning, flexible learning* and *student-centred learning*. Whilst each has a common denominator in that the focus of learning is decentralised (Evans, 1993: 18), each concept answers a more distinct gravitational pull from the particular sphere of influence from which it emanated. Thus, for example, independent learning derives its force from a need to develop long-term learner strategies which will be of use in current or future learning situations where a teacher may not be available. An example of this might be in Higher Education where student–teacher ratios are, in the UK at least, subject to deterioration. Flexible learning, on the other hand, comes more from the vocational stable, where the emphasis is on the need to develop a broader range of student outcomes including the 'core skills of enterprise learning, study skills and information skills' (TVEI, 1988: 6). Student centred learning draws its rationale from theories of *individual learner differences* and proposes a learning environment which might best cater for those differences.

Behind these concepts is a broader based philosophy which argues that man is as much a producer of a society as a product of it. Therefore the exercise of responsibilities implies a degree of autonomy from educational structures and processes, an autonomy which will enable the adult to undertake a process of lifelong learning (Council of Europe, 1980). In addition, the replacement of behaviourist learning theory by cognitive theory in the sphere of applied linguistics has contributed to a perception of the language learner as an intelligent, discriminating decision-maker (James, 1990).The freedom which autonomy brings, therefore, should not be associated only with external organisational considerations but with the relation between the learner, the content and the process of learning (Gathercole, 1990). This involves learner-teacher negotiation, involvement in decision making, learning contracts and participation in the organisation of working groups. We should not conclude from this that autonomy is a set of recognisable behaviours which once observed are taken as acquired (Council of Europe, 1980). Autonomy is an ability which is learnt through knowing *how* to make decisions about the self as well as being *allowed* to make those decisions. It is an ability to take charge of one's own language learning and an ability to recognise the value of taking responsibility for one's own objectives, content, progress, method and techniques of learning. It is also an ability to be responsible for the pace and rhythm of learning and the evaluation of the learning process. In this respect 'distance learning', for example through television programmes, only enables autonomy of pace and rhythm, not of objectives or content. Moreover, the presence or the absence of the teacher is not the yardstick by which one can judge autonomous learning skills. Indeed, it may be that, paradoxically, a teacher has to be present merely to demonstrate the degree of autonomous distance that the learner is able to interpose between himself/herself and the teacher. Ironically whereas the traditional teacher might have been replaceable with a machine, the facilitator teacher becomes irreplaceable (Council of Europe, 1980).

These propositions and aspirations, deriving as they do from older/ advanced or adult learner contexts, may again seem somewhat remote from the secondary FL classroom. Cook (1991: 151) sees an incompatibil-ity between the individual nature of instruction and the collective

nature of most classrooms in mainstream educational systems. Autonomy is therefore not at a very advanced stage. Indeed HMI (1988)
(quoted in Gathercole, 1990) reported very little shift, in a decade, across
all subjects in the curriculum, in terms of moving towards greater
learner autonomy. The reasons that the authors say were given by
teachers for this inertia are: the influence of exams, large classes, rigid
timetables, insufficient support and inadequate resources. As we shall
see from the Tarclindy data, only some of these constraints are reported
by language teachers and the overall response to a movement towards
autonomy is a positive one. It is, furthermore, encouraging that a
number of small-scale classroom based projects have been developing
recently, some with a research component. Grenfell and Harris (1994)
report on a project in London schools which concentrated, as we have
seen in earlier chapters, on developing and evaluating learner strategies. Evans (1993: 19) describes a project in a Coventry school designed
to encourage increased autonomy in the selection of activities from a
range of decentralised resources and greater independence in the
learning process. Tumber (1991: 24) describes the process of bringing
about a gradual change in a department in a school in Essex, a change
towards greater pupil responsibility for their own learning and a voice
in defining both the objectives and the programme.

   As I have tried to argue throughout this book, we should always
analyse critically theories or principles of second language acquisition
that have sprung from studies and practices carried out in very
different institutional learning contexts. Having made that analysis
we should, however, willingly test their applicability to our own
language learning context. The above initiatives show that experimentation in practice need not be confined to those geographical areas
of the world from which language pedagogy theory principally
emanates. Chambers and Sugden (1994: 51) whilst being realistic of the
possibilities of English teachers of German being able to emulate Leni
Dam teaching English in Denmark, nevertheless rightly warn against
'hiding behind excuses' and advocate 'one step at a time'.

   In this chapter I want to concentrate on a functional definition of
learner autonomy, one which puts the emphasis on autonomy *as
developing potential* in the learner, on how s/he can use it to operate
more effectively, rather than as a reaction to difficulties. I would also
want to argue that all language learners are already to a lesser or greater
degree autonomous in that they are able to accept, partially reject or
circumvent an imposed learning style. What is in question is through
which opportunities and to what extent we can develop further those
abilities and skills.

Functional Autonomy

For the purposes of this chapter I will subdivide autonomy into:

(1) *Autonomy of language competence.* The main development in the learner here is the ability to communicate having acquired a reasonable mastery of the L2 rule system. In addition s/he should be able to operate by and large without the help of a more competent speaker of the target language (in most classroom cases, the teacher). We have already touched on this issue in our discussion on communicative strategies and on the progression from formulaic output to freer, individualised and extended output. We might illustrate this last point, the extended output, by the example of a class of learners being given the task of creating a 'forever extending sentence' using link words like: qui (who), que (what), où (where), dont (of which/whose), etc:

Pupil 1: le chat noir
Pupil 2: qui n'aime pas le poisson
Pupil 3: entre dans l'hôtel
Pupil 4: où il n'y a pas d'éléctricité
Pupil 5: et où le patron dort
Pupil 6: sur un lit sans couvertures
Pupil 7: dont les oreillers sont cachés

(The black cat who doesn't like fish goes in the hotel where there is no electricity and where the owner is asleep on a bed without blankets and whose pillows are hidden.)

Whereas in this activity not only the teacher would be prompting the link words but also fellow learners would be supplying all but one of the clauses, in the development of this one aspect of autonomy of language competence, the individual learner would be able to deploy by himself/herself all the skills deployed collectively by class and teacher.

(2) *Autonomy of language learning competence.* The main development in the learner here is the reproduction and transference of L2 learning skills to many other situations including a possible future L3. Thus, we would emphasise the function of learner strategies in general and the metacognitive strategies proposed by O'Malley and Chamot (1990: 47) in particular. Quoting Lachman *et al.* (1979) they give a computer analogy where declarative knowledge is the stored data and procedural knowledge is the software program that does things with the data. Thus whereas a cognitive strategy is a learner using a dictionary for words s/he does not know, a metacognitive (or planning or procedural) strategy might be deciding in advance how much time to allocate to

dictionary use in a timed exam. In other words *if* I only have 60 minutes to complete the test, *then* I will not spend 55 minutes looking up every word.

There are many other examples of how learners can develop autonomy in their language learning competence. Clearly one of them has to be in the carrying out of homework tasks where, independently of the teacher, they need to develop strategies and systems for getting the most out of the time devoted to language homework whatever its nature. Another must surely be the ability to cope with access to target language sources and resources not planned or 'mediated' by the teacher.

(3) *Autonomy of choice and action.* In the classroom situation, learners (particularly adolescents) need to be given the opportunity to develop autonomy of choice if the required skills are to be developed. By this I mean the ability to:

- develop a coherent argument as to why they are learning a foreign language even if they may not have the choice of not learning that language;
- perceive their immediate or *short-term* language learning objectives (e.g. 'I can't seem to get to grips with talking about the town I live in, I'll spend some time this lesson practising that');
- perceive their *long-term* language learning objectives (e.g. 'I want to use languages in my future work, therefore I'll really concentrate on telephone skills);
- perceive the range and types of TL materials and have access to the range and types of materials which will help them fulfil those personal objectives;
- come to an understanding of the ways in which they learn best ('I remember best if I write words down no matter *what* the teacher says!').

In the Appendix, Figure A.7 is a unit of work elaborated in some detail. Many teachers of all experience levels will recognise it as being common to their own practice. There are not meant to be any implied criticisms of the procedures contained in this unit of work. Indeed, they are procedures which I have many times adopted myself often, due to lack of time, with less elaboration! However, it clearly demonstrates what little decision making we give to learners. At the end of this chapter I propose a 'practical idea to try out' in order to redress this heavy emphasis on teacher decision making.

It is at this point opportune to review what the National Curriculum says about learner autonomy. A characteristic of good practice, say the authors of DES (October 1990), is where 'learners become increasingly independent in their work'. It may be just a casual lexical oversight otherwise it would surely be interesting that the word 'work' is used, rather than 'learning'. It would be a contradiction, would it not, if autonomy in language learning were confined to classroom behaviour rather than learning outcomes. The authors go on to explain that this independence includes linguistic and general skills such as:

> using language in unrehearsed situations;
> using a range of sources to get linguistic and factual information;
> planning work either alone or with a partner;
> from quite an early stage, choosing some topic or aspect to be studied. (DES (October 1990): 61)

The above recommendations would all appear to sit very comfortably in any interpretation of learner autonomy. Unfortunately, very little support is given in the *Non Statutory Guidance* (NCC, 1992) on how to implement a programme of learner autonomy. We have a brief reference to it in the section on use of Information Technology where it is acknowledged that it 'gives ownership to pupils by enabling them to create, store and retrieve their own information' (an exercise book, of course, does this too!). We find a fleeting reference to autonomy in the section on differentiation where 'pupils can work on different activities at different times, i.e. in a carousel arrangement'.[1] However, the prospect of pupils choosing from 'quite an early stage' a topic or aspect to be studied, or negotiating agendas, or ground rules, or planning work, is fairly unlikely given that we are told that teachers should use the TL from day-one-lesson-one in order to establish good practice. In other words, in the domain of developing learner autonomy there is yet again a display of the inherent tension in CLT, a tension continually brought into being by the testing (through classroom practice) of how far L2 learning is like L1 learning. In a brief study involving pupils who had been learning German for a year Mitchell and Swarbrick (1994) found that learners were able to decode a great deal of the language of a difficult German text through such strategies as: seeing what went before and what went after; breaking big words down; looking words up; remembering having seen the word in another context (yoghurt pot); by intelligent guessing from context. The study noted that not all pupils were using the same strategies and that there were some strategies that none had considered. This example of awareness raising and training for learner autonomy was, given the language competence of the pupils, carried out in L1.

To summarise then, a framework for developing a programme of learner autonomy opportunities exists within the NC document, but no coherent strategy is proposed for its implementation. What might appear to some as its fundamental contradictions are not discussed let alone resolved. One contradiction which seems to emerge and which might have been sustained through further analysis is that there is a procedural incompatibility between the strong advocacy of the teacher as the major source of target language input and the promotion of learner autonomy.

We will now investigate if some of these contradictions are indeed borne out by the Tarclindy data.

Tarclindy Project Data

An appropriate starting point are the results illustrated in Table 6.1. The teachers surveyed show clear positive attitudes to three of the fundamental tenets of learner autonomy. That is to say that it provides learners with a sense of self-esteem which becomes intrinsically motivating, that it provides a more flexible learning environment in which teachers can perform certain tasks which benefit the learners, and that choosing among a range of learning activities is a desirable aspect of autonomy. Clearly there are reservations, particularly on the question of giving pupils choice; but the overall response is positive. Questionnaire comments and interview data will furnish us with greater insights on these views.

Table 6.1

	Agree	Partly agree	Disagree
Independent learning is motivating	57.6	35.5	0.6
Independent learning gives teacher flexibility	55.8	31.4	12.2
Independence means giving pupils choice[2]	52.3	39.9	8.1
Independent learning leads to less TL use by pupils	22.7	52.9	23.8
Independent learning leads to less TL use by teacher	17.4	40.7	41.3
Learning objectives – possible in TL	12.8	65.1	20.9
Tutorial work – possible in TL	8.1	41.9	49.4

The question of whether autonomy brings about more or less L2 use in the classroom is not so clear. On the one hand, teachers appear to disagree that there is a conflict between independent learning activities and teacher use of L2. On the other hand, they perceive major obstacles in discussing individual learner progress in the target language and they perceive some difficulty in outlining and discussing learning objectives with pupils in L2. How is this explained? Firstly, we could assume that, given the score on flexibility, teachers are using the independent work as an occasion to use L2 on a more one-to-one basis with learners, or alternatively with small groups. This approach is advocated by Gathercole (1990) argues that the key element is the teacher-led small group tutorial 'and all the class management that can support and lead to that'. In other words set up carousel-type situations in order to free the teacher to work on oral work with smaller groups. This deduction from the data is further substantiated by Table 6.1 and from comments made by the teachers. Whilst no one would want to criticise this procedure or argue against its value as a strategy among others available to the teacher, we are entitled to ask if the cause of autonomy is furthered by it or whether it is just a further opportunity for teacher-led learning. Can learner autonomy be nothing more than a flexible lesson strategy, one which facilitates classroom management, a means of reducing the teacher–pupil ratio, rather than a means of developing what some would postulate as key learning strategies in pupils. To what extent are teachers providing opportunities for learners to discuss (let alone have a hand in setting) learning objectives? To what extent is individual progress being monitored by the learner himself/herself? Teachers' comments suggest that the last of these issues is being addressed within the school's overall profiling or record of achievement system. Learners might have progress cards in L2 where they commented briefly on their work ('I can do statements') but their real self-evaluation work was carried out in L1 especially as some of this was then documented and sent home as information for parents. L2 could be maintained where evaluation was limited to whether objectives had been achieved; it was much more difficult to sustain L2 when exploring feelings and setting targets.

Returning to the issue of *teacher's use* of L2, an experienced teacher, commenting on carousel-type activities, said:

With so many different activities going on, I find I am having to move from group to group quickly. At the moment this means explaining quickly in English. I hope, as we and pupils become more relaxed with independent learning more TL will be used.

Teachers' definitions of learner autonomy

When in the interviews teachers were asked what they felt was meant by independent learning the following were the definitions most often mentioned. They are ranked approximately in the order of most often mentioned:

(1) Advancing at the learner's own pace (particularly the more able through extension work).
(2) Separate activities – e.g. going to a resource centre or resource area in the classroom, computer, etc.
(3) Independence from the teacher.
(4) Home learning as opposed to classroom learning.
(5) Giving pupils time to think about what they are doing (both during task and in post-task evaluation).
(6) Working independently is not synonymous with working individually.
(7) Learner ownership of materials (e.g. study packs).
(8) Choice of activities.

In fact only one teacher mentioned an instance of learner choice and that is the 'three columns' described below. As one other teacher commented: 'The degree of freedom of choice might need restriction and/or guidance in order to ensure that pupils work to stretch themselves.'

The above definitions, when considered collectively, do amount to a fairly clear understanding of what the literature argues are some of the fundamental principles of learner autonomy. Particularly welcome is the observation that independence does not mean a return to silent classrooms where learners beaver away at individual reading and writing tasks. Nevertheless, some respondents gave justifiable warnings in this respect, for example:

My gut reaction is that language is about communication and that independent learning might reduce the amount of TL. However, I'm open-minded on this and happy to be convinced otherwise.

Teachers to some extent echoed Gathercole (1990) that learners require time and psychological space in which too learn. There is the notion that if we are too 'insistently interventionist in our pedagogic practice'(Gathercole, 1990: 9) we are in fact depriving them of that time and space. What seems to be missing, however, from the definitions the teachers gave is a belief, referred to earlier, that independent learning is about a process which *emancipates the language learner from the classroom*. Whilst few teachers would subscribe to the following comment:

> ... writing happens at home anyway, reading will happen at home anyway, when you're in my class you're going to be speaking and listening because that's the only chance you're going to have to do it ...

there is little evidence to suggest that teachers were deploying a coherent programme of autonomy development. The definitions above refer to moving away from teacher centredness towards learner centredness but as *behaviours within the classroom* which may or may not stimulate a process of autonomy of language competence, language learning competence and competence in choice/action. A simple test of this is for teachers to ask themselves these two questions: (1) If I am away from my year 10 class for two weeks and they are supervised by a non-linguist supply teacher, to what extent are they, as learners who have been engaged in the process of learning a language for four years, still able to make *some* progress? (2) Would I be able to measure that progress not only in language competence terms but also in terms of language learning competence (evidence of how they went about learning). In other words, to what extent has *my* teaching enabled my pupils to learn *without* me?[3]

Teachers' examples of independent learning activities

Again, the following list is given in approximately the order of 'most often mentioned' in the interviews

(1)   Use of dictionaries and textbook glossaries.
(2)   Extra reading or reading sessions.
(3)   Carousels.
(4)   Pupils recording own progress on paper/grids etc.
(5)   Information Technology.
(6)   The school library as a resource.
(7)   Pupils using the learning support assistant as a resource (i.e. going to for help).
(8)   Pupils using the teacher as a resource (surprisingly low).
(9)   Pupils making recording in non-class time.
(10) Individual work/study packs.
(11) Giving pupils choice through three columns of activities.

It would be fair to say, however, that each of these independent learning activities was not mentioned that often by teachers. Indeed, some had to think at some length before offering an example of an activity which was not either teacher centred or collaborative but teacher directed. The observation logs also rarely recorded activities which seemed directly geared to developing autonomy. It is to be noted that the data collected from the LEA advisers suggest that not a great deal of attention was paid to independent learning (see Table 1.2, page 27). Many teachers were limiting their pupils' skills development to being able to use a dictionary and/or a textbook glossary. No doubt the increase in this practice resulted from a direct reference to such sources as opportunities for independent learning in DES (October 1990b) and DES (1991). Indeed, the very fact that dictionaries are also mentioned in the Attainment Targets may have led to an increased use of dictionaries. Interestingly the authors of both these documents suggest the use of exercise books (back of) or textbook glossaries at level 2 of the Reading Attainment Target, but not until level 5, a level which a considerable percentage of learners will not be able to go beyond, do they suggest the use of a dictionary.

The 'three column of activities' described by one teacher in the above list worked as follows (this is a teacher description of the activity, it was not observed and recorded). A unit of work would be structured such that there were in the first column activities which the pupils *had to do* in order to 'acquire the language'. In the second column there were activities which pupils *should do* in order to 'support' the things that they had to do. Then there was a third column of activities from which pupils could choose any activity they wanted to do. They *didn't have to do* any of the third column but if they didn't they would *have to do* all of the first two columns. At the end of the unit of work teacher and pupils would do some collective revision and then a further activity which used the language they had learnt. Although the researchers had no evidence as to the success or otherwise of this approach in terms of motivation and improving language competence, it would seem to contain a number of elements which develop both autonomy in language learning (selecting activities which reflect personal competence) and autonomy of choice/action. At the very least it is offering learners a negotiated syllabus.

Issues Relating to Independent Learning

We have already explored to some extent issues relating to teacher target language use, learners exposure to L2 and independent learning. There was a general consensus that teachers were likely to use less L2 in order to specify objectives, set up student-centred activities and to evaluate progress where, as one beginner teacher recognised: 'The target language can appear to be a "play" language and therefore may not be taken as seriously as mother tongue when assessing (evaluating) progress'.

Moreover, resources, especially in the early years of learning, had to have some instructions in L1 and offer bilingual glossaries in order to help the learners work independently, whereas in the teacher-led situation the teacher could at least attempt to sustain L2 in order to put across meaning. On the other hand, most teachers felt they were more free to use L2 with individual learners or small groups once the activities were under way. A feeling came through strongly that once the lesson moved from the teacher centred to the student centred situation, there was a release of tension and the problems associated with sustaining use of L2 or recourse to L1 were much reduced. This would appear to be logical for a number of reasons. Firstly, not all learners are struggling with comprehending procedural instructions at the same time. Some understand and want to get on, others need more support before they can do so. A teacher can therefore target L2 support more individually. Secondly, the individual interaction crucial to supplementing input is more likely to occur naturally in the teacher–individual or teacher–small group situation. Lastly, if recourse to L1 does occur in the individual or small group situation it can be done so quietly, less obviously and is therefore less likely to undermine the possibility of restarting with L2 when the teacher moves on to another individual or small group. Some teachers believed that this *quality* of exposure would outweigh the decrease in *quantity* of exposure – the target country environment brought about by extensive teacher fronted input and fellow-learners' answering of questions. The question remains to be answered by future research as to whether teacher-fronted learning promotes more learner 'thinking in L2' than independent learning.

Teachers felt that their own role would have to change considerably if they were to move towards promoting greater learner autonomy. A beginner teacher admitted: 'It's very difficult actually to relinquish control. You feel a bit useless wandering around even though you're being asked questions'.

Interestingly this teacher also believed that when leading from the front and, as it were, doing the work with the whole body of the class, one was much more part of the process and much more intimate with what every learner was doing. As we have seen from Chapter 4, pupils may be very adept at giving the impression that they are all 'moving together' in a learning process whereas in fact they are not. Some would argue that intimacy with the learning process is more likely to result from student centred activities.

The data provided a clear indication that a gradual move towards greater degrees of independent learning entailed resource implications for teachers both in terms of materials and financing in-service. A number of teachers alluded to attempts to set up independent learning centres or areas within their classrooms but could not do so for lack of space. Resources had to be of high quality if they were to prove successful. Others felt they were just not adequately trained or mentally prepared for it. One teacher felt her own language learning experience at school, where, for example, using a dictionary was frowned upon, was a barrier to change. On the other hand, there were instances when, for teachers, success in partial implementation of flexible and independent learning one year was leading to optimism about further development the next.

Another issue that surfaced in the data was whether sufficient time was available to complete the languages syllabus if independent learning activities were being adopted. This was especially the case if choice were being offered to the learners. Some teachers were yet to be convinced that this was the most effective and efficient way of teaching skills to pupils when there was not enough time to complete the syllabus. Clearly there is a need for a debate about how learner autonomy can be placed squarely and unashamedly in the process of language learning rather than being a bolt-on when time from the supposed main business of covering the syllabus allows.

Lastly, but as always not least, surfaced the question of learners' ability levels and its relationship to the success or otherwise of developing learner autonomy. Some teachers felt only the most motivated and/or 'clever' were able to benefit linguistically from it. Others felt that some pupils could be made responsible for their own learning whilst others 'just need spoon feeding – they need telling every little step'.

One of the strong claims made in favour of a student centred classroom (and one made more tentatively above) is that it is more likely to cater for *individual differences* in learners. But what are these differences and are they discrete, easily recognisable entities? If so, are they measurable? Only if they are can a strong claim be made that they are not being catered for in the traditional teacher-fronted classroom.

Individual Differences

We have discussed *Learner Strategies* and *Communicative Strategies* at some length in earlier chapters. Clearly these are individual differences in learners both in terms of quantity of use and consistency of application to a particular activity or language task.

Intelligence, in the narrow sense of IQ, seems to play an important part only in those aspects of L2 acquisition which could be described as formal, for example analysis of language structure. In this sense it mirrors L1 learning in that acquired oral language has only a weak link with the notion of intelligence but development of formal L1 language learning (e.g. reading and writing) has a strong link. Thus a communicative classroom, with an emphasis on oral and aural skills, should theoretically reduce the impact of intelligence (if taken in isolation from other factors), on success.

The elements which separate *aptitude* from other success-linked measurements are that: aptitude is not necessarily synonymous with IQ; aptitude varies from subject to subject and discipline to discipline; aptitude is not affected by previous learning or current teaching; aptitude does not seem to change according to the learner's age. In other words, aptitude in language learning is fairly stable and it varies between people (Skehan, 1991: 276). Aptitude is the theoretical basis for class setting as opposed to banding by cross-subject ability/success.

Learning styles, on the other hand, may be affected by factors such as previous and current teaching styles since there is no evidence that they are immutable. Nevertheless, the theory is that the learner will operate at the most efficient level when the teaching style matches his/her most prominent (current) learning style. Learners who prefer to interact with teachers or other learners will perform better than learners who prefer to analyse texts and concentrate on the language as medium. Learners who prefer to be spectators at interaction will be badly served by a teacher who constantly directs the spotlight on them. There are, however, a number of unresolved questions relating to this hypothesis about learning styles. (a) individual *learning styles* are neither discrete nor constant. They may be affected by mood swings, the security or otherwise of the learning environment, peer pressure, the learner's self-concept in relation to events taking place in the classroom; (b) whereas with *aptitude* it may be possible to take certain steps to compensate for a deficiency, with *learning styles* the only remedy possible is a change in teacher style *or* a change in learner style. For example, if memorisation and recall of vocabulary is an example of *aptitude*, learners with low scores on this aspect can be helped to make lists, use dictionaries, devise word-image associations and so on (Skehan, 1991). It is possible, therefore, that training for *learner strategies* (an individual difference discussed in Chapter 4) can compensate for low level of aptitude. What is the effect of a highly interactive classroom on a learner who prefers a passive style? Does that learner change over time or does s/he grow to reject language learning? There are justifiable reservations about the relationship between learning styles, teaching styles and success. More research needs to be done. However, research so far should, at a minimum, make us sceptical of claims that a particular teaching method will suit the needs of all learners (Lightbown & Spada, 1993).

Linked to the notion of *learning styles* is that of an individual's *personality*. Ellis (1985) suggests that *personality* is a factor in second language acquisition listing three aspects: (a) extroversion/introversion – as having some influence on oral production; (b) social skills – affecting the quality of L2 interaction though not necessarily the quantity; (c) inhibition – having a negative effect on pronunciation. Thus, it would seem that personality variables are at least linked to communicative competence. Given that language learning is internationally recognised as being primarily for the purpose of practical communication, which implies interaction, does the teacher have any choice but to encourage a change in the learning style of passive learners even if this conflicts with their personality traits? Whilst there may be some truth that learner types are born but not made, as Tumber (1991: 24) suggests, there is as yet no evidence that attempts to increase the range of learner styles in individuals is either a lost cause or psychologically damaging.

We have already discussed *motivation* as an individual learner variable. One of its problems is the chicken and egg conundrum of: does success bring motivation or vice versa? Two important observations need to be made here in the context of general learner differences. Firstly, most if not all of these learner differences appear to be interdependent. It is therefore difficult to address the causes of one variable without taking into consideration another. Secondly, we know from experience that events, behaviour and other participants in the classroom (i.e. the classroom atmosphere) can make a difference to an individual learner's motivation. Thus, if we can create the conditions whereby a majority (if not all) of learners can achieve success then we can bring about some changes in motivation if this is the, as yet, undiscovered causal link. If motivation is the starting point, then we have to provide opportunities for learners to at least consider changing their predisposition to language learning. In other words, pending more definitive answers to the questions of individual learner differences, teachers are forced, as always, to adopt a compromise. A more small-group and student-centred approach which nevertheless produces sufficient levels of oral interaction, would seem to be the best solution. Whilst it is certainly not necessary to put learners into boxes labelled according to cognitive styles (Richards & Lockhart 1994: 62), it is useful to try to identify the range of learning styles contained within a class and try to accommodate these as much as possible without losing sight of the ultimate goal of communicative competence. But what would this move towards greater learner-centredness look like structurally? That is, if a department were planning a scheme of work (or programme) where would the elements which provided scope for individual learner variables and developing autonomous skills fit?

A possible answer is in a further learner variable, that of *age*. A pattern began to emerge through the analysis of the Tarclindy interview and comment data on independent learning. Most teachers felt that older learners could be directed towards greater autonomy. We can speculate here as to whether it was the older learners themselves who, being more assertive, were adopting willy-nilly more independent learning strategies or whether teachers were actively employed in providing opportunities and developing these in the learners. Clearly the increased homework loads brought about by the approaching exams at 16 would suggest some premeditated teacher input in this process. Despite these uncertainties, might it be possible to propose some progression towards autonomy based on age related factors? What might that progression contain and what might be its points of reference?

Autonomy and Age Appropriate Teaching

We have seen right through this book that one of the significant variables that teachers reported in the Tarclindy project was the age of the learners. Research into L2 acquisition would tend to support this belief even though it would not support a straight correlation between younger learners and eventual success. Nevertheless, some things are clear. L1 learners do not differ that much in their eventual success at language acquisition. L2 learners differ a lot from each other and they have more individual differences.

I have already suggested that autonomy springs from an interrelationship between the learner, the content and the process of learning. We could add to this tentative model by attempting to relate each of the participants in the FL classroom to content and process. In this relation we may see emerging a situation where the boundaries *between the participants* as well as the boundaries between *participants and content* become increasingly blurred into a single overarching process of learning or system of inter-relationships. This system and process would attempt to be both collective and individualised. Figure 6.1 is an attempt at an illustration of such a process where emphasis shifts between year 7 to year 12, over a period of six years of language learning.[4]

According to the model proposed in Figure 6.1, the following would be the age related characteristics of a process towards autonomy.

In year 7, when pupils in England are, in most cases, first encountering a foreign language, it may well be that it is the *teacher* around which much of the learning process revolves. In these early stages, the presentation of new language, particularly classroom language, will need a high level of mediation by the teacher and will be fairly medium oriented despite its message oriented appearance. In addition, the language will probably be more graded and selected, less authentic with a high emphasis on repetition and formulaic expressions. The part which *other learners* will play will be important but in terms of language competence development, it may well be limited to practice in a variety of structured pair work situations. New information type communication will be fairly minimal. Materials will have the least important part to play at this stage. The teacher's own language, supported by visual materials and the language of the classroom playing the largest part of the content and process input. Learners are highly motivated in this first year and will be able to tolerate fairly

	most emphasis			least emphasis
year 7	teacher	other learners	learner	materials
year 8	other learner	learner	teacher/materials	
year 9	learner	other learners	materials/teacher	
year 10	learner	materials	other learners	teacher
year 11	learner	materials	other learners	teacher
year 12	materials	learner	other learners	teacher

Figure 6.1

lengthy (but not too lengthy!) periods of teacher centred activities as well as the command/directions nature of classroom language. Simultaneously, there must also be some focus on the learner. An awareness of language (discussed below), a development of personal cognitive strategies applied to specific recognisable tasks in an activity, a predisposition to learning the language of the target culture, all these must feature in these early stages.

After a year or so of language learning (probably less, and in any case with much less clear boundaries than presented in this model), *other learners* begin to play an increasingly greater part. For all the reasons outlined in the chapter on collaborative learning, the classroom becomes increasingly a crucible for the exchange of information, for the performance of oral activities involving real interaction and where faith is built up in the value of learning from others, both socially and linguistically. The *teacher* begins to take a slightly less prominent position in the input of language and consequently *materials* begin to complement the role played by *other learners*. In terms of the learner's developmental stage of maturity, it is in this year that the challenges to authority and/or an early disillusionment with language learning can start. Teachers will therefore want to reduce the emphasis on classroom language in L2 and encourage the drawing up of learners' own ground rules. These may have to be done partly in L1. In order for the learner to be able to develop the capability to operate in this collaborative environment in L2 s/he must be helped to develop communicative strategies thus encouraging more lengthy exchanges and sustaining a conversation more effectively.

By year 9 it may be that individual differences in aptitudes and learning styles, conflicting attitudes to the target culture and unequal success rates are at their most prominent. A move to placing the individual leaner as the central participant in the process is probably wise at this stage. This learner focus operates on two levels. The first is a reduction in the amount of teacher-direction in task setting. There is an introduction of choice, limited at first. Tasks become longer with age-appropriate goals. Materials *have* to reflect the learner's physical and psychological development stage no matter how slow has been his/her language competence development: 14-year-olds cannot be fed a diet of topics such as pets or classroom objects. Topics which need to be revisited (for example introductions and personal identification) must be re-cast in age appropriate contexts. Other learners are utilised not just as opportunities for practising oral language or even merely as participants in interaction, but as collaborators in the mechanics of the learning process: accessing materials, checking and evaluating, pooling information, asking for feedback, proposing group work-patterns. An increase in group work should enable the teacher to circulate more freely and give individual or small group support. Secondly, there is a substantial increase in the focus on learner strategies, particularly those which can develop the *emancipation from the classroom* type of autonomy: developing a home-based set of listening cassettes and a related programme of revision; a tidy folder of letters to imaginary pen-friends with a consistent system of re-drafting in order to improve accuracy; devising a personal system of note taking/vocabulary listing perhaps divided into 'items understood' and 'items to be looked up later'.

In years 10 and 11 we see a continuation of a process towards greater autonomy rather than a deliberate shift to preparing for an exam. However, with the introduction of new Areas of Experience (*The World of Work, The International World,* DfE, Jan. 1995: 4) there will necessarily be a shift of focus to text both written and aural and of a much longer and substantial nature. The presentation, practice and use sequence, already being phased out in year 9, is now a rare feature of the classroom. In its place there is a system of helping learners to access written and spoken text both collaboratively and individually. The teacher is on hand to help with this accessing process. Once text is understood it forms the basis of creative output by offering groups of learners the increased range of vocabulary and idiom which they can use to prepare and perform dialogues, discuss opinions, feelings and facts. In addition, learners will be encouraged to look outside the classroom for opportunities in language learning: listening to foreign radio; watching foreign films; seeking out target language nationals in the community; developing exchange links;

By year 12 learners should be in a position whereby most of their personal strategies for studying and learning have been considered and developed.[5] With the reduction in student numbers, they should be in a better position to operate almost autonomously of the teacher with access to resource banks which they may even have helped to create.

The age related model which I have proposed is the most likely one to succeed from the position of relatively little independent learning which we are starting at. More radical models of learner autonomy could be proposed but it is likely that in the secondary FL context they would be rejected out of hand. It may seem contradictory to suggest that year 7 classes be those in which there is most teacher centredness given that learners may well be coming from primary schools (year 6) where group work and learner centred activities may have featured prominently. The problem is that, unfortunately, the National Curriculum is not providing language learning before the age of 11. There is no gradual progression in language acquisition from the early years which would enable a parallel progression in pedagogy. Some readers may object to the individual learner's position in year 7 of the model. To claim that the individual learner is *always* the most important participant in the process of learning may be true in principle but unachievable in the reality of a densely populated classroom, with the current lack of initial and in-service training provision and within the current institutional framework.

Summary

In this chapter I have argued that the 'push and pull' of autonomy (the teacher's intention to develop autonomy and the learner's desire to take it) existed in the past and is not absent from the present. Nor are pedagogical developments in autonomy confined to North America, Scandinavia or adult education learning environments. In England, however, where different sources have given rise to different emphases, it maybe that a re-evaluation of its purpose and a rationalisation of its approaches is necessary.

I have tentatively proposed such an emphasis for autonomy in secondary foreign language learning in the form of emancipation from the classroom and the teacher. This emancipation needs to be realised because two hours a week of language teaching is not going to produce highly competent speakers of the FL. The classroom cannot be the only place where language is learnt. I have therefore proposed three functional subdivisions of autonomy: language competence, language learning competence and autonomy of choice/action.

The National Curriculum, in its original form, gave a powerful impetus for the development of independent learning. However, it did not attempt to resolve the conflicting nature of autonomy when conjoined with the pedagogical implications of statements on target language use and the implications of part 1 of the Programmes of Study (DES, 1991).[6] We have seen, on the other hand, that in England the ground is fertile for a more rapid growth of the autonomous learning culture even though not much may be happening at the moment. A clearer focus is needed in order to separate the desire to increase learner autonomy from classroom practices and behaviours which appear to involve independent learning. That is, activities which enable autonomous development rather than those which are merely a better opportunity to control the learner.

I have tried to suggest a realistic model of gradual increase in learner autonomy based on age appropriateness, one which should cater at the same time for individual differences. We must remember, however, that as yet we do not fully understand these differences.

Practical Ideas to Try Out

(1) Look at the unit of work in the Appendix (Figure A.7). Are there any aspects of autonomy being developed here? Think of the three development types described on pages 170–1.

Autonomy of choice and action. For each 'decision' in the unit of work, consider (or discuss with other colleagues) whether responsibility could be given to a learner or a group of learners).

Autonomy of language competence. In what ways could learners initiate language rather than merely respond to the teacher's language? Can the sequence of 'activities' be modified with the input and presentation of new language not coming from you the teacher? Think of the other 'participants' - the other learners, the materials, the learner himself/herself.

Autonomy of language learning competence. Which of the 'decisions' and 'activities' could a learner (or group of learners) make or do in a place other than the classroom? To what extent is the unit of work preparing the learner for making those decisions and doing those activities?

(2) Look at the age appropriate proposals on page 183. Compare this with you own scheme of work in your school or the way you were taught a foreign language at school.

(3) Give the Learner Strategies Questionnaire (Appendix, Figure A.8) to a class in year 8 and also to a year 10 class. Are there any significant differences in their answers? How do you explain these? Are there significant differences between boys and girls? To what extent does high strategy use correlate with your estimation of their language ability/success?

Notes

1. A further marginalisation of autonomy is brought about by the revised NC documents in whose programmes of study there is no longer a specific section on independent learning, even though the authors do include some of its elements in Section 3: language-learning skills. There are also references to the use of dictionaries and glossaries in the Attainment Targets.
2. The actual phrasing for this question is: pupils working independently should be allowed to choose among a range of learning activities.
3. In this scenario I am excluding the question of laziness or misbehaviour

(even though they are obviously a factor).

4. I have deliberately omitted year 13 as it may be so linked to preconceptions associated with individual examination systems that it would mask what is relevant here, namely a language learning process for its own sake.

5. I would argue that the so-called gap to be bridged between the current GCSE and A level is much more one of lack of learner autonomy than the often cited one of lack of grammar.

6. For example compare in terms of implications for methdology the sections: Communicating in the Target Language and Understanding and Responding, with the other four sections: Language Learning Skills and Awareness of Language; Cultural Awareness; Ability to Work with Others; Ability to Learn Independently.

7 Is a National Methodology Desirable?

In Chapter 1 we examined how curriculum designers in England and Wales erected a framework to bring about change in teaching styles. Alongside the framework and the characteristics of good practice, the NC provided actual descriptions of good practice in the classroom (DES, 1990b: 63). The 20 descriptions of good practice offered are, by and large, isolated activities and they would not appear to be offered as components of a coherent methodology. We have, for example:

(a) a reading scheme (KS3 and KS4);
(b) a practical activity involving making solids from cards (year 7);
(c) an environmental project involving a trip abroad (year 8);
(d) a combined French, history and geography visit to Nantes (years 10 and 11);
(e) a Foreign Languages at Work lesson (years 10 and 11);
(f) homework using tape recorders (KS3 and KS4);
(g) An 'applied French course' with less able pupils (year 11);
(h) An Urdu lesson where the learners have a range of home languages (year 9);
(i) A modern languages poetry writing project (KS3, KS4 and post-16).

Whilst there is nothing unacceptable about these activities, indeed, all would seem highly desirable, it is impossible to assess them in terms of a recognisable scheme of work stretching over three or five years. They are described in a vacuum. Apart from the age group, language taught and description of the school, we know very little except that the activity took place and that the observers thought it represented 'good practice'. We do not know what the teacher's objectives were at the time, his/her beliefs about approaches, the pedagogical changes s/he made because of the knowledge s/he had of the children. No detailed observation of the lesson is provided. We are told that: 'All the modern languages lessons were conducted entirely or almost entirely in the target language' (DES, 1990b: 62)

Thus, we are presented with a fragmented picture of practice but one rigidly underpinned by the tenet of L2 exclusivity. L2 exclusivity seems to be giving the activities the seal of approval. However, we are given little indication of how difficulties regarding comprehensibility of teacher input, readiness to speak or promoting interaction were overcome. There are no examples of lessons in years 8 and 9 (apart from the Urdu lesson) where classroom management, activity change, activity explanation and feedback might present difficulties in L2. Indeed, readers might speculate as to how activities (d) and (g) we conducted 'almost entirely in the target language'. In other words, these examples of practice address few of the issues we have raised in this book.

Descriptions of good practice, at the very least, should contain detailed observation of more than one lesson by the same teacher in order to make comparisons. They should be backed up with an account of what the teacher believes and how this is translated into observable practice. In addition, it would be preferable for there to be some learners' reaction to the teaching. Ideally there should also be some measurement of pedagogical progression – how the teacher adapts principles of practice to ongoing learner outcomes. Evidence of successful learning, achievement in value added terms, would help to complete the picture.

I therefore offer, as part of our conclusion, a profile of three teachers from the Tarclindy project and try to include as many of the above criteria for reporting practice as the data offers. The names of the teachers have been changed. This is not because the description in any way portrays anything they should be ashamed of. Quite the contrary! On the other hand, I do not offer them up as exemplars. This is a practice that rarely encourages emulation in others. More often than not it demotivates. Rather they have been chosen because they demonstrate the range of views and practices which struggle to find a coherence in the sometimes conflicting elements of the NC framework and operate within the tensions inherent in CLT. Table 7.1 reports their respective responses to the attitude questionnaire. As this is given in full, it is not reproduced in the Appendix.

A Profile of Three Teachers

Christine

Christine is 36 years of age, has taught French for 10 years, for the past two years as a Head of Department in a large, mixed comprehensive in the Midlands. She describes the catchment area of the school as 'challenging' even though it is not in an inner city, the pupils coming

Table 7.1 Attitude statements

		Christine	Alex	Viv
1	Good language teachers use the target language almost exclusively.	3	1	2
2	Good language teachers use the TL to organise language activities: e.g. pair work.	2	1	1
3	Good language teachers use the TL to give instructions in class: e.g. 'close books, pack up'.	1	1	1
4	Good language teachers use the TL to evaluate/comment on pupil performance: e.g. 'well done'.	2	2	1
5	Good language teachers always use the TL to correct pupils' oral performance.	3	1	1
6	Good language teachers use the TL for disciplinary interventions: e.g. 'stop tapping that pencil!'.	2	2	1
7	Good language teachers use the TL for building up relationships with individual pupils.	3	2	2
8	Good language teachers use the TL as appropriate to the language ability level of the pupils.	1	1	1
9	Good language teachers use the TL when there is little or no risk of pupil misbehaviour.	3	3	3
10	It's easier to use the TL with younger pupils, e.g. years 7 and 8.	2	2	3
11	It's easier to use the TL with older pupils, e.g. years 10 and 11.	2	2	3
12	To use the TL you have to be very fluent yourself in the language.	1	2	2
13	You've got to start pupils off right at the beginning using the TL.	1	1	1
14	You have to build up your use of the TL slowly	1	3	1
15	You can't teach grammar in the TL	3	3	2
16	Too much use of the TL by the teacher can reduce the use of TL by the pupils.	1	3	3

Table 7.1 (*continued*)

		Christine	*Alex*	*Viv*
17	Too much use of TL by the teacher makes it difficult to set up active-learning.	1	2	3
18	Pair work encourages a lot of TL use by pupils	2	1	1
19	Pair work encourages a lot of TL use by *some* pupils	1	3	2
20	Pair work encourages real communicative exchanges	2	1	2
21	Pair work encourages a lot of TL use by pupils *only if* carefully monitored by teacher(s).	1	2	2
22	Pair work encourages a lot of TL use by pupils if they are allowed to work independently.	2	3	2
23	Pair work encourages a lot of TL use by *some* pupils if they are allowed to work independently .	1	2	1
24	Pair work encourages a lot of TL use by pupils if highly structured (e.g. clearly defined tasks and guided use of language.	1	1	3
25	Pair work encourages a lot of TL use by pupils if *no* highly structured.	3	1	1
26	The amount of structuring needed for pair work depends on the language ability of the pupils.	1	2	1
27	The amount of structuring needed for pair work depends on the difficulty of the task.	1	1	1
28	Pair work lets pupils' error go by uncorrected.	1	2	1
29	Pair work can allow error to become a habit.	2	3	2
30	group work (i.e. when three or more pupils are talking to each other) is a worthwhile activity.	1	2	1
31	Group work is a worthwhile activity but is difficult to set up in the TL.	1	2	2

32	Group work (general – e.g. composing a poster collaboratively) is a worthwhile activity.	1	1	2
33	Group work (general) is a worthwhile activity to assess.	1	2	3
34	Group work (general) means a lot of TL is used by pupils.	3	2	2
35	The opportunity for groups of pupils to work independently is a motivating factor in language learning.	1	2	1
36	Pupils working independently allow the teacher greater flexibility.	1	2	1
37	Pupils working independently should be allowed to choose among a range of learning activities.	1	2	1
38	Independent learning leads to less TL use by pupils.	2	2	2
39	Independent learning leads to less TL use by teacher.	1	2	2
40	Learning objectives can be explained and discussed in the TL.	2	2	2
41	Tutoring (discussing individual pupil progress) can be carried out in the TL.	1	2	2

1 = agree; 2 = partly agree; 3 = disagree

mostly from white working class council estates where unemployment is well above the national average. From her attitude questionnaire we can see that she does not consider 'almost exclusive use of TL' as the main criteria for describing a good language teacher. She believes that 'good teachers have a repertoire of skills which they call on to enhance learning' and that too much use of anything is detrimental to good learning. For Christine the ability level and motivation of the pupil is a major factor in TL use, much more so than age. When it comes to pair and group work, Christine believes that it should be highly structured and that learners 'always need to know what to do'. Nevertheless the real value of pair and groupwork for Christine is that it has high potential for learners' personal and social development, particularly for the less able. She says that she and the department have had to move towards a much less teacher-led style of learning in order to cope. But it's not just a reaction to de-motivation. She says: 'It's about getting it right for the individual learner'. Independent learning is, on the one hand, about groups being able to collaborate without the strong presence of the teacher and on the other about 'creating opportunities for them to exercise their study skills, to use any sources of information including reference sources and to use machinery' (tape recorders and computers).

Despite Christine's reservations about linking L2 use with 'a good teacher', she believes that the NC's stance on use of the TL was effective in opening up the debate and focusing teachers on how to maximise opportunities to exploit the medium of the target language even if 'the pendulum swung too far towards having to do it all the time'. She believes some teachers have experienced feelings of guilt about not staying in the TL. Some of these are teachers who aren't 'reflective enough and just think it's an imposition'. Others are the ones who want to 'push forward the frontiers of learning' and do care and, like her, do feel guilty. But for her, the reasons why RL1 occurs are substantial pedagogical and psychological reasons, linked to how learners perceive a foreign language and the constant need for a variety of activities to motivate them. The greater the variety and authentic value of the activity the more difficulty in sustaining L2 use.

Christine does not see too much of a problem (at a theoretical level) with target language testing of listening and reading skills because these are artificial skill distinctions anyway, mixed skill reflecting much more a true foreign language competence. She is very worried, however, that pupils will not understand what is required of them. Consequently she had very mixed feelings about the issue.

The researchers observed three of Christine's lessons lasting 50 minutes each: one top set year 8 and two mixed ability year 7s. Christine's own L2 competence is high, somewhere between very fluent and near-native. The year 8 group were very co-operative but rather shy even though they very much gave the impression of being happy to be in the classroom with Christine and not afraid to speak French. Chairs were arranged in a horseshoe shape with no tables (the tables were behind the pupils and against the walls of the classroom). Christine says this is now the layout she prefers (it facilitates inter-action) even though it does have its problems. The topic was about introducing food items which Christine did by using flashcards and overhead projector. In addition to the oral presentation of the food items there was some listening (teacher input–pupil matching) some reading and writing activities. The lesson was 50 minutes long with about 80% of it being teacher centred. Christine had recourse to L1 mostly for explaining how to do the activities (10 instances of recourse to L1 being recorded in different lesson segments) and when ensuring meaning of individual items. In fact Christine, right at the beginning, gave the English word for each food item. When asked afterwards why she did this, she replied that sometimes pupils went through whole lesson appearing to understand what the item (e.g. on the flashcard) was but in fact being right off the mark. Christine did this with a 'planned time out' approach, although some individual items were explained in English with an 'unplanned RL1' (see Chapter 4). Very few other instances of RL1 were recorded. Pupils interviewed after this lesson said they liked it when Christine spoke in French (L2) and tried to explain in TL at least a couple of times before resorting to English. Generally they preferred to speak in pairs and groups because people wouldn't laugh at them and Christine gave them lots of opportunities to do this. They did go into English (L1) when working collaboratively but kept an eye on the fact that Christine might be coming round to listen in! When the idea of support cards for learner–learner interaction to help them stay in L2 was suggested, they reacted favourably. They thought Christine should tell naughty pupils off in English (L1).

The two year 7 lessons (Topic: classroom objects) produced very much the same pattern of RL1, with an even higher rate on the explaining of activities which included pair work activities. The lessons were both judged to be about 60% teacher-led, 40% learner centred. This is a relatively high level of learner centredness for year 7 lessons. Other RL1s occurred when Christine was making management (rather than disciplinary) interventions and when 'parroting' (see Chapter 3). When this feature was pointed out to Christine, she commented that she wasn't aware she was doing it. Christine also used a mixture of French and English to talk quietly to individual pupils during the pair work activities. These year 7 pupils were not interviewed because of time tabling restrictions. One of Christine's colleagues' year 9 classes was interviewed. These were more uncomfortable when they didn't understand the teacher and were keen for her to explain in English after a few failed attempts in L2. Apart from this there was virtually the same response from these pupils as from the year 8 pupils on all other issues.

Alex

Alex is a teacher of German and has taught for 17 years, seven years as a head of department in a suburban comprehensive on the edge of a large town in the South of England. Alex describes the school as fairly easy to teach in although there are 'some difficult elements'. As we can see from Table 7.1, Alex very strongly equates 'almost exclusive use of

TL' with being a good teacher. He feels that an 'amazing amount of language can be learnt by pupils by daily and regular repetition of phrases which are used for instructions and explanation'. There are very few occasions when Alex justifies RL1. At the end of a lesson, perhaps, particularly with less able pupils, 'it is a good idea to talk to individuals in English (L1) when special praise is warranted, otherwise they might miss out on the message'. He is unsure about the age-related factor. He doesn't feel that target language with older pupils should be a problem although a wide range of ability within a group can make it difficult, as does the fact that they have not been used to a high level of TL beforehand. The ability factor was also not significant. L2 input had to be tailored to suit the ability level of the learners. He finds that in many cases teaching grammar through the L2 medium is easier. Alex is a firm believer in short bursts of pair work resulting from short periods of teacher input. He recognises that these are highly structured, pupil–pupil exchanges on clearly delineated tasks with not much freedom to experiment, but he reports high success in this type of situation and comparatively low success when learners are 'left to devise their own situations'. Alex is a very efficient and reflective practitioner, capable of self-criticism and always demonstrating open-mindedness to ideas and issues. He is, consequently, aware that he (and the department) need to consider developing extended output and 'open ended use of language' in the learners and to 'investigate the possibilities of the methodology of independent learning'. Nevertheless, his 'gut reaction', although he is happy to be convinced otherwise, is that independent learning would reduce the amount of target language use in the classroom. Both he and the department had been using the TL extensively before the advent of the NC. The documentation was thus only an added impetus.

Alex recognises problems with Target Language testing of comprehension but is unhappy with the GCSE's use of English (L1) because it 'becomes almost impossible to keep in the TL'. TL testing would thus improve the quality of teaching. 'Whether it would be a better exam is another question'.

Researchers observed a year 9 top set. Alex's own L2 competence is comparable to that of Christine's. The year 9 class, working on the topic of telephone conversations, was very co-operative. Dialogues were first done in open pairs then in closed pairs. The pace was fast and Alex gave pupils only a short amount of time to practise their closed pairs before moving back to the 'whole class' situation. The lesson was judged to be about 75% teacher-led with the learner centred proportion being pair work and some reading in groups (telephone dialogues from the coursebook). Alex's recourse to L1 occurred under only one category and that was *when translating or asking for translation*; 12 instances of this were recorded. When asked afterwards about this, Alex commented that translation of words of lesson content was to 'speed things up' and to 'ensure everyone knows what's going on'. Although only this lesson was recorded, several others were observed where the teaching style was similar: short bursts of whole class activities, followed by intensive but highly regulated pair work. Another feature of Alex's lessons was frequent vocabulary tests. These involved L1.

This year 9 class, generally, said that they didn't mind it when Alex used L2, even if sometimes they didn't understand. They had been used to that style of teaching since year 7. They guessed at meaning and felt strongly that they learned more because he conducted virtually the whole lesson in L2. They would 'be missing something if he spoke in English'. However, they pointed out that Alex went into English if they really didn't understand. They also reported that Alex only tells them off in English if 'it's something really bad!' Whilst most felt reasonably happy about speaking in front of the class, they did prefer speaking in pairs – for example because 'if your partner's having difficulties you can help'. Some said they did go into English (L1) in pair work, others made an effort not to. Support cards might help them stay in TL for interaction but only if the teacher was there to enforce it. To help them remember language Alex gives them lots of tests, rhymes and mnemonics.

Viv

One of the reasons Christine and Alex were chosen as case studies is their very different reaction to question one – the 'global attitude' question. Viv's reaction takes the middle position.

Viv, like Christine, has been teaching for 10 years, three years as a HOD in a comprehensive in a small town in the South of England. The school, however, has the top ability range 'sliced off' by nearby selective schools. The pupils are generally co-operative and interested in language learning. Viv would like to achieve 'a totally German environment' where even the children talked to each other in German. 'I'm far from achieving that', she comments. She feels she can stay in the TL about 80% in a 'successful lesson' and she achieves this by informing the pupils of what she is trying to do. She uses L1 when she wants to give pupils a piece of work which is going to be assessed and wants to make sure 'that they know exactly what they're doing for homework'. Otherwise the pupils panic. She also has RL1 when she has tried two or three times to explain an activity in L2 and thinks: 'this is silly, I could spend forever doing this!' The only other time is when explaining a point of grammar to older pupils. She believes that this ties in also with the older learner's emotional development when 'the last thing they want to do is speak a foreign language anyway'. When it comes to quantity of L2 use, Viv takes very much the 'failed maximalist' position described in Chapter 3 whereas Christine and Alex take more of an assertive stand on the amount of TL they use in class though, of course, this varies considerably between them.

Viv is highly critical of various other aspects of her teaching. For example, she feels she does not give them enough choice in their learning and she puts this down to a fear of not achieving the comparatively high results her department has enjoyed over recent years. The pupils she teaches tend to be average to lower ability because of the intake and she has to compensate for this by teaching to the exam. She feels that she is yet to be convinced that autonomous learning is 'the most effective and efficient way of teaching skills to pupils'. Moreover, she feels she has been unsuccessful in giving pupils the language they need to organise groupwork in L2, something she would like to do.

Researchers observed two of Viv's lessons both 35 minutes in length. The first, a year 8[1] mixed ability class, was very co-operative and worked hard despite sporting dramatically bloodstained shirtsleeves, the result of measles inoculations! In the classroom, the children sat in rows. They worked on the topic of personal identification. Viv issued the children with false identities and they had to go round the class 'finding each other'. A German assistant was also in the lesson and helped model answers and worked with children in pair work. Viv used very little English (L1). Most instances of RL1 resulted from her trying to set up this fairly complicated pair work activity where she commented for example: 'You still haven't got the hang of this have you?'. She also had RL1 for translating individual words to ensure comprehension. The lesson was judged to be about 50% teacher-led. The second was a year 9 class, set by ability (set 2). Pupils were, again, very co-operative. The lesson was based around a visit to a tourist information centre. They had to prepare a short sketch involving asking what there was to visit in the town. There are two interesting observations to be made about this lesson. Firstly, it was judged to be 75% learner-centred. Secondly, Viv used virtually no English at all as she moved from group to group of children. Her RL1 was as a result of having to translate individual words and phrases into English that pupils were having difficulty with (three instances), when talking quietly with a group of pupils (two instances only) and when explaining the home-work at the end. The type of activity, without the emphasis on the teacher, clearly did not create difficulties in sustaining L2 use on her part. Pupils were observed to use L2 only when monitored by Viv. Viv has a strong and lively personality with a good sense of humour. She was able to express these personality traits through the L2.

The pupil interviews produced very mixed responses. Some year 8 pupils said that the teacher using L2 was OK as long as they could understand it. Some really objected to it, others saw the learning value in it. The year 9 pupils felt secure that they could ask the teacher if they didn't understand and felt that they learnt more from exposure to L2. They expected the teacher to use English if they really didn't under-stand. Other year 9 pupils reported feeling quite frustrated when they didn't understand. Some pupils felt reasonably happy about speaking in front of others but the majority reported feeling uncomfortable and said they preferred small groups. One can speculate as to whether Viv's greater indecision about L2 use led to a much greater mixture of reactions than was recorded from pupils taught by Christine and Alex.

What conclusions can we draw from these three teacher profiles? Firstly, it is apparent that their methods and techniques, whilst differing quite radically at the 'belief level' are not hugely dissimilar when it comes down to actual quantity of L2 use. For example, Christine's ability to modify her input is higher than perhaps she herself estimates and she recognises that her pairwork activities are highly structured and controlled. By contrast, Alex's 'short cuts' to comprehension are strongly defended and bring to mind (a little ironically) the German Länder recommendations that we saw in Chapter 1. Moreover he is now preparing to turn his attention to greater learner independence. Nevertheless the different ways of conceptualising the learning process and different emphases are sufficient at both the belief and the practical levels to suggest that a prescriptive national methodology is unlikely to gain much of a foothold. Viv's prioritising of the testing and examination process contrasts sharply with Christine socialising function of teaching. Alex's intensity of input and controlled output is at variance with Christine's avowed espousal of more student-centred learning. Yet, all three are confident, successful teachers and middle managers. What we witness, in fact, is the principled prioritising of approaches and activities according to local circumstance. Even more importantly we witness the constant interdependence of target language use with other pedagogical imperatives such as collaboration and autonomy.

The Professional Need for a Rigid Framework

We can now ask whether the prescriptivism of the NC framework was necessary *professionally*? There is evidence from the above (and what teachers generally in the Tarclindy project said) that an increase in teacher L2 *was desirable* in some schools. Was the presentation of the framework and its enforcement the most effective way of bringing that increase about and what have been the consequences of this approach? To what extent can a national framework, enforced by national agencies, act as a fulcrum for change? Green (1990: 80) points to the lack of incentive for methodological change in the classroom brought about by advancement being more closely linked with management skills than pedagogy. By contrast, therefore, top down pressure on classroom styles would suggest a greater likelihood of success. Yet we have also seen that grass-roots innovation (e.g. Graded Objectives, and Language Awareness) *was* readily taken on by teachers in the 1980s and only lacked coherence and opportunities for refinement because it never received backing at the national level. I would argue that with a top-down approach it is, in fact, unlikely that teachers will participate creatively in adopting new styles, designing new courses and pursuing imaginative methods of assessment. They are more likely to give the grudging minimum as laid down by law (Green, 1990: 80).

OFSTED (1993b: 6) reports an increase in teacher use of L2 in Keystage 3 within one year of the implementation of the NC. One is forced to ask to what extent that increase is impressionistic given that the newly formed inspection teams had nothing rigorous to compare observations with. There is also anecdotal evidence that some teachers considerably increase their L2 use during inspections. There is, moreover, some evidence from the Tarclindy project that the potential for innovation in teaching styles is being suppressed by focusing so emphatically on this aspect of the National Curriculum. Comments made by LEA advisers betray the degree of failure of the NC top-down approach. When asked what they felt now needed to be developed through INSET, by far the issue most cited by advisers was pupil use of L2 and development of target language proficiency – the very essence of FL learning! The fact that learner initiated dialogue, learner independence and IT[2] were also cited by advisers as needing attention only serves to reinforce the interdependence of teacher L2 use with other aspects of teaching and learning. OFSTED (1993) and OFSTED (1995) add their weight to the call that much work still needs to be done in terms of encouraging and developing pupils' (a) length of L2 utterance; (b) spontaneous use of L2 and initiative taking; (c) ability to work collaboratively; and (d) ability to operate independently of the teacher.

It is not unreasonable to conclude from these judgements on the progress of change that teacher input in the secondary FL context has not, of itself, produced greater learner proficiency.

Of course, teachers in the Tarclindy project welcomed the greater emphasis on teaching and learning styles. The majority, however, saw its value in terms of the start of a debate about issues rather than the conclusion or the stifling of that debate. The introduction of the National Curriculum for MFL was a unique opportunity for a re-appraisal of teaching and learning. Indeed the 14 characteristics of good practice (particularly the three characteristics we have examined closely in this book) offer excellent parameters within which to conduct a debate on teaching and learning styles which fit the needs of a multi-faceted and multi-cultural society.

The Pedagogical Need for a Rigid Framework

Was the prescriptivism of the framework necessary *pedagogically*? What is the case for L2 exclusivity in the FL secondary context? It is useful to remind ourselves, once again, that the designers of the framework appear to have adopted this methodological tenet from ELT. Yet its validity is being robustly challenged even in the inter-national ELT sphere (Phillipson, 1992: 185). We also need to remind ourselves that the message behind L2 exclusivity is that: learners learn best from the native speaker teacher model; that you can compensate for lack of curriculum time allocated to L2 learning (and lateness of starting L2 learning) by increasing the intensity of the L2 exposure; that you can coerce all adolescents into abandoning and denying, albeit for relatively short periods of time, the existence of their mother tongue. The conclusion from the Tarclindy project and that of other studies is that exclusivity is not justifiable pedagogically. That is *not* to say that extensive exposure to the teacher's L2 is not necessary. Indeed I have argued that it is essential for the development of many aspects of language proficiency. What is challenged by the data is the notion that quantity alone develops proficiency or that quantity should, as it were, always have hegemony over other aspects of learning. There is a place for contrastive analysis in conceptualising meaning and for making up the language exposure deficit. I have therefore proposed an *optimal* teacher use of L2 founded on the overarching principle that it must be seen to contribute to learner interaction and learner output. There are many indicators, throughout this book, that an emphasis on teacher input is problematic. There are also recurring indicators that teacher centred learning may be an obstacle to learner proficiency. We have seen that lock-step teaching makes meaning negotiation difficult. Early production of language and learner initiated dialogue, essential for the development of language proficiency and confidence, appear to be inhibited by whole class oral exchanges. We have therefore explored collaborative learning and autonomy as alternative strategies. In Chaper 6 we have explored the interdependence of L2 use, collaboration and autonomy through an age related model of learning. In this chapter we have seen this interdependence exemplified in the profile of three teachers' practice. Our concept of autonomy is underscored by the notion of working towards eventual emancipation from the language classroom. Teacher L2 use must be seen to promote learner use of L2. It must facilitate (and operate efficiently in) more learner centred activities and in turn facilitate emancipation from the classroom. If it isn't doing this, it isn't doing its job!

Target language use must also take into consideration the variables located amongst the learners themselves. We have seen that ability is one crucial variable which cannot be ignored in deciding on TL use. Yet there is a need to explore further what 'low ability' actually is in the FL context and what it represents to teachers. Is it observable demotivation, notions of language inaptitude, lack of effective strategies for learning, reactions to a teaching style, lack of parental involvement or masked peer pressure? In other words, we need to have a much firmer grasp on the characteristics of the successful and unsuccessful language learner before we can be confident of using it as a variable for optimal teacher use of L2. An irreducible notion of learner ability cannot be an acceptable differentiating criterion for quantity of teacher use of L2. Yet there is a danger that it may be the easiest solution adopted in the long run[3] even though it would be a solution which could deny equal opportunities to all learners. Our current notions of ability can only operate as a *temporary* working variable of teacher L2 use.

The second crucial variable, we have seen, is learner age. Another appraisal of the benefits of starting a FL before the age of 10 needs to be made in the new and dynamic European context. We need to ascertain whether achieving a threshold of FL competence early will both propel the learner towards greater fluency and avoid those demoralising returns to talking about their 'name and appearance' at the age of 16. Imaginative initiatives in other European countries will hopefully provide British educators with the arguments with which to confront their national government. It is hoped that those arguments will not be formulated too late for them to have an impact. In the meantime, matching the learning content and style to the psychological developmental stage of the learner must be an important consideration.

In this book we have discussed in detail the quantity and quality of teacher L2 use and its effect on FL language acquisition and FL learning. We have explored in what ways teacher L2 use might impact on learner attitudes to peoples and cultures. Any language curriculum which opts to turn so much of its attention to learning processes rather than learning outcomes must be vigilant of the effects it may have on attitudes.

As a case study of one country's introduction of a new curriculum, I hope that this book offers planners, designers and teachers elsewhere some insights into how best to proceed with the implementation of change. As we have seen, the majority of teachers consulted demonstrated that they were open to change. But when asked if they thought a national methodology was desirable they responded by alluding to a search for a basic structure, a set of core principles about collective approaches balanced by an individualised response to individual needs. I hope that this book has shed some light on what those core principles might be. I believe these core principles hold for other FL learning contexts. Indeed, there is a need for the debate about core principles and about purposes, approaches and methods to continue and for it to be held within the context of continued European integration.

'Internationalising' the FL classroom, through a combined analysis of SLA and FL literature/research has, throughout the writing of this book, been a challenging and sometimes daunting task. Where the links have proved successful it has been extremely rewarding. Second Language Acquisition literature and research do seem to have something to offer the secondary FL context. Where the links have failed they have either exemplified a need for further context-specific research or the need for the links to be made by a more able author. In any event, I hope that the reader has found that the cross-fertilisation of ideas has illuminated and demystified the issues rather than rendered them incoherent.

Internationalising the debate has also gone some way towards exorcising the spectre of the monoglot English learner. Through observing and talking to colleagues in other European countries it has brought home to me the realisation that teachers in the UK are not alone in confronting the complex issues presented by the monolingual classroom and that they are also not alone in rejecting unidimensional solutions to them.

Notes

1. In this area of Southern England pupils transfer to secondary school in year 8 having done at least one year of MFL in their 'middle school'
2. It could be argued that the greatest value Information Technology can offer the language learner is the ability to work co-operatively but independently of the teacher.
3. As I write there is a suggestion that examining boards will use up their permissible percentage of L1 use in the lower levels of exams at Key stage 4.

Appendix

The Tarclindy Project

The following is a lengthy description of the study which contributes in fair measure to this book's evidence. I describe it in full as I believe it may offer others, usually through the difficulties it encountered, what it has offered me, a valuable insight into empirical research methodology and a better understanding of some of the issues.

Research population

It was hypothesised by the researchers that one of the independent variables was the experience level of the teachers being studied. Accordingly, three categories of teachers were devised: Experienced (more than two years since qualifying); Beginner (either at end of first year or in second year since qualifying); Student teacher (at or near the end of the Post Graduate Certificate of Education Course of 36 weeks duration). I am aware that these classifications do not match those in other studies. For example, Nunan (1992b) defines *experienced* as over five years. However, it could be argued that definitions of experience are either arbitrary or related to the professional context the teachers are working in. In the UK it is not uncommon to find teachers with posts of responsibility after only three years. Whilst Experienced teachers were selected at random (but see criteria below) from schools in England, the Beginner teachers and Student teachers were selected from only two UK teacher training institutions. That is, the Beginner teachers were followed up in-post from the records kept by those two institutions. One of the researchers was familiar with one of the institutions, thus in order to avoid a bias or desire to please in the responses, the questionnaires (which were anonymous) were administered to the Student teachers but they were not interviewed.

Teacher questionnaires

The questionnaires were devised on an adaptation of the standard attitudinal questionnaire with a three-point scale answer. The decision to adopt a three choice rather than five choice answer was due to the fact that in the pilot a number of respondents commented on the difficulty of 'agreeing *strongly*' and 'disagreeing *strongly*' with attitudinal statements. A four-point scale was considered but rejected on the grounds of respondents not being able to differentiate semantically between 'partly agreeing' and 'partly disagreeing'. These were felt to be stronger arguments than the one which claims that in a three-point scale respondents will opt for the middle. The three-point scale was then also piloted.

The final version of questionnaires with space for comments (referred to as Teacher Questionnaire Comment data), were sent to teachers in England (200 schools for the Experienced and Beginner teachers) with an attempt at covering a cross-section of inner-city, suburban, small town and rural schools. In the case of the Student teachers, this was judged according to where they had carried out their 12 week (approximately) block teaching practice and they completed their questionnaire anonymously at the end of that practice. Almost all the schools used in the survey were comprehensives.

Of the total of 173 completed and returned questionnaires, the largest number is made up of Experienced teachers (see Table A1). Of the Experienced teachers the span was between three years and 32 years in service, although the vast majority had taught for more than five years. Table A.2 gives a breakdown of respondents' schools in terms of where they were located. These categories are, of course, only approximate, evidenced by the fact that 10 teachers felt the categories were not appropriate to them.

Table A.1 Teaching experience

Experienced	83
Beginner	45
Student teacher	45

Table A.2 Location of school

Inner City	35
Suburban	42
Small Town	54
Rural	27
Other	10

The Teacher Questionnaire Comments generated categories amounting to some 26 pages of typed A4.

The teacher interviews

Experienced and Beginner teachers were selected for interview on the basis of their responses in the questionnaire so that in the interview data we have a representation of views on the three issues of target language use, collaborative learning and autonomy. In addition, care was taken to interview teachers in a variety of socio-economic 'locations'; 21 teachers were interviewed of which 10 were Experienced and 11 were Beginners. Of the 21 teachers, two were native speakers although they had lived in England a long time. Interviews were conducted using a semi-structured schedule and were taped. The transcribed interviews generated 147 pages of typed A4.

The observation logs

The same Beginner and Experienced teachers who agreed to the interviews were also observed and logged. The Student Teachers were also included in this part of the study. The main purpose of these logs (see Figure A.1) was to record teachers' instances of recourse to L1 (RL1) during a lesson. Teachers were not informed in advance of this main purpose although they knew from the previously completed questionnaire, of course, that the project was about (amongst other things) the use of Target Language in the classroom. If this produced any 'effect' or 'bias' at all it will be in the direction of *less use of L1*, teachers naturally not wanting to go out of their way to demonstrate a teaching technique contrary to contemporary trends. However, it was made quite clear to participants as to the objectivity of the research and of its assured anonymity. The categories in the logs caused some difficulties. Firstly, a decision had to be made as to what constituted an *instance*. In the end it was decided that the two observers separate the lesson into activity segments such as: teacher giving instructions for an activity; teacher giving directions or changing focus; teacher giving feedback on a reading comprehension. Thus, even if this segment was broken by several RL1s it would only count as one instance. This by no means solved the problem of accurately recording all instances of RL1 although it does give a fairly clear idea of what areas cause the most difficulties in trying to sustain L2. In order to record RL1 accurately there would seem to be a need for a more sophisticated model of lesson categorisation, one which will have a discourse analysis structure as its scaffolding. Some details about the observation are given in Tables A.3–A.6.

Table A.3 Experience level of teachers observed

Experienced teacher	10
Beginner teacher	11
Student teacher	16

N = 37

Table A.4 A total of 62 hours of observation were carried out

Experienced teachers	21 hours
Beginner teachers	14 hours
Student teachers	27 hours

N = 37

Table A.5 Breakdown by year group. No. of different classes

year 7	14
year 8	26
year 9	22
year 10	7

Table A.6 Proportion of mixed ability to setted groups expressed in total number of lessons

Mixed ability	23
Setted	46

The pupil interviews

The majority of schools where interviews were carried out with pupils were ones where teachers had also been interviewed and observed. A total of 196 pupils were interviewed. Most pupils were either in year 8 or year 9. The data were gathered by a number of approaches, however. In the beginning, the researchers started off by interviewing individual pupils during a quiet moment in the lesson. This technique was quickly discarded as being too intrusive – in any case there was a tension brought about by talking to pupils in the presence of the teacher. Individual pupils were then interviewed *outside* the classroom. This felt better but produced what appeared to be very inhibited and in any case short (sometimes monosyllabic) responses. It was therefore decided to adopt a group interview approach, lasting about 15 minutes, with four being the usual number. This worked much better but there were either long silences or one pupil tended to dominate. The next approach tried was to give members of the group a card to read out with a statement on it (see Figure A.8). This enabled each pupil to 'break the ice' and at least say something. After each card had been read out pupils were invited to comment on which card they thought best matched what they felt about an issue. Again there was an improvement but it was still felt that the most interesting data was coming out when interaction among the pupils resulted from individual differences. As a last refinement it was decided to first ask the group of pupils to rank the cards in order of preference before going on to discuss each issue more openly. Whilst it may be objected that what was collected here was a group reaction rather than an individual reaction, the amount of talk and interaction which resulted from these groups was so informative as to make researchers feel reasonably confident that this 'focus group' approach was the best one. Moreover, as the analysis will show, there was a high degree of individual differences within the groups. Recording of the interviews was again done by a mixture: taped recording and note taking, with tapes being used in the group interviews. The pupil interviews were probably the most fascinating part of the whole study, partly because of what was learnt about interviewing youngsters. A future recommended refinement, if possible, would be to have two researchers, one conducting the proceedings and the other making notes both on the visual interaction as well as the content interaction of the participants. The pupil interviews (transcriptions and field notes) produced 63 pages of typed A4.

Pupil questionnaires

Partly to counterbalance the group data, but also to plug a few gaps that appeared as the project went on, a questionnaire was administered to 271 pupils in 16 year 8 classes in nine schools. The Pupil Questionnaire Comments produced five pages of typed A4.

Local Education Authority (LEA) questionnaires

In order to provide a context for the target language debate, a questionnaire with space for comments was sent to 90 LEA advisers or inspectors of Modern Foreign Languages in England and Wales. The questionnaire sought to investigate what LEAs had been able to provide in terms of INSET during the period concurrent with the start of the National Curriculum for Modern Foreign Languages; what issues they had focused on, what had been the difficulties and constraints; what had been their advice or 'attitude'; and what they thought still needed to be achieved. Fifty-two replies were received. The LEA Questionnaire Comments produced 15 pages of typed A4.

Action research cycles

As these were (a) limited and still continuing and (b) different in research methodology orientation from the above they do not, in that sense, form part of the research project. They are, however, described in Chapter 5.

Description of School	inner city [ ] small town [ ] suburban [ ] rural [ ] other [ ]

Description of class
Approximate number in class [ ]   mixed ability [ ]
year group [ ]   set: 1 2 3 4 5 6
     other ability grouping: . . . .

general response of class: (e.g. cooperative)

. . . .

. . . .

Does **the teacher** describe himself/herself as fluent in the TL [ ] fairly fluent
[ ] not fluent [ ]

Description of lesson
length in mins [ ]   topic:

teacher centred	[ ]	oral presentation	[ ]	writing/reading alone	[ ]
pupil centred	[ ]	pair work	[ ]	writing/reading in groups	[ ]
about half of each	[ ]	group work	[ ]	listening to tape	[ ]
				listening to teacher	[ ]

Figure A.1 Target Language Logs (Beginner and Experienced)

Instances of teacher reverting to English (tick boxes to indicate approximate number of instances)

when giving instructions for an activity or when giving clarification
[ ] [ ] [ ] [ ] [ ] [ ] [ ] [ ] [ ] [ ] [ ] [ ]

when giving instruction for an activity *which some pupils seemed not to understand*
[ ] [ ] [ ] [ ] [ ] [ ] [ ] [ ] [ ] [ ] [ ]

when giving directions or changing the focus of the lesson (e.g. 'close books', 'now let's do a listening')
[ ] [ ] [ ] [ ] [ ] [ ] [ ] [ ] [ ] [ ] [ ]

when making disciplinary/management interventions (e.g. 'stop talking'; 'don't tap that pencil', 'listen all of you' 'don't shout out')
[ ] [ ] [ ] [ ] [ ] [ ] [ ] [ ] [ ] [ ] [ ]

when talking on a one-to-one basis with a pupil *with* rest of class being able to hear (e.g. 'have you done your homework, Emma?' 'have you brought the worksheet, John?'
[ ] [ ] [ ] [ ] [ ] [ ] [ ] [ ] [ ] [ ] [ ]

when talking on a one-to-one basis with a pupil *without* rest of class ostensibly being able to hear (e.g. 'are you feeling OK?' 'how are you getting on with that?' 'if you don't stop that now you'll be in trouble')
[ ] [ ] [ ] [ ] [ ] [ ] [ ] [ ] [ ] [ ] [ ]

when praising, encouraging
[ ] [ ] [ ] [ ] [ ] [ ] [ ] [ ] [ ] [ ] [ ]

when correcting an oral response
[ ] [ ] [ ] [ ] [ ] [ ] [ ] [ ] [ ] [ ] [ ]

when commenting or giving feedback (e.g. on a listening)
[ ] [ ] [ ] [ ] [ ] [ ] [ ] [ ] [ ] [ ] [ ]

when confirming (e.g. parotting)
[ ] [ ] [ ] [ ] [ ] [ ] [ ] [ ] [ ] [ ] [ ]

when translating or asking for translation (e.g. comment est-ce qu'on dit *factory*)
[ ] [ ] [ ] [ ] [ ] [ ] [ ] [ ] [ ] [ ] [ ]

when, in your judgement, the teacher did not know the L2 phrase or word
[ ] [ ] [ ] [ ] [ ] [ ] [ ] [ ] [ ] [ ] [ ]

when talking about the culture of the target country
[ ] [ ] [ ] [ ] [ ] [ ] [ ] [ ] [ ] [ ] [ ]

when teaching a more 'Language Awareness' part of the lesson
[ ] [ ] [ ] [ ] [ ] [ ] [ ] [ ] [ ] [ ] [ ]

when attempting to explain a grammatical point
[ ] [ ] [ ] [ ] [ ] [ ] [ ] [ ] [ ] [ ] [ ]

Figure A.1 (*continued*)

Teachers should stay in the TL when: giving instructions for a simple activity. For example asking pupils to get into pairs and read a dialogue Variable?	**Teachers should stay in the TL when:** giving instructions for a complex activity. For example when asking pupils to get into groups of 5, choose a waiter and 4 customers and act out a role-play based on cue cards Variable?
Teachers should stay in the TL when: giving instructions *that have been used before with that class* in order to manage the lesson. For example *close your books; write the date here* Variable?	**Teachers should stay in the TL when:** giving instructions. For example *close your books; write the date here* even though *some pupils seem not to understand* Variable?
Teachers should stay in the TL when: giving instructions that the teacher knows the pupils have not heard or learnt before. Variable?	**Teachers should stay in the TL when:** they are commenting on or evaluating a pupil's oral performance for example *well done*, or *yes, nearly* . . . Variable?
Teachers should stay in the TL when: making minor disciplinary interventions for example: *not quite so noisy!* Variable?	**Teachers should stay in the TL when:** making difficult disciplinary interventions for example: *John and Andrew, if I hear that word ever again there's going to be trouble!* Variable?

Figure A.2 Statement squares

Teachers should stay in the TL when:	Teachers should stay in the TL when:
trying to build up a relationship with individual pupils for example: *Jane what's the matter today?* *Something happened?* Variable?	changing the focus of a lesson for example: *now we're going to do a listening exercise* Variable?
teaching a grammatical point for example: *if it's a plural you have to ...* Variable?	asking pupils for a translation of a word or phrase for example: *How do you say 'voiture' in English* Variable?
talking about the culture of the target country for example: *discussing the eating habits of French people* Variable?	teaching 'language awareness' For example: *we can communicate by using speech ... how else can we communicate information or feelings?* Variable?

Figure A.2 (*continued*)

Teachers should insist: **that pupils ask each other for things in the target language** For example: *can I borrow your felt tip?* *Variable?*	**Teachers should insist:** **that pupils socialise in the target language when they are in the classroom (at an appropriate level)** For example: *can I come round your house tonight?* *Variable?*
Teachers should insist: **that pupils ask for help in the target language** For example: *Sir . . . how do you say in Italian . . .* *Variable?*	**Teachers should insist:** **that pupils volunteer information in the target language** for example: *I'm late because the bus was late . . . sorry* Variable?
Teachers should insist: **that pupils ask them for things in the target language** for example: *can I go to my music lesson please?* Variable?	**Teachers should insist:** **that pupils interact with them in the target language** for example: Miss, *I went to see Gemma in hospital last night.* Variable?

Figure A.3 Statement squares – learner initiated dialogue

- Pupils' response to teacher taking the register.
- Pupils announcing problems to the teacher
- Pupils asking to leave the lesson early and giving the reasons
- Pupils recording a role play on a cassette recorder (press rewind/pause, etc.)
- Pupils playing a game of pelmanism (games seem particularly to generate pupil–pupil classroom language)
- Pupils' response to teacher checking on homework
- Messages from other teachers/interruptions
- Preparing a restaurant scene: checking group organisation (tu as les assiettes? etc.)
- Teacher trying to set up a complex activity
- Making a 'contract' with a class
- A dice-throwing game
- Teacher giving pupils feedback (oral and written)
- Learner strategy training sessions
- Pupils' asking or commenting about the language content and progress of a lesson

Figure A.4 Topics for classroom language

Card 1

In a language lesson the teacher may want you to do a listening exercise using a taped recording. The teacher will probably explain *how to go about doing this* in French.

If I can't understand what the teacher is saying to me I get frustrated.

Card 2

In a language lesson the teacher may want you to do a listening exercise using a taped recording. The teacher will probably explain *how to go about doing this* in French.

Even if I can't always understand what the teacher is saying it's good for the teacher to speak in French because I learn more.

Card 3

In a language lesson the teacher may want you to do a listening exercise using a taped recording. The teacher will probably explain *how to go about doing this* in French.

If I don't understand what the teacher is saying all I have to do is ask the teacher. Or I can ask a friend.

Figure A.5 Focus group cards for pupils

Card 4

> Teachers should give important information, like homework, in English.

Card 5

> In a language lesson the teacher may call out questions in French and expect pupils to answer in French.
>
> Answering the teacher's questions, in French, in front of the rest of the class is embarrassing.

Card 6

> In a language lesson the teacher may call out questions in French and expect pupils to answer in French.
>
> Answering the teacher's questions, in French, in front of the rest of the class is OK but you have to put up with people making fun of you.

Card 7

> In a language lesson the teacher may call out questions in French and expect pupils to answer in French.
>
> Answering the teacher's questions, in French, in front of the rest of the class is no problem. That's what the lesson's all about.

Card 8

> In a language lesson pupils sometimes need to ask the teacher for information. For example: 'Do we do this in rough books?' The teacher may want you to do this in French.
>
> Asking the teacher questions in French feels awkward.

Card 9

> In a language lesson pupils sometimes need to ask the teacher for information. For example: 'Do we do this in rough books?' The teacher may want you to do this in French.
>
> Asking the teacher questions in French is OK as long as you know what to say.

Card 10

> In a language lesson pupils sometimes need to ask the teacher for information. For example: 'Do we do this in rough books?' The teacher may want you to do this in French.
>
> Asking the teacher questions in French makes me feel good.

Figure A.5 (*continued*)

Card 11

> In a language lesson the teacher may ask you to work in pairs.
>
> Working in pairs makes me feel comfortable and confident.

Card 12

> In a language lesson the teacher may ask you to work in pairs.
>
> Sometimes my partner doesn't want to work with me.

Card 13

> In a language lesson the teacher may ask you to work in pairs.
>
> I don't like working in pairs. I prefer answering the teacher.

Card 14

> In a language lesson the teacher may ask you to work in pairs.
>
> When I work in pairs I learn a lot and remember a lot.

Card 15

> In a language lesson the teacher may ask you to work in pairs.
>
> Working in pairs is a waste of time.

Card 16

> In a language lesson the teacher may ask you to work in pairs.
>
> Working in pairs is OK but we tend to chat in English.

Figure A.5 (*continued*)

Oral work in pairs or groups encourages a lot of target language use by pupils Variable?	Oral work in pairs or groups encourages real-life communicative exchanges Variable?
Oral work in pairs or groups encourages a lot of TL use by pupils only if carefully monitored by the teacher or FLA Variable?	Oral work in pairs or groups encourages a lot of TL use if pupils are allowed to work independently of the teacher Variable?
Oral work in pairs or groups allows error to become a habit Variable?	Oral work in pairs or groups lets pupils' errors go uncorrected Variable?

Figure A.6 Statement squares – collaborative learning

Teacher	Pupils might ...
chooses a topic	
decides what the learning objectives will be	
decides on structures and vocabulary	
selects materials: textbook; text; cassette; video; visuals; realia	
makes additional materials: worksheets; OHTs; gamecards	
decides which will be classwork and which will be homework	
decides whether *all* pupils will do *all* the activities	
decides upon and devises some activities which will extend the more able	
decides how the classroom will be organised	
decides on any groupings: friendship; ability; gender; random	
decides how much (if any) L1 will be used	
decides what L2 the learners will use; how often; how structured the sequences; in what order; medium or message oriented	
introduces some new language using own voice	
plays tape recordings	
practises structures and vocabulary using teacher–pupil question and answer	
organises a game	
organises communicative oral exchanges (e.g. pair work)	
organises non-communicative writing	
organises communicative writing	
monitors language learning	
assesses language learnt	
diagnoses learning difficulties and problems	
evaluates unit of work and teaching	

Figure A.7 A unit of work

	Often	Sometimes	Not often	Rarely	Never
Guess what words mean					
Think if words look like English words					
Ask teacher to clarify or repeat things					
Repeat words to myself					
Do silent practice (thinking in my head)					
Practise saying new words out loud					
Practise saying new words under my breath					
Answer (in my head) questions directed at other people					
Look up words in the dictionary or coursebook (at home)					
Make a note of new words; write language down (in class or at home)					
Make word links (e.g. animal – dog) or make up a word web					
Make a mental association when trying to memorise difficult words (perhaps with something funny)					
Learn vocabulary by a system which suits me (e.g. look; hide; say; write)					
Practise with a friend					
Ask parents, other adults, siblings for help					
Turn language into songs, rhymes, raps or mnemonics					

Figure A.8 Learner Strategies Questionnaire

Try to use the foreign language when I'm outside the classroom					
Act out language					
Listen to FL cassettes at home					
Watch FL videos at home					
Listen to FL songs					
Use a computer to help me re-draft some written work					

Figure A.8 *(continued)*

References

Adelman, C. and Macaro, E. (1995) Curriculum theory and citizenship education: A comparison between England and Italy. *Curriculum* 16 (1), 36–46.

Alderson, J.C. and Wall, D. (1993) Does washback exist? *Applied Linguistics* 4 (12), 115–130.

Alexander, L.G. (1974) *New Concept English*. London: Longman.

Allen, P. *et al.* (1990) Aspects of classroom treatment: Towards a more comprehensive view of second language education. In B. Harley, P. Allen, J. Cummins and M. Swain (eds) *The Development of Second Language Proficiency*. Cambridge: Cambridge University Press.

Allwright, D. and Bailey, K.M. (1991) *Focus on the Language Classroom*. Cambridge: Cambridge University Press.

Asher, C. (1993) Using the target language as the medium of instruction in the communicative classroom: The influence of practice on principle. *Studies in Modern Languages Education* Vol. 1. University of Leeds.

Asher, J. (1969) The total physical response approach to second language learning. *Modern Language Journal* 50, 3–17.

Atkinson, D. (1993a) Teaching in the target language: a problem in the current orthodoxy. *Language Learning Journal*. September 1993, No. 8.

——(1993b) *Teaching Monolingual Classes*. London: Longman.

Austin, J.L. (1962) *How To Do Things With Words*. Oxford: Clarendon.

Bauckam, I. (1995) A Vygotskyan perspective on foreign language teaching. *Languages Forum* 1 (4).

BOEN (1991) (*Bulletin Officiel*) Nos. 9 and 10. Paris: Ministère de l'Education nationale.

——(1994) (Bulletin Officiel) No 8. Paris: Ministère de l'education nationale.

——(1995) (Bulletin Officiel) Enseignement elementaire et secondaire No. 19. Paris: Ministère de l'education nationale.

Breen, M.P. (1985) Authenticity in the language classroom. *Applied Linguistics* 6 (1).

——(1991) Understanding the language teacher. In R. Phillipson, E. Kellerman, L. Selinker, M. Sharwood Smith and M. Swain (eds) *Foreign/Second Language Pedagogy*. Clevedon: Multilingual Matters.

Briggs, L., Goodman-Stephens, B. and Rogers, P. (1992) *Route Nationale 1*. Walton: Nelson.

Brumfit, C. (1984) *Communicative Methodology in Language Teaching*. Cambridge: Cambridge University Press.

Buckby, M. *et al.* (1992) *Auto*. London: Collins Educational.

Bullock Report (DES, 1975) *A language for Life*. HMSO.

Burstall, C. (1970) *French in the Primary School: Attitudes and Achievement*. Slough: NFER.

Byram, M. (1992) Foreign language learning for European citizenship. *Language*

Learning Journal. September 1992, No. 6.

Cajkler, W. and Addelman, R. (1992) *The Practice of Foreign Language Teaching.* London: Fulton.

Canale, M. and Swain, M. (1979) Theoretical bases of communicative approaches to second language teaching and testing. *Applied Linguistics* 1, 1–47.

Chambers, F. (1991) Promoting use of the target language in the classroom. *Language Learning Journal.* September 1991, No. 4.

Chambers, G. (1992) Teaching in the target language. *Language Learning Journal.* September 1992, No. 6.

——(1994) A snapshot in motivation at 10+, 13+ and 16+. *Language Learning Journal.* March 1994, No. 9.

Chambers, G. and Sugden, D. (1994) Autonomous learning – the Danes vote yes! *Language Learning Journal.* September 1994, No. 10.

Chamot, A. (1987) The learning strategies of ESL students. In A. Wenden and J. Rubin (ed.) *Learner Strategies in Language Learning.* NJ: Prentice-Hall.

Chaudron, C. (1988) *Second Language Classrooms.* Cambridge: Cambridge University Press.

Chomsky, N. (1965) *Aspects of the Theory of Syntax.* Cambridge, MA.: MIT Press.

Cicurel., F. (1989) La mise en scène du discours didactique dans l'enseignement des langues étrangères. *Bulletin CILA* 49, 7–20.

Clark, A. (1993) Bridging the gap: GCSE to 'A' level. *Language Learning Journal,* September 1993, No. 8.

CNDP (1993) *Anglais: classes des collèges, 6e, 5e, 4e, 3e.* Paris: Centre Nationale de Documentation Pédagogigue.

Cohen, A.D. (1991) Strategies in second language learning: insights from research. In R. Phillipson, E. Kellerman, L. Selinker, M. Sharwood Smith and M. Swain (eds) *Foreign/Second Language Pedagogy Research.* Clevedon: Multilingual Matters.

Comenius (cited in Evans 1993) *The Analytic Didactic of Comenius,* translated by V. Jelinek (Chicago and Cambridge, 1953) p. 166.

Convery, A., Evans, M., Green, S., Macaro, E. and Mellor, J. (1996) *European Citizenship and Identity: The Shaping of Pupils' Perceptions.* London: Cassell: (forthcoming).

Cook, V. (1991) *Second Language Learning and Language Teaching.* London: Edward Arnold.

Corder, S.P. (1981) *Error Analysis and Interlanguage.* Oxford: Oxford University Press.

Council of Europe (1980) *Autonomy and Foreign Language Learning.* Strasbourg: Council of Europe.

Cross, D. (1985) The monitor theory and the language teacher. *British Journal of Language Teaching.* 23, 75–78.

Dam, L. (1990) Learner autonomy in practice. In I. Gathercole (ed.) *Autonomy in Language Learning.* London: CILT.

Debyser, F. (1989) Pédagogies venues d'ailleurs – Transferts de didactique et cultures. In P. Bertocchini and E. Costanzo (eds) *Manuel d'Autoformation.* Paris: Hachette.

Department for Education (DFE) 1995, *Modern Foreign Languages in the National Curriculum.* London: HMSO.

Department of Education and Science (DES) (1986) *Foreign Languages in the School Curriculum.* London: HMSO.

——(1987) *Modern Foreign Languages to 16: Curriculum Matters 8.* London: HMSO.

——(1988) *Modern Languages in the School Curriculum: A Statement of Policy.* London: HMSO.

——(1990a) (Feb) *National Curriculum Modern Foreign Languages Working Group: Initial Advice.* London: HMSO.

——(1990b) (Oct) *Modern Foreign Languages for Ages 11 to 16.* London: HMSO.

——(1990c) *A Survey of Language Awareness and Foreign Language Taster Courses.* London: HMSO.

——(1991) (Nov) *Modern Foreign Languages in the National Curriculum.* London: HMSO.

Di Pietro, R.J. (1987) *Strategic Interaction.* Cambridge: Cambridge University Press.

Dickson, P. (1992) *Using the Target Language in Modern Foreign Language Classrooms.* Slough: NFER.

Dodson, C.J. (1985) Second language acquisition and bilingual development: A theoretical framework. *Journal of Multilingual and Multicultural Development* 6 (5), 325–347.

Duff, P.A. and Polio, C.G. (1990) How much foreign language is there in the foreign language classroom? *The Modern Language Journal* 74 (ii), 154–166.

Ellis, R. (1984) *Classroom Second Language Development.* Oxford: Pergamon.

——(1985) *Understanding Second Language Acqusition.* Oxford: Oxford University Press.

——(1992) *Second Language Acquisition and Language Pedagogy.* Clevedon: Multilingual Matters.

Evans, M. (1993) Flexible learning and modern language teaching. *Language Learning Journal.* September 1993, No. 8.

Faerch, C., Haastrup, K. and Phillipson, R. (1984) *Learner Language and Language Learning.* Clevedon: Multilingual Matters.

Franklin, C.E.M. (1990) Teaching in the target language: problems and prospects. *Language Learning Journal*, September 1990, No. 2.

Freeman, D. (1992) In D. Nunan (ed.) (1992a) *Collaborative Language Learning and Teaching.* Cambridge: Cambridge University Press.

Gardner, R C. (1985) *Social Psychology and Second Language Learning: The Role of Attitudes and Motivation.* London: Arnold.

Gardner, R.C. and Lambert, W.E. (1972) *Attitudes and Motivation in Second Language Learning.* Rowley, MA: Newbury House.

Gathercole, I. (ed.) (1990) *Autonomy in Language Learning.* London: CILT.

Gattegno, C. (1972) cited in D. Nunan (1991) *Language Teaching Methodology.* Hemel: Prentice-Hall.

Green, S. (1990) The letter kills but change deskills. *Language Learning Journal,* March 1990, No. 1.

Grenfell, M. (1991) Communication: Sense and nonsense. *Language Learning Journal,* March 1991, No. 3.

——(1992) Process reading in the communicative classroom. *Language Learning Journal,* September 1992, No. 6.

Grenfell, M. and Harris, V. (1993) How do pupils learn? (Part 1). *Language Learning Journal,* September 1993, No. 8.

——(1992) Process reading in the communicative classroom. *Language Learning Journal,* September 1992, No. 6.

———(1994) How do pupils learn? (Part 2). *Language Learning Journal*, March 1994, No. 9.

Hagen, S. (1992) Language policy and strategy issues in the new Europe. *Language Learning Journal*, March 1992, No. 5.

Håkansson, G. (1992) The role of the teacher in the second language classroom. *Revue de Phonétique Appliquée*, 103–4; 163–80.

Håkansson, G. and Lindberg, I. (1988) What's the question? Investigating questions in second language classrooms. *AILA Reviews* 5, 101–16.

Halliday M.A.K. (1975) *Learning How To Mean*. London: Edward Arnold.

Halliwell, S. and Jones, B. (1991). *On Targe*. London: CILT.

Harbord, J. (1992) The use of the mother tongue in the classroom. *ELT Journal* 46, (4), 75–90.

Harley, B., Allen, P., Cummins, J. and Swain M. (eds) (1990) *The Development of Second Language Proficiency*. Cambridge: Cambridge University Press.

Harris, V. (1995) Differentiation: Not as easy as it seems. *Language Learning Journal*, September 1995, No. 12.

———and Noyau G. (1990) Collaborative learning: Taking the first steps. In I. Gathercole (ed.) *Autonomy in Language Learning*. London: CILT.

Hawkins, E. (1987) *Modern Languages in the Curriculum*. Cambridge: Cambridge University Press.

HMI (1988) (quoted in I. Gathercole (1990) *Autonomy in Language Laearning*. London: CILT).

Honnors, S., Holt, R. and Mascie-Taylor, H. (1978) *Tricolore 1*. Walton: Nelson.

Hope, M. (1987) GCSE: Back to the future in a school department. In D. Phillips, *Languages in Schools: From Complacency to Conviction*. London: CILT.

Hymes, D. (1972) On communicative competence. In J. Pride and J. Holmes (eds) *Sociolinguistics*. Harmondsworth: Penguin.

James, C. (1990) State of the art article: Learner language. *Language Teaching*. Cambridge: Cambridge University Press.

James, C. and Garrett, P. (1992) *Language Awareness in the Classroom*. London: Longman.

Kellerman, E. (1991) Compensatory stategies in second language research: A critique, a revision and some (non-) inplications for the classroom. In R. Phillipson, E. Kellerman, L. Selinker, M. Sharwood Smith and M. Swain (eds) *Foreign/Second Language Pedagogy Research*. Clevedon: Multilingual Matters.

Kharma, N.N and Hajjaj, A.H. (1989) Use of the mother tongue in the ESL classroom. *IRAL*. Vol. 27.

Kohonen, V. (1992) In D. Nunan (1992a) *Collaborative Language Learning and Teaching*. Cambridge: Cambridge University Press.

Krashen, S. (1981) *Second Language Acquisition and Second Language Learning*. Oxford: Pergamon.

Krashen, S.D. (1987) *Principles and Practice in Second Language Acquisition*. London: Prentice-Hall

Krashen, S.D. and Terrell, T.D. (1988) *The Natural Approach*. London: Prentice-Hall.

Kultusminister des Landes Schleswig-Holstein (1986) *Lehrplan Hauptschule, Realschule, Gymnasium* (Englisch). Kiel: Schmidt & Klaunig.

Lachman, R. *et al.* (1979) cited in J.M. O'Malley and A.U. Chamot (1990) *Learning Strategies in Second Language Acquisition*. Cambridge: Cambridge University Press.

Lightbown, P.M. (1991) What have we here? Some observations on the influence of instruction on L2 learning. In R. Phillipson, E. Kellerman, L. Selinker M. Sharwood Smith and M. Swain (eds) *Foreign/Second Language Pedagogy Research*. Clevedon: Multilingual Matters.

Lightbown, P.M. and Spada, N. (1993) *How Languages are Learned*. Oxford: Oxford University Press.

Little, D. (1994) Autonomy in language learning: Some theoretical and practical considerations. In A. Swabrick (ed.) *Teaching Modern Languages*. London: Routledge.

Littlewood, W.T. (1984) *Foreign and Second Language Learning*. Cambridge: Cambridge University Press.

Long, M.H. (1983) Native speaker/non-native speaker conversation in the second language classroom. In M. Clarke and J. Handscombe (eds) *On TESOL '82 Pacific Perspectives on Language Learning and Teaching*. Washington, DC: TESOL.

Macaro, E. (1995) Target language use in Italy. *Language Learning Journal*, March 1995, No. 11.

——(1996) Teacher use of the target language. *Languages Forum*. 1 (5).

MacArthur, T. (1983) *A Foundation Course for Language Teachers*. Cambridge: Cambridge University Press.

Macdonald, C. (1993) *Using the Target Language*. Cheltenham: Mary Glasgow Publications.

Medgeys, P. (1992) Native or non-native: Who's worth more? *ELT Journal* 46 (4).

Mellor, J. and Trafford, J. (1994) National Curriculum in modern foreign languages – the first year of implementation: The ALL survey. *Language Learning Journal*, September 1994, No. 10.

Ministero Della Pubblica Istruzione (1979) *Nuovi Programmi, Orari di Insegnamento e Prove di Esame per la Scuola Media Statale*. Roma: Istituto Poligrafico e Zecca Dello Stato.

Mitchell, I. and Swarbrick, A. (1994) *Developing Skills for Independent Reading*. London: CILT.

Mitchell, R. (1986) An investigation into the communicative potential of teacher's target language use in the foreign language classroom. PhD thesis, University of Sterling (quoted in R. Mitchell 1989).

Mitchell, R. (1988) *Communicative Language Teaching in Practice*. London: CILT.

——(1989) Second language learning: Investigating the classroom context. *System* 17 (2), 195–211.

——(1994) The communicative approach to language teaching: An introduction. In A. Swabrick (ed.)*Teaching Modern Languages*. London: Routledge.

Müller, K. (1987) Zur Rolle des native speaker beim Fremdsprachenerwerb. *Die neureren Sprachen* 86 (5), 383–407.

Naiman, N., Frohlich, M., Stern, H. and Todesco, A. (1978) *The Good Language Learner*. Toronto: Ontario Institute for Studies in Education.

National Congress on Languages in Education (NCLE) (1985) *Papers and Reports 6*. London: CILT.

National Curriculum Council (1989) *An Introduction to the National Curriculum*. York. NCC.

——(199) *National Curriculum Council Consultation Report: Modern Foreign Languages*. York: NCC.

——(1992) *Modern Foreign Languages Non-Statutory Guidance*. York: NCC.

——(1993) *Target Practice: Developing Pupils' Use of the Target Language.* York: NCC.

Neather, T., Woods, C., Rodriguez, I., Davis, M. and Dunne, E. (1995) *Target Language Testing in Modern Foreign Languages.* Report of a project commissioned by the School Curriculum and Assessment Authority. London: SCAA.

Nunan, D. (1991) *Language Teaching Methodology.* Hemel Hempstead: Prentice-Hall.

——(ed.) (1992a) *Collaborative Language Learning and Teaching.* Cambridge: Cambridge University Press.

——(1992b) *Research Methods in Language Learning.* Cambridge: Cambridge University Press.

Nystrom, A. (1978) *French as a Foreign Language.* Stockholm: Almqvist and Wiksell.

O'Malley, J.M. and Chamot, A.U. (1990) *Learning Strategies in Second Language Acquisition.* Cambridge: Cambridge University Press.

Office for Standards in Education (OFSTED) (1993a) *Handbook. Inspection Schedule.* London: HMSO.

——(1993b) *Modern Foreign Languages.* Key Stage 3 'First Year' 1992–1993. London: HMSO.

——(1995) *Modern Foreign Languages: A Review of Inspection Findings 1993/94.* London: HMSO.

Oxford R.L. (1989) Use of language learning strategies: a synthesis of studies with implications for strategy training. *System* 17 (2), 235–247.

Page, B. (1993) The target language and examinations. *Language Learning Journal.* September 1993, No. 8.

Page, B. and Hewitt, D. (1987) *Languages Step by Step.* London: CILT.

Pattison, P. (1987) *Developing Communication Skills.* Cambridge: Cambridge University Press.

Paulston, C. (1990) Educational language policies in Utopia. In B. Harley, P. Allen, J. Cummins and M. Swain (eds) *The Development of Second Language Proficiency.* Cambridge: Cambridge University Press.

Peck, A. (1988) *Languages Teachers At Work.* Hemel Hempstead: Prentice-Hall.

Phillips, D. (1988) *Languages in Schools: From Complacency to Conviction.* London: CILT.

Phillipson, R. (1992) *Linguistic Imperialism.* Oxford: Oxford University Press.

Phillipson, R., Kellerman, E., Selinker, L., Sharwood Smith, M. and Swain, M. (eds) (1991) *Foreign/Second Language Pedagogy Research.* Clevedon: Multilingual Matters.

Pica, T. and C. Doughty (1985) Input and interaction in the communicative classroom: a comparison of teacher fronted and group activities. In S. Gass and C. Madden (eds) *Input and Second Language Acquisition.* Rowley, MA: Newbury House.

Pomphrey, C. (1994) The 'knowledge about' and 'use of ' dichotomy. *Languages Forum* 1 (2/3).

Porter, P.A. (1986) How learners talk to each other: input and interaction in task-centred discussions. In R. Day (ed.) *Talking to Learn: Conversation in Second Language Acquisition.* Rowley, MA: Newbury House.

Prabhu, N.S. (1987) *Second Language Pedagogy.* Oxford: Oxford University Press.

Ramage, K. (1990) Motivational factors and persistence in foreign language study. *Language Learning* 40 (2), 189–219.

Richards, B. (1994) 'It won't come in the bath, will it?' What children can teach us about complex questions. *Early Years* 14 (2), 24–29.

Richards, J. (1984) The secret life of methods. *TESOL Quarterly* 18 (1) 7–23.

Richards, J.C. and Rodgers, T.S. (1986) *Approaches and Methods in Language Teaching*. Cambridge: Cambridge University Press.

Richards, J.C. and Lockhart, C. (1994) *Reflective Teaching in Second Language Classrooms*. Cambridge: Cambridge University Press.

Richardson, G. (1983) (ed.) *Teaching Modern Languages*. Kent: Croom Helm.

Rivers, W. (1983) *Speaking in Many Tongues: Essays in Foreign Language Teaching*. Cambridge: Cambridge University Press.

Roberts T. (1994) Grammar: Old wine in new bottles? *Languages Forum* 1 (2/3), 2–5.

Rubin, J. (1981). Study of cognitive processes in second language learning. *Applied Linguistics* 2, 117–131.

Sato, C. (1982) Ethnic styles in classroom discourse. In M. Hines and W. Rutherford (eds) *ON TESOL '81*. Washington, DC: TESOL.

School Curriculum and Assessment Authority (SCAA) (1994) *Modern Foreign Languages in the National Curriculum: Draft Proposals*. London: SCAA.

Searle, J. (1969) *Speech Acts*. Cambridge: Cambridge University Press.

Selinker, L. (1972) *Interlanguage*. IRAL. Vol 10.

Sharwood-Smith, M. (1994) *Second Language Learning: Theoretical Foundations*. Harlow: Longman.

Sinclair and Coulthard (1975) *Towards an Analysis of Discourse*. Oxford: Oxford University Press.

Skehan, P. (1991) Individual differences in second language learning. *SSLA*, 13, 275–298.

Skinner, D. (1985) Access to meaning: the anatomy of the language/learning connection. *Journal of Multilingual and Multicultural Development* 6 (5), 369–389.

Slimani, A. (1987) The teaching/learning relationship: Learning opportunities and the problems of uptake – an Algerian case study. (Cited in D. Allwright and K. Bailey (1991) *Focus on the Language Classroom*. Cambridge: Cambridge University Press.)

Smalley, A and Morris, D. (1992) *The Modern Language Teacher's Handbook*. Cheltenham: Stanley Thornes.

Strong, M. (1983) Social styles and the second language acquisition of Spanish-speaking kindergartners. *TESOL Quarterly* 17, 241–258. (Cited in C. Chaudron (1988) *Second Language Classrooms*. Cambridge: Cambridge University Press.)

Swain, M. (1985) Communicative competence: Some roles of comprehensible input and comprehensible output in its development. In S. Gass and C. Madden (eds) *Input and Second Language Acquisition*. Rowley, MA: Newbury House.

Swarbrick, A. (1994) (ed.) *Teaching Modern Languages*. London: Routledge.

Towell, T. and Hawkins, R. (1994) *Approaches to Second Language Acquisition*. Clevedon: Multilingual Matters.

Tumber, M. (1991) Developing learner autonomy. *Language Learning Journal*, September 1991, No. 4.

TVEI (1988) *Flexible Learning*. Sheffield: The Training Agency.

Ur, P. (1981) *Discussions that Work: Task Centred Fluency Practice*. Cambridge: Cambridge University Press.

Varonis, E and Gass, S (1985) Non-native/non-native conversations: A model for negotiation of meaning. *Applied Linguistics* 6 (1), 71–90.

Waterhouse, P. (1990) Supported self-study across the curriculum. In I. Gathercole (ed.) *Autonomy in Language Learning.* London: CILT.

Wenden, A. and Rubin, J. (1987) *Learner Strategies in Language Learning.* New Jersey: Prentice-Hall.

Westgate, D. (1991) Modern foreign languages 11–16: A too cosy consensus? *Language Learning Journal,* September 1991, No. 4.

White, L., Spada, N., Lightbown P.M. and Ranta, L. (1991) Input enhancement and L2 question formation. *Applied Linguistics* 12 (4), 416–432.

Wilkins, D. (1976) *Notional Syllabuses.* Oxford: Oxford University Press.

Woods, C. and Neather, T. (1994) Target language testing at Key Stage 4. *Language Learning Journal,* September 1994, No. 10.

Wringe, C. (1989) *The Effective Teaching of Modern Languages.* London: Longman.

Index